COLLEGE COUNSELING ~ ~~
ADMISSIONS PROFESSIONALS

College Counseling for Admissions Professionals is a much-needed resource to guide college admissions professionals in helping students navigate the college choice process. This research-based book prepares college admissions professionals to not only be marketers of their institution, but also disseminators of knowledge about the college choice process. Arguing that the most effective retention tool for an institution is to provide prospective students with the best possible information to choose the right institution, this book provides the full set of tools that every college admission professional needs today to ensure students applying to their institutions are making informed choices and will more likely achieve success while in college.

Coverage includes:

- The role of college access professionals—including school counselors, pre-college outreach providers, and independent consultants—and how to effectively work with these groups
- The shifts in financial aid at the federal, state, and institutional levels and the implications of these trends for students' and families' ability and willingness to pay for college
- The abundance of college access tools on the Internet and those that are most useful for students and families

Nathan J. Daun-Barnett is an Assistant Professor of Higher Education Administration in the Educational Leadership and Policy Program at the University at Buffalo, USA.

Carl W. Behrend is a retired school counselor, former chair of the guidance department at Orchard Park High School, and founder of Behrend Consulting in Buffalo, New York, USA.

Cory M. Bezek is Assistant Director of Admissions at the State University of New York at Fredonia, USA.

COLLEGE COUNSELING FOR ADMISSIONS PROFESSIONALS

Improving Access and Retention

Nathan J. Daun-Barnett, PhD

Carl Behrend

Cory M. Bezek

Routledge
Taylor & Francis Group

NEW YORK AND LONDON

First published 2014
by Routledge
711 Third Avenue, New York, NY 10017

and by Routledge
2 Park Square, Milton Park, Abingdon, Oxon OX14 4RN

*Routledge is an imprint of the Taylor & Francis Group,
an informal business*

Library of Congress Control Number: 2013950818

ISBN: 978-0-415-53697-4 (hbk)
ISBN: 978-0-415-53698-1 (pbk)
ISBN: 978-0-203-11097-3 (ebk)

Typeset in Sabon
by Apex CoVantage, LLC

CONTENTS

PREFACE

In this book, we recognize that there are four groups of college access professionals who work with students during the transition from high school to college—higher education admissions professionals, school counselors, pre-college outreach providers, and independent consultants—and collectively, they hold the key to helping more students think about, plan for, and gain admission to college. But we also recognize that all of these professional groups operate from different sets of knowledge, assumptions, expectations, and priorities. As a consequence, we have found that they generally have limited understanding of each group's roles, what their work entails, and how their incentives work. That lack of understanding, in our estimation, allows each group to operate from a different playbook—the consequence of which is that students and parents may receive contradictory or inconsistent messages from different professionals.

Intended Audience

While volumes could be written for each of these groups, we have chosen to focus our attention in this volume on admissions professionals. College admissions professionals are the face of the institution both for students and parents, and they are the professionals that support students in the college choice process. In many cases, admissions counselors are the primary source of information about college for school counselors, pre-college outreach providers, and to some degree independent consultants. If we hope to bridge the gap between high schools and colleges, then we must prepare the next generation of college admissions professionals to balance two key roles—as advocates and marketers of their respective institutions and as proponents of college access for students least likely to pursue education after high school.

On one hand, admissions counselors are ideally positioned to serve these two roles because they spend much of their time talking with school counselors and students. They are on the road—visiting schools, meeting with students, and talking with counselors about the admissions process and related issues. On the other hand, they are inadequately prepared to educate their K12 college access counterparts because they lack the requisite knowledge and training. Admissions counselors typically receive no formal training in college counseling or higher education administration. Frequently, they are recent graduates of the institution who can sell their experience, but are required to adapt to the other demands of the profession as they go. Personal experience at the institution is useful, from a marketing perspective, but it is limited in terms of helping school counselors, pre-college outreach providers, and independent consultants understand the vagaries of the higher education landscape. Even among the college admissions staff with degrees in higher education administration, most are unlikely to have any formal training in college counseling or very much familiarity with college access as a body of knowledge. Few higher education administration programs offer a course in college access or college counseling, and none that we know of require it as a central part of their curriculum. We hope to address this gap in training by providing insights into the key issues facing admissions professionals and their work with other college access professionals.

Contributions to the Admissions Profession

The purpose of this book is to provide college admissions professionals a solid foundation upon which to build their admissions career—the information they need to help students and their parents navigate the college choice process and achieve success as they transition to college. We believe the best retention tool for an institution is to provide prospective students with the best possible information to choose the right institution—whether or not it is that particular institution. It sounds simple, but we have to recognize that this is not how most institutions currently operate. From an institutional perspective, admissions professionals are responsible for marketing the college, first and foremost. They serve on the front line, engaging prospective students as they decide whether or where to attend. However, as we discuss in the first chapter, the incentive structure currently places greater emphasis on what is best for the institution rather than what is best for the student.

We should be clear that we are not proposing a book about college retention. There are many volumes written on that topic, and while it remains a critical challenge for colleges and universities, this volume is not intended to fill those gaps. Instead, we believe that one of the gaps in the existing conversations around college access is the recognition that access to college and successful completion of a degree are inextricably linked and that even the best informed high school students are not always prepared for what lies ahead. Consider the growth of independent consultants in the college admissions process. Many of the students enrolled in these services have access to all the resources one might expect—a knowledgeable counselor, college-educated parents, and peers enrolling in postsecondary education—and yet they continue to seek out the services of professionals who can provide individual guidance and support as they make the most important investment of their young lives. This is a high-stakes environment for prospective students and parents—a college education may cost families as much as a home, and most would not go through the process of buying a home without the help of a real estate agent. The higher education community recognizes how substantial this investment is for families, but collectively, it has not developed an effective model to ensure that the right support exists to help families weigh all relevant information and make informed decisions.

In this volume, we hope to empower admissions counselors with the knowledge, insight, and resources to see themselves as college access professionals over and above their role as promoters of their respective institutions. In so doing, we expect that counselors will be better able to serve the needs of students they meet and to provide better, more reliable information to school counselors, pre-college outreach providers, and independent consultants. Currently, school counselors, pre-college outreach providers, and independent consultants rely on college admissions counselors for access to the information they need to help students plan, prepare, and attend college—the utility of those relationships, relative to improving access to college, is predicated upon two factors: (a) the quality of the information admissions counselors possess and are able to share with others and (b) the degree to which schools and programs are capable of helping colleges identify students who will be successful at their institutions.

As we discuss in the first chapter, admissions professionals are rational economic actors, and, when their time is limited, they focus their time, energy, and resources on cultivating the networks most likely to send students to their institutions. As a result, the counselors who are already successfully positioning students for college have greater access to admissions staff, and those for whom access is a real issue are left largely on their own. Some might suggest it is foolish to think that modifying the role of admissions counselors will make any difference in terms of their behavior or ultimately the chances that an increasing number of students will attend college. We suggest that the recent experience of Harvard University is instructive. In 2008, Harvard elected to replace loans with grants for every admitted undergraduate student whose family income fell below $60,000 (Avery et al., 2006). They found, perhaps surprisingly, that while the numbers of low-income students enrolled at the university increased, the percentage of the low-income applicant pool admitted to the institution remained unchanged. Researchers found that, while the guarantee of grants for loans may have had some impact, the more important difference was found in the practice of the admissions office. Rather than simply increasing the yield (an admitted student's decision to accept the offer and enroll at the institution) of the existing pool, the admissions staff expanded its reach to a larger number of schools that had not previously sent students to Harvard. We suspect that if simply changing the priorities at Harvard can expand to high-achieving low-income students across the country, then it is possible to achieve something similar in other sectors of postsecondary education.

For the academic community, we expect this volume to respond to increasing calls to improve alignment between high schools and colleges and by extension, improve the quality and delivery of signals to students and parents regarding the college choice process. Educators have attempted for more than a century to align high schools with colleges, but both have very different histories and have developed along different trajectories, making a system approach difficult to achieve in practice. We suggest, beginning with admissions professionals, that in order to align this complex network of comprehensive high schools, magnet schools, and charter schools with a heterogeneous mix of postsecondary institutions, we must focus on the professionals that routinely span the boundaries of these organizations. We focus on college admissions staff because they are best positioned to influence school counselors, pre-college outreach providers, and independent consultants. We believe this sort of alignment will result in clearer, more consistent signals to students and parents and will allow these professionals to work more effectively together in complementary ways.

Organization of the Book

The book begins with three chapters that give college admissions professionals a foundation for understanding college access in the United States. The first chapter develops the case for helping more students go to college and the important role of a range of college access professionals including admissions professionals, school counselors, pre-college outreach providers, and independent consultants. It also lays the foundation for using signaling theory as a way to think about the alignment of these four groups of professionals to streamline and simplify the messages students and parents receive about how to navigate the college choice process. The chapter also discusses, by way of analogy, what motivates each group of professionals and how their incentives work. Chapter 2 provides a brief overview of the history and evolution of both K12 and higher education in the United States. It is important for college admissions professionals to recognize that these two systems have unique histories in the United States and that their trajectories have frequently made alignment difficult to achieve—even when the demand for it was clear.

Chapter 3 discusses the roles of admissions counselors relative to the roles of other college access professionals. Admissions counselors play a critically important role in the college choice process, but as a whole, their role has been modest in terms of increasing access to college—with the possible exception of those working in community colleges and other open enrollment institutions. They may work directly with a handful of students at each school in their region, but these students generally come to them with established college aspirations and are already likely to attend college. In these cases, admissions professionals operate as marketers, where their job is to help informed students understand why their institution is the right fit for them. We believe that their more important role has not been fully realized as a primary source of information for counselors and pre-college outreach professionals working with students who are less likely to attend college. School counselors have long served as the front line of college access for students and parents, but, as the numbers suggest, there are simply too few of them to meet the growing demand for college. We suggest that much less is known about pre-college outreach providers or independent consultants, and as a result they remain largely on the periphery of the choice process. As a result, these two groups may hold a good deal of potential to help more students successfully navigate the college choice process—but first, admissions counselors must understand the role each of these groups plays.

Chapter 4 examines the importance of academic preparation—arguably the primary barrier students face at the intersection of high schools and colleges. High schools are charged with the task of preparing graduates for both employment and postsecondary education. Unfortunately, there is no single standard for what constitutes "academically prepared." Policy makers, testing agencies, and education advocates have pushed for greater alignment between high school requirements and admissions expectations—an idea that resonates with many educators and policy makers but may be difficult to achieve in practice, given the complexity of the two systems. Chapter 5 provides a thorough discussion of the cost of college—which may be the most important barrier for low-income, first-generation, and underrepresented minority students and parents. It is also among the most important concerns for families already likely to send their sons and daughters to college. Educators and policy makers recognize that the growing costs of college far outpace rates of inflation as well as growth in family income. States have been unable to keep pace with funding demands for public higher education, and financial aid strategies have been shifting toward creating incentives for academic achievement in high school (merit aid) and providing loans (instead of grants) to help families pay for the cost of college. As a result, students and parents assume a greater proportion of those costs. We pay particular attention to recent changes in federal student loan programs and increased efforts to increase FAFSA completion rates.

Chapter 6 is the first of three chapters that examines the lack of information and support many low-income, first-generation, and underrepresented minority students face as they attempt to navigate the choice process. Access to information is a necessary but insufficient condition for gaining access to college. It is equally important that students have adequate support from parents, counselors, teachers, and other adults who are familiar with the process. This chapter examines the theoretical foundations for understanding the role information plays in the college choice process, and it explores the importance of the social network to which students belong. In many ways, pre-college outreach programs and the range of college access interventions— including the Federal TRIO and GEAR UP (Gaining Early Awareness and Readiness for Undergraduate Programs)—were designed specifically to provide more reliable sources of information and support. Chapter 7 begins with a discussion of the array of outreach programs at the federal, state, and local levels. One of the recent trends in college access work is the proliferation of programs designed to place paraprofessional staff in high-need schools to help more students plan and prepare for college. Chapter 7 also examines the increasing prominence of National College Advising Corps (NCAC) and AmeriCorps and the growth of these paraprofessional, school-based strategies. These programs increase the numbers of professionals prepared to help students navigate the college choice process, but those who serve in these roles are not trained counselors and are prepared to serve in a very narrowly focused capacity. These paraprofessionals may be important partners for college admissions professionals, particularly as they work with schools that have traditionally not sent as many students to college.

Chapter 8 is an extension of the prior two chapters on information, support, and navigation of the college admissions process, and it pays much more specific attention to the burgeoning presence of the Internet in the college choice process and the increasingly confusing array of social marketing campaigns, recruitment strategies, college access web portals, and other web-based resources. The great irony is that at the very point when information is more readily and democratically accessible to the greatest proportion of students and families, it has become more complicated for many to navigate—particularly families of students who are the first to attend college, who may not know where to begin or what questions to ask. We examine the range of web-based strategies designed to help facilitate the college choice process and discuss how to sort through these tools, identify those most likely to be of some assistance, and to leverage those tools to expedite the work of college access professionals Admissions professionals have moved much of their process online, but they should recognize that they have a good deal of competition for students' attention in this virtual environment, and they need to be aware of what is available and how complicated that space has become for students and parents.

In Chapter 9, we address a dimension of the information challenge that we believe has been underexamined relative to its importance as a barrier to college—anticipating success in college. We believe that first-generation students and those with little exposure to college are ill equipped to anticipate what it will require to be successful in college and what supports are available to help them on most college campuses across the country. In this chapter we examine the range of transitional issues students face that mirror those we discuss in the college choice process—(a) academic preparation and the role of placement testing and remediation; (b) college affordability, working while in school, and student loan debt; (c) social integration into the campus community and the range of orientation strategies; and (d) the growing importance of technology in higher education. We conclude the book in Chapter 10 by returning to the importance of alignment and the simplification of the signals sent to students, as well as the potential benefits of moving these four groups of college access professionals toward a shared vision for the college choice process.

1

INTRODUCTION

Understanding the Role of Admissions Professionals in the Context of College Access

When high school students are asked if they plan to go to college, the answer is overwhelmingly yes. Surveys suggest that more than 80% of all high school seniors today plan to attend some sort of postsecondary education (Ingels, Planty, & Bozick, 2005), and that number has changed by only a few percentage points in more than a decade (Ingels, Curtain, Kaufman, Naomi Alt, & Chen, 2002). Our experience talking to high school students is very much the same—most indicate that they plan to go to college and that they understand, at least generally, the potential benefits. Contrary to what some might expect, students attending lower performing schools and from less economically advantaged backgrounds respond in the same way as their more affluent peers. However, once we ask them where they plan to go or how they plan to get there, fewer students are as certain, particularly among lower income and first-generation students (Adelman, 1999).

It is not surprising that most students plan to attend college. President Barack Obama (2010) has made college access and success a national priority, proclaiming that the United States should once again lead the world in terms of the proportion of adults with some form of postsecondary education. Twenty-five years ago, the United States was second only to Canada in terms of the proportion of adults with a postsecondary degree (Barro & Lee, 2011). Today, the United States is third overall for adults (25–64) but has fallen to 10th in the world among young adults (25–34) with a 2-year or a 4-year degree (Organisation for Economic Co-operation and Development, 2010). The difference between these two numbers suggests that the rest of the world has caught up and in many cases surpassed the United States in terms of educational attainment in recent years. The gaps are even more pronounced in science, technology, engineering, and math (STEM), where the United States ranks near the bottom among advanced industrial nations in terms of the production of new engineers.

Many of the traditional jobs high school graduates once filled are no longer available, or the expectations have changed for entry into those positions. Consider the recent evolution of the manufacturing sector. In 1950, manufacturing comprised 30% of employment in the United States; by 2006, that proportion dropped to just over 10% (Lee & Mather, 2008). In 2002, reports suggested that manufacturing had lost more than 1.9 million jobs in just two years (Hagenbaugh, 2002). Manufacturers are quick to point out, however, that the decline is at least in part the result of improved technologies. Over the past 30 years, as employment opportunities have declined, manufacturing output in the United States has risen (Housel, 2011). The result is twofold with respect to manufacturing employment—more employees require postsecondary education to operate new technologies, and new manufacturing sectors will grow to meet the demand for these new technologies. In both cases, a postsecondary education will be necessary for a growing number of employment opportunities.

Students and parents have gotten the message that a college education opens a world of career opportunities that may not be available to a high school dropout or even a graduate. The Bureau of Labor Statistics (2012) reports that on average, adults with a Bachelor's degree earn nearly 60% more than a high school graduate, which translates to more than a million dollars over a lifetime (Long & Riley, 2007). Each additional level of education achieved results in higher average wages and lower rates of unemployment—patterns that have remained consistent, even throughout the tumultuous economic downturn during the early part of the 21st century. These numbers are so compelling and nearly ubiquitous that it has become the most effective marketing strategy for higher education. What better investment than earning a degree that will accrue economic benefits over one's lifetime? Of course, every investment involves a degree of risk, and a college degree is no different. A Bachelor's degree may open some doors but, in and of itself, will not guarantee a job upon graduation, and it certainly does not guarantee that an employee will keep his or her job. In 2007, only 2% of adults with a Bachelor's degree were unemployed; three years later, that number rose to 5.4% (Baum & Ma, 2007; U.S. Bureau of Labor Statistics, 2012).

It is perhaps more surprising that, despite what we know about the changing nature of economic and employment opportunities and students plans to attend college, more traditional age high school graduates and returning adults are not attending college and earning degrees. Today, approximately 41% of adults over age 25 in the United States have earned at least a Bachelor's or Associate's degree—a number that has not changed in recent years (Organisation for Economic Co-operation and Development, 2010). We suspect, as others have, that one of the critical barriers to greater college participation and degree completion is access to information. It is in some ways ironic that information is a barrier in an age when access to information has never been greater—particularly via the Internet. As we have found in earlier work (Daun-Barnett & Das, 2011), the proliferation of college access information on the Internet has improved access for many families, but in the process has made it more difficult for students to find what they need if they do not have guidance and support. So while information is more readily available, students and parents who don't know where to begin the process may be at an even greater disadvantage than in years past. And of greater relevance to this book, there are too few educators and professionals prepared to help students and parents ask the right questions, identify appropriate data, and find the answers they need as they navigate the college choice process.

One key strategy to level the information playing field in the college choice process is to rethink the role of the college admissions professional as part of a larger network of college access professionals. We identify three key groups of professionals who complement admissions staff—school counselors, pre-college outreach programs, and independent consultants all play an important role decoding and demystifying the college choice process for students and families. We contend that today, there are simply too few of these professionals to meet the growing demand. Many of these college access professionals serve students with the greatest needs, and yet most have never been formally trained in college counseling. We argue that these four groups operate in relative isolation and in many ways lack an understanding and appreciation for what the other college access professionals know and, more to the point, what they do and how they do it. We also believe this is a problem for students and parents because it may lead to competing and inconsistent messages to students and parents about how to make good decisions regarding college and careers.

We pay particular attention to the role of college admissions counselors and suggest the key to aligning these four professional functions rests in their hands. First, they have access to school counselors, pre-college outreach providers, and independent consultants. They travel to high schools, visit programs, and respond to requests for information on a regular basis. No other group of access professionals routinely interacts with the others like admissions counselors. Second, they already possess some of the information the other three groups need, particularly regarding their specific institutions, requirements, and admissions processes. More important is the fact that they are perceived to be sources of information among school counselors, pre-college outreach providers, and independent consultants. Admissions counselors are already cast as providers of information to the others, so it is not necessary to change the nature of the relationships—but rather, the scope of the network and the breadth of information shared. Third, they have more ready access to one piece of information that we believe has been absent from many efforts to improve college participation. With the possible exception pre-college outreach providers located on college campuses, admissions professionals are the only group with some familiarity with what happens in postsecondary education and what students should be prepared to know about how to successfully navigate this new educational terrain.

First-generation, low-income, and underrepresented minority students are less likely to have access to this information, and admissions counselors are best positioned to provide it, either directly through their individual meetings, campus visits, and admissions fairs, or indirectly through their conversations with other college access professionals. This book provides college admissions professionals with the information they need to understand their role more broadly, in terms of college access, and to help them rethink the role they play providing information to school counselors, pre-college outreach providers, and independent consultants. By extension, it standardizes the signals sent to students and parents by providing a common framework for college access professionals who send those messages to students and parents.

Framework for the Book

We recognize that access to information is not a new problem from a college choice perspective. In fact, most of the major theories developed to better understand whether and where students go to college rely, at least in part, on access to accurate information, the presence of informational asymmetries, or the dissemination of information across networks of professionals, families, peers, and communities. The difference today is that the stakes are higher and the process for navigating college admissions is more complex and idiosyncratic than ever before. Job growth is occurring at faster rates in knowledge producing sectors where college is expected, and many careers that did not require postsecondary education in years past are changing. For example, automotive manufacturing plants that once hired high school graduates with no formal postsecondary education now expect advanced technological training. And mechanics today require similarly advanced technological training to work on hybrid and alternative fuel vehicles. In years past, high school graduates with some vocational/technical training could have entered directly into these well-paying careers, but today that is less and less the case.

Understanding the Role of Information in College Access

In this section, we consider the role information plays across a range of theoretical and disciplinary perspectives. We do not attempt to provide an exhaustive review of these of these areas, but our goal is to expose the reader to a range of alternative approaches to understanding what information students and parents need and how institutions can provide the right information and support. Next we examine the incentive structures for all four groups of college access professionals beginning with admissions professionals. If P16 alignment is an achievable goal and, as we suggest, primarily an issue to be addressed at the local level, then admissions professionals must understand both expectations and constraints of their own roles and the incentives guiding the work of school counselors, pre-college outreach providers, and independent consultants.

The Economic Perspective

Economists have generally assumed that students and parents are rational consumers whose goal is to maximize the return on their investment. They weigh the costs of attendance (tuition, fees, books, cost of living) and the opportunity costs (primarily wages sacrificed from immediate post–high school employment opportunities) with the anticipated benefits of attending college and earning a degree. From this perspective, students must understand what college costs, how financial aid works, and whether they are likely to qualify for various sources of economic support. Equally, they must have some sense of possible career opportunities and the monetary and nonmonetary benefits of each. Economists recognize that consumers seldom operate with full information, so they anticipate that the "rational" choices students and parents make are bounded by the quality and availability of the information they weigh to make those decisions. Additionally, consumers are not always prepared to assess the quality of information, nor do they have sufficient time to consider all options. From a rational choice perspective, then, if we can eliminate or minimize constraints, students and parents will be better equipped to choose whether and where to go to college.

Sociological Perspectives

While economists assume students are rational actors whose decisions will reflect the best information they have given the constraints described above, sociologists seek to understand how social structures influence social and economic stratification. Status attainment models assume that parents' social status is the strongest predictor of their children's future career choices and that family background combined with academic performance influence the choices students make about postsecondary education (Hossler, Schmit, & Vesper, 1999). These models typically recognize that the most important predictors of college attendance are family income and parents' education and occupation, followed by academic achievement. Parents who have attended college and work in occupations requiring a college degree often value postsecondary education differently than families without the same background, and they instill in their children aspirations for college attendance. The information college-educated parents share with their sons and daughters is different from non-college-educated parents. The result is more apparent in students' plans for college than in their aspirations. Simply put, students whose parents have gone to college have greater access to information regarding how to get to college, what the college experience is like, and how to succeed once they arrive.

To the extent that information is a critical barrier, status attainment theory suggests that students need to be better informed about what is expected of them to succeed in school and what will be required of them academically when they go to college. They will also require better information about career opportunities, given that parent's occupation is a critical predictor of students' future college and career plans. From this perspective, better-informed students will have higher aspirations for college and will develop more specific plans for college attendance.

Cultural capital theory, used widely among education researchers, suggests that all families transmit knowledge, attitudes, and skills associated with successful navigation of their uniquely situated cultural context. Middle and upper class families possess and transmit a particular form of cultural capital that values postsecondary achievement and occupational prestige. This form of capital provides a mechanism by which those with wealth and prestige maintain privilege by ensuring their sons and daughters access to postsecondary opportunity and entry into lucrative and prestigious careers. The fact that those from different socio-economic strata possess different forms of cultural capital would not pose a concern except that the transmission of cultural capital results in the inequitable distribution of postsecondary education and, as an extension, social and economic prestige. As Lareau and Horvat (1999) note, "[A]ny form or type of capital derives value only in relation to the specific field of interaction. Particular types of social capital do not have inherent value exclusive of what is accorded in a specific field" (p. 53). In this case, the field of interaction is the college choice process, and students from middle and upper class families tend to inherit this sort of capital from their families. The information parents and families transmit as part of cultural capital may include a clearer understanding of the college experience, more specific guidance on career opportunities, and a set of expectations regarding whether and where to attend college. It is likely that parents of upper- and middle-class backgrounds are able to help students understand how to successfully navigate the college experience.

Although cultural capital flows directly from families, social capital theory recognizes that students and parents participate in networks of relationships—all of which have some value depending upon the context. Social capital recognizes that peers, educators, and community members, in addition to families, may all influence the opportunities available to students (Stanton-Salazar & Dornbusch, 1995). Like cultural capital, the value associated with social capital depends largely upon the context and the nature of the relational networks. Students who are well connected with college graduates will derive different benefits during the college choice process from their networks than similar students who may be equally well connected in other types of networks. Each set of relationships has value dependent upon the situation, and in our efforts to level the playing field, we increasingly rely on teachers, counselors, and other "institutional agents" to help connect low-income and underrepresented minority students to the resources they need to navigate the college choice process. Implicit in both the social and cultural capital frameworks is that there is a particular type of capital that is valued, and those without it are at a deficit. A more recent line of inquiry attempts to build upon the cultural assets each student possesses. The cultural integrity framework, for example, suggests that when interventions are designed to celebrate and recognize the inherent value of family and culture, students and parents may be more responsive to the program and more likely to attend college (Tierney, Corwin, & Colyar, 2005).

Each of these theories—taken up in greater detail in Chapter 6—help us to better understand what factors affect students' opportunities for college and, in different ways, they all rely upon the transmission or acquisition of knowledge and the mechanisms by which students are connected to the information they need. We expect that in working with high school students, all of these theories provide useful ways for us to think about what information students need and how to provide them with it. From an economic perspective, students and parents care a great deal about what college costs, and college access professionals need to be equipped to help students understand differences in college price, financial aid strategies, tuition discounting, loans, and the notion of opportunity costs. From a sociological perspective, students need access to the social support networks and specific forms of cultural capital to navigate the path into and through college.

System Alignment Perspective as an Alternative Framework

In this volume we develop a P16 framework for thinking about the barriers students face and for helping college access professionals understand how best to assist their students. P16 (also seen variously as K16, P20, etc.) has become public policy jargon for aligning PK12 and higher education in ways that allow students to more seamlessly transition from high school to college. We draw upon the insights of economists and sociologists who have examined students' transitions from high school to college, but we use the P16 alignment as a way to organize our thoughts around what admissions counselors and college access professionals need to know to work with a generation of students who will increasingly expect to go to college and may need greater support to get there. K12 educators should expect that all students will attend some form of postsecondary education at some point in their lifetimes, and they should know what students will need in order to be successful in college. At the same time, postsecondary institutions need to be more transparent about their expectations and spend more time thinking about how to partner with and support the work of educators in primary and secondary education.

Signaling theory as adapted by Kirst and Venezia (2004) provides a useful theoretical lens for thinking about how information is transmitted to students and parents that specifically addresses the high-school-to-college transition. Kirst and Venezia borrow their notion of signaling theory from communication, suggesting that K12 and higher education systems send messages to students regarding what is expected of them to succeed and that those messages are not consistent, largely because the two systems are not well aligned. For example, high schools send one set of messages regarding what students must do to complete high school. Admissions offices may provide some information regarding the minimum course requirements, GPA, and admissions test scores, but gaining entry to the institution does not guarantee that a student is prepared for college-level work. When these signals are poorly aligned, some proportion of high school graduates that go to college will be required to complete non-credit-bearing remedial courses in order to be prepared to complete college-level work.

At least part of the problem is the misalignment of high schools' requirements and postsecondary expectations, but we suggest that it may not be either desirable or even possible to achieve alignment at the system level—to do so would require a far more centralized system common in other nations around the world. A nationalized approach to P16 alignment is not practical or even desirable in a decentralized and highly diversified system of education. Students attending a community college or a regional, 4-year public institution will face a different set of expectations than students attending a public flagship university or a selective private college. Instead of attempting to align systems at the state level, we focus on alignment at the local level where professionals work with students to navigate the transition from high school to college. We believe that college admissions staff, school counselors, pre-college outreach professionals, and independent consultants play a critical role in college choice that requires a different set of tools and a new framework for thinking about their roles in a 21st-century knowledge economy.

We acknowledge that while information may be a critical barrier for some students, it may not be the most important barrier students or families face. Both college cost and the lack of academic preparation for college-level work are arguably more direct and substantial barriers to access and success. We may be able to help students identify the costs of college and their earning potential with a degree, but with better information, students may come to the conclusion that college is still far too expensive. Educators should be concerned about the rising cost of college, but that is not something most college access professionals can change. They can, however, help students and parents understand the actual costs and how to manage those costs most effectively. Inadequate academic preparation is a very real concern for a large proportion of college attenders, but to address this problem in a significant way will require nothing less than comprehensive school reform. Ultimately, we believe that knowledge is power and that for some, better information will increase the likelihood they will attend college where, for others, it may improve their choice of institution.

When we think about alignment, then, we are referring to local systems of professionals who play both complementary and, in some ways, competing roles in the college choice process. It is confusing for students and parents to receive inconsistent messages at the system level, but it can be even more problematic when a student's school counselor provides different information than an admissions counselor or a pre-college outreach provider. We are less optimistic that policy makers and system leaders will be able to simplify the complex array of educational opportunities on either side of the K12/higher education divide, and we are not entirely certain that doing so is advantageous. But we believe the goal of alignment can be achieved when we focus greater attention at a local level where school counselors, admissions staff, pre-college outreach providers, and independent consultants interact with and engage some of the same students.

Our experience suggests that each of these four professionals operates largely independent of the others with little knowledge or understanding of the role of the other three. We suggest that these roles are necessarily complementary from the perspective of students and parents, but in order to achieve real alignment, college access professionals must develop the same shared understanding and find ways to connect and collaborate with their professional peers. This begins by understanding how their work is structured and the role that each group plays in the college choice process. To that end, we highlight the perspectives of each of these four groups throughout the text, beginning in the next section of this chapter and then continuing with a more complete discussion of these roles in Chapter 3.

Second, from an alignment perspective, these four professional groups should develop a shared understanding of the nature of the problem and potential solutions. Admissions counselors are in the best position to disseminate that information broadly, given the nature of their work and their access to the other three groups of professionals. College access professionals come to the work from different backgrounds and disciplines, and in many cases, they are not trained in college counseling. School counselors, for example, are commonly trained in the tradition of mental health counseling and as such are well equipped to deal with students' developmental challenges throughout schooling. However, in most cases they will never be exposed to the rich body of research related to the factors influencing students' transitions from high school to college. Admissions counselors, on the other hand, are more likely to have pursued a degree in higher education administration and have some understanding of the college choice process, but they know much less about the school context and frequently have little training as counselors. In the next section, we talk about the roles each of these individuals play and examine the incentives that guide their work. The next section discusses the organization of the book and the layout of the subsequent chapters.

Understanding the Players in the College Choice Game

At the beginning of *Freakonomics*, Steven Levitt and Stephen Dubner (2005) reveal the inner workings of economic incentives by illustrating how experts utilize information to their advantage. They note that

> as the world has grown more specialized, countless such experts [like real estate agents] have made themselves indispensable. Doctors, lawyers, contractors, stockbrokers, auto mechanics, mortgage brokers, financial planners: they all enjoy a gigantic informational advantage. (p. 5)

Real estate agents are hired because they are experts at identifying the value of a home, assessing trends in the market, and understanding both the buyer and seller. While most of us will purchase a home a few times in our lives, real estate agents engage in these transactions daily. In fact, this is why we hire them. Real estate agents are experts so that we do not have to be. Levitt and Dubner point out, however, that experts respond to incentives, and in many cases, those incentives are at odds with the very people they are expected to represent. They recount a study of home sales records that found real estate agents who sold their own homes kept them on the market an average of 10 days longer and sold them for 3% more. As the seller of their own home, they will make an average of $10,000 more, assuming a $300,000 home, where they would only clear an additional $150 to do the same for a consumer. Clearly, the incentives do not favor the consumer.

Students and parents trying to navigate the college admissions process are very much like the real estate consumers. Students apply to college only a few times in their lifetimes, on average, and parents may only engage in the process slightly more frequently. They are novices to the college admissions process, and they rely upon experts to help show them the way. A college education is among the largest investments either students or parents make during their lifetime—second perhaps, to purchasing a home. Students and parents are at a decided disadvantage because they lack the information they need to make informed decisions, and the experts respond to different incentives that may not always have the best interests of the student in mind. In one way, purchasing a home is easier than going to college because the experts are readily identifiable. Who are the comparable experts in the college admissions process?

Admissions Professionals

The closest corollary to the real estate agent is the college admissions counselor who promotes postsecondary education but is effectively engaged in sales. They know their institutions' product, they can read the college market, and they can assess fairly quickly whether or not a student is likely to attend their institution by virtue of what they look like on paper and how they engage the institution. For example, we know that students who visit campus are more likely to accept an offer of admission. As a result (and depending upon other aspects of their application package), that student may be offered less institutional aid in their overall financial aid package. Why is this? Simply put, institutional aid is frequently used as an incentive to attract students who might not otherwise choose to accept an offer of admission to that particular college. A student who visits campus has demonstrated two things—they are serious enough about college to engage actively in the process, and this particular institution has made the crucial first cut of possible colleges. Everything else being equal, students who visit the campus are more likely to attend, so additional incentives are not necessary.

The incentive for an admissions counselor is to enroll a class that achieves all of the institutional priorities. If they enroll the right number of students and attract the appropriate mix of international students, out-of-state students, athletes, musicians, legacy students, honors students, men, women, and students of color, then they have done their job. The value proposition for school counselors is slightly different because they are not paid a commission for each student they enroll or box they check. The admissions staff as a group, however, will be evaluated based upon these criteria, so they will work to meet those goals whether or not doing so is best for each individual student.

Admissions counselors differ from real estate agents in at least one important way. In real estate, agents sell many different homes and frequently even different types of homes. They may specialize in certain types (e.g. condominiums or high end family homes) or focus on particular neighborhoods, but only rarely do they sell the same home more than once. Admissions counselors do exactly the opposite. They sell the same institution every day. They derive their expertise from their experience at a single institution first and foremost. Many admissions counselors have worked at other institutions, but at any given time, they are expert in a single institution. Their expertise generalizes to the extent that the process is similar at other institutions, but that may extend only as far as their postsecondary sector. For example, an admissions professional at one of the 64 State University of New York (SUNY) campuses may be able to speak with great facility about the virtues of public higher education, and if they have been on the job long enough, they may be knowledgeable about each of the SUNY campuses to discuss the differences with a student or a parent. They will also know the process for applying to and enrolling in a SUNY institution. They may not, however, know much about private liberal arts or proprietary for-profit institutions.

School Counselors

While admissions counselors are the equivalent of a seller's agent, school counselors are thought to represent students as buyers, except they do not have the same time to devote to the admissions process, and they lack access to the same information as the admissions counselor. In this transaction, school counselors are at a competitive disadvantage. Unlike in real estate where realtors frequently play both the seller's and the buyer's agents, school counselors only ever represent the student. As a result, they do not have the same knowledge and insight into the college choice process as the admissions counselor. For counselors that focus greater time, energy, and attention on the college admissions process, much of their information comes from personal experience and the insights gleaned from professional meetings and interactions with admissions staff. School counselors frequently receive little or no training on college counseling, and when they do, it is frequently on their own initiative and not through formal credentialing programs.

So what is the incentive of the secondary school counselor? Most would argue that their incentive is to help students maximize their potential as they navigate high school and transition to college or work. We trust and believe that this is what motivates school counselors. However, when we consider what counselors are actually expected to do, it is clear that college counseling cannot be given the time it requires or even that counselors might prefer. According to a study by the National Center for Education Statistics (Parsad, Alexander, Ferris, & Hudson, 2003), 43% of school counselors report spending 20% or more of their time on college counseling—which is their highest reported priority. In real hours, that means school counselors spend approximately 8 hours per week during a 40-week year assisting students in college admissions, for a total of 320 hours. In an average school with 463 students per counselor, that translates into 41 minutes per student per year (McDonough, 2005). In those 320 hours, school counselors will be asked to write letters of recommendation for most of their college-bound students, respond to transcript requests, register students for college admissions tests and administer those tests, and organize visits of admissions counselors. All of this could easily take 320 hours, and notice that we have not even mentioned talking with students about college choices or career plans. As a consequence, any given school counselor will not have a lot of time to devote to helping students and their parents make arguably the most important life decision and financial investment. We expect that the actual amount of time the average counselor commits to college counseling is much less because they are increasingly asked to assume a greater range of responsibilities—an issue we discuss in greater detail in Chapter 3.

In an era of accountability and increasing public scrutiny, the incentive for school counselors, like all educators in schools, is to graduate the greatest proportion of students and to increase the proportion of students who demonstrate proficiency in math, English, science, and social studies. They will be evaluated on this metric above all others. Unfortunately, these modest goals are anything but simple to achieve. Students arrive in high school with vastly different levels of preparation and yet, increasingly, states are expecting students to complete a similarly rigorous core academic curriculum by the time they leave. Coupled with a dizzying array of postsecondary standards for preparation, it is difficult to define a common standard or to move the majority of students toward it. The top institutions in the United States today set a standard for grades, test scores, and curricular rigor that is only achievable by a select few. Even the best school counselors dedicated to college counseling will find it difficult to keep up with the information students and parents need to find their way through the maze.

Pre-College Outreach Providers

The third expert—the pre-college outreach professional—is specifically committed to helping students achieve their postsecondary goals. Unlike school counselors who have a wide range of administrative responsibilities in addition to serving the needs of students, pre-college outreach counselors exist only to help students and parents navigate the college choice process. We liken this group of professionals to doulas in the childbearing process. The doula is hired (or serves as a volunteer) to help pregnant mothers plan for the birth of their children, prepare for their future role as mothers, manage the pain of the actual birth, and deal with the initial transition into motherhood. In short, they are knowledgeable about the birthing process, but they are entirely focused on the needs of the mother. Pre-college outreach programs provide supplemental counselors to assess the needs of their students, work with them to identify possible postsecondary options, develop strategies to improve their academic preparation, provide services and support for parents, and assist students as they visit colleges, sit for admissions tests, and choose the best fit of postsecondary institution.

In most cases, these programs serve the most challenging high-need schools or districts or they focus on very high-achieving students who have thrived despite their circumstances. These programs are typically funded by private philanthropy and public grant opportunities. Even those that have demonstrated success find it difficult to scale up to the larger population at their current costs. While these professionals are committed to understanding both high schools and colleges, they tend not to be experts in either. In some cases they started as either admissions professionals or school counselors, but many others come from related areas like social work, public administration, and higher education administration. They bring a different set of skills and experience to help students complete high school and manage the admissions process, but they will not know high schools or colleges quite like school counselors or admissions professionals. Pre-college outreach professionals' expertise is derived from their commitment to the students they serve, but they are constrained by their degree of access to either school counselors or admissions staff.

Unfortunately, the incentives for these programs often are in conflict with the real or perceived needs of the schools they serve. For example, an

Upward Bound program may be expected, according to federal guidelines, to serve low-income, first-generation, and underrepresented minority students in high-need districts while also ensuring that those students graduate at high rates and complete a prescriptive college preparatory curriculum. In many cases, students in the high-need district will not have access to the full curriculum of courses. The incentives, then, encourage these programs to admit students likely to be successful, and fewer of the highest-need students receive the services.

Independent Consultants

The fourth and final player in the college admissions game is the independent consultant—some refer to professionals in this area as counselors, but to avoid confusion through this text, we will call them consultants. In many respects, this group plays a similar role as the pre-college outreach program and operates in a manner similar to the buyer's agent. Instead of being funded by a grant, these individuals are paid by families to help students navigate the choice process. Parents and students increasingly recognize the importance of the college application and choice process, and they have sought out professionals to help maximize their opportunities. Their services typically include career and college searches, career guidance, preparation of application materials, information gathering, and consultation about college costs. These professional consultants supplement the role of school counselors and often provide greater depth to all facets of the experience prior to the actually transmission of the application—at least in part because that is what they are hired to do.

One of the challenges parents and students face is how to choose the right independent consultant. Like in real estate, there is no regulating body or certification program required for individuals to become college advisers. Real estate agents may choose to become part of the national association of realtors, but they are not required to do so in order to sell real estate. Independent consultants may join a professional organization with a set of guidelines for professional practice. Individuals who become independent consultants are from a variety of backgrounds. Some are practicing or retired school counselors or college admission personnel, while others are financial and career planners. An early complaint about independent consultants was the lack of training and regulation of the business. As the number of independent consultants has grown, primarily in larger urban areas, professionals in the field have begun to form professional associations, ethical guidelines, and ongoing professional development support for these businesses.

Families seek out independent consultants for a number of reasons. Many public school counselors have excessively large caseloads of students and are only able to spend a small amount of their precious time around the college admission process with individual students. Recognizing this situation, families concerned about finding a good fit college for their children, coupled with a large personal financial investment, look for additional help and support in the process. Other families, in districts where counseling services are virtually nonexistent, also look to independent counselors/consultants to guide them through the process. Still others, hoping for a competitive edge in the admission process, seek out experienced independents to help them present their student in the best possible manner. The reasons families use independents are as varied as the students themselves.

The early suspicion of independent consultants has given way to a much broader acceptance of these individuals as part of the ever-changing landscape of college admission. Parents, however, need to assess the level of training and experience of anyone they hire to work with their children. In some ways, the incentives are clear—profit. Like colleges and universities, independent consultants make money by enrolling clients who are successful in the college choice process. It is likely that some proportion of independent consultants is motivated by the opportunity to make money. Given the growing demand for college credentials in the workforce and the value of a college degree, we suspect that some are motivated to earn a higher salary by marketing their expertise to those willing to pay for personal attention. We also suspect that a number of independent college advisers are motivated to help students and parents. Former school counselors, for example, might pursue this route in retirement because they want to share the knowledge and expertise they have developed over a career. Others might pursue this path out of frustration for a system that does not allow sufficient time to advise students on the college choice process. The advantage of this approach is that professional advisers spend a great deal of time with each student. The downside is that it can be a costly service that can only reasonably reach a small number of students.

We contend that it is not possible, nor is it necessarily preferable, to consolidate the responsibility of college counseling role in a single individual. All four sets of college access professionals play a critical role, and they bring different strengths, information, and perspectives to the table. We believe the bigger problem is that, for a variety of reasons, admissions professionals, school counselors, and pre-college outreach staff are unaware of the roles others play, or they rely on incomplete information and faulty perceptions. We hope to bridge this gap by articulating these differing roles while helping an increasing number of students plan, prepare for, and navigate the transition from high school to some form of postsecondary education.

College Marketing and the Accessibility of Information

Experts derive their power from the complexity of the problem and the availability and accessibility of information to identify possible solutions. Researchers have acknowledged in a variety of ways the importance of information to all stages in the admissions process, and to some extent, the problem may be that students and parents lack the information they need to make informed decisions. That is different from saying that the information is not available. The greatest irony is that, in our efforts to simplify the admissions process by making more information publicly available in a variety of forms, we have actually made the process more complicated for some. Today, if you search for "going to college" in Google, you will find more than 5.8 million results. Anything you could possibly want to know about colleges and universities, the admissions process, or student financial aid is available at the click of a button. But how can a parent or student be reasonably expected to sort through the volumes of information to find the right information presented in the right ways and at the right times along the way? The World Wide Web, like the encyclopedia or the dictionary, is a tremendously powerful tool for anyone who knows what questions to ask. However, it is virtual paperweight for anyone who does not know where to begin. We believe this is the essential problem with the current availability of information. Simply put, there is no shortage of available information. The problem is that trying to get the right information for novice parents and students is akin to filling a tea cup with a fire hose—if you can hold on to the cup, you are certain to catch some water, but you will get soaked in the process.

The second problem is assessing the quality of available information. Just because there are 5.8 million hits on Google does not mean those sites are equally valuable. In that mix, you will find institutional admissions offices, pre-college outreach programs, social marketing campaigns, comprehensive college access Web portals, and sophisticated search tools. You will also find personal blogs, YouTube video reflections, newspaper articles, for-profit college advising services, and an array of costly online services. It is difficult to assess the quality of any source of information, and while search engines try to fill this gap with sophisticated algorithms and covert data collection on individuals' Web behaviors, it is difficult to know what each individual will find valuable. Assessing the value of any information in this context is only partly a matter of understanding the source of that information. For example, it is good to know whether SAT test preparation materials were created by College Board, Kaplan, or the Princeton Review. It is relatively easier for an individual to judge the potential value of these resources. But what if parents are looking for advice on where to begin the process, or what if they know their primary concern is college cost? Different sources of information will be more or less valuable.

The third problem we face, then, is to identify which information is most important and at what times. This is the role of the expert. Ultimately, we do not expect the proliferation of new and increasingly sophisticated college access web-based tools to eliminate the need for experts. No matter how good the tool, students and parents will still need someone to help them make sense of the information. Consider increased access to credit scores as an illustration. This may be the most important piece of information about individuals' personal economic situations that for many years was only accessible to creditors. Now that credit scores are more readily available to individual consumers, people have the opportunity to use that information to change their spending behaviors and to increase their credit worthiness. Access to credit scores does not diminish the potentially important contributions of financial planners, but again, it may inform the conversation consumers have with this group of professionals. We assume that increasing access to information and changing the nature of those conversations is a positive development. We also suspect that those changes have required some adjustments on the part of individual consumers and financial professionals.

If we hope to improve access to postsecondary education for a generation of students who clearly indicate their desire to attend college, then we must contend with the barriers preventing some students from making the transition successfully. Information is one of the critical barriers, and the college access professionals who work with that information every day are the key to improving access to information for students and parents. We believe that the first step toward effective and meaningful collaboration is to develop a shared understanding of the different roles college access professionals play and how those roles affect their opportunities to work with students through the college choice process. Once we understand the roles of others involved in the process, we can begin to appreciate the linkages across professional groups and establish a degree of trust that is necessary to share in the ways we describe in this volume. That trust will strengthen the relationships among these groups and allow information to flow more freely across the social network that students and parents rely so much upon to navigate the college choice process.

2

UNDERSTANDING THE BASIC
STRUCTURE OF P16 EDUCATION
IN THE UNITED STATES

In colleges and universities across the country we face a set of difficult choices regarding the admission of new college students. One the one hand, the majority of American postsecondary institutions are enrollment driven and tuition dependent, meaning they rely on the supply of high school graduates and a growing population of returning adults. The incentive for institutions is to increase enrollments while simultaneously managing academic profile—what we think of as the quality of the incoming class. On the other hand, the higher education community clamors about the lack of adequate preparation among the graduating classes of high school seniors and expresses frustration over substantial investments made in remedial, developmental, and non-credit-bearing college courses designed to address the gap in a student's level of preparation. Colleges blame schools for failing to provide the education students need to succeed beyond high school. Schools blame parents for not effectively engaging in the educational process and intervening to ensure their sons and daughters receive that high quality education. Along the way, many students do what is minimally required to earn their high school diploma.

In this chapter, we trace the evolution of these two separate systems in American education, from the early days of Harvard College to the passage of the No Child Left Behind (NCLB) Act. We pay particular attention to the 20th century and recent developments at the beginning of the 21st century because the issue of aligning high schools and college has been a frequent, if not consistent, theme throughout the entire time period. We begin by considering the early history of postsecondary education in the United States, followed by a discussion of the early roots of public high schools. We focus much of our attention on the moments throughout the late 19th and early 20th centuries when the alignment of high schools and colleges was a focal point for educational leaders. Next, we examine developments throughout the 20th century that brought alignment to the forefront of educational practice and policy. We conclude by suggesting that we may need to rethink what alignment looks like and how we accomplish this task from the perspective of those most impacted—students, parents, and families.

Specifically, we must recognize that the professionals operating at the intersection of high schools and colleges hold the key to aligning the signals sent and the messages received by students about how to navigate the transition from high school to college.

A History of Colleges and Universities

The United States is home to more than 4,000 colleges and universities, ranging from small private junior colleges to large multicampus public research universities to the relatively nascent for-profit sector of proprietary schools and distance education providers (National Center for Education Statistics, 2012). In 2010, more than 16 million students attended these institutions of higher education (National Center for Education Statistics, 2011b), and 40% of all adults over age 25 had earned degrees from one of these colleges or universities (U.S. Census Bureau, 2010). The establishment of colleges has been an important part of the American tradition since the founding of the nation—Harvard College received its charter in 1636 and began granting degrees by 1650 (Rudolph, 1962). The oldest public institutions trace their roots nearly as far back. The College of William and Mary in Virginia was established in 1693, and the Rutgers University of New Jersey was founded as Queens College during the 18th century. According to Thelin (2004), by 1781 and prior to the formal establishment of the United States of America as a sovereign nation, 10 colleges had already been founded, including most of the institutions comprising the Ivy League colleges and the first two public universities.

In the early history of colleges and universities, communities built colleges as the nation expanded westward, and the government created incentives for that expansion. The Northwest Ordinance of 1787, for example, set aside portions of land for the establishment of colleges. As Frederick Rudolph (1962) noted, ". . . the institution that did the most to change the outlook of the American people toward college-going was the landgrant college, creation of the Morrill Federal Land Grant Act of 1862" (p. 247). The act provided the equivalent of 30,000 acres per U.S. senator and representative for the express purpose of providing a more practical education in agriculture and the mechanical arts. The lands were to be sold, and the proceeds went to the establishment of one or more colleges to address these agrarian and industrial purposes.

Access for Whom?

The issue of college access is largely a 20th-century phenomenon, fueled, in part, by the connection between postsecondary education and labor market success. Figure 2.1 shows that, prior to 1920, fewer than 20% of teenage students were enrolled in high school. College participation lagged behind;

19

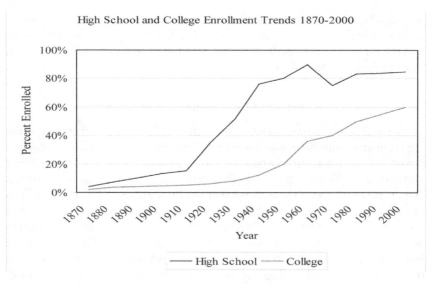

Figure 2.1 High School and College Enrollment Trends, 1870–2000
Source: Data for 1870 to 1960 are from the Carnegie Commission on Higher Education (1973). Data for 1970 to 2000 are from the U.S. Census Bureau (2000). Note: High school enrollment for 1970 reflects completion numbers, while the previous are enrollment numbers, which explains the rapid decline between 1960 and 1970.

it was not until the mid-1950s that more than 20% of the traditional age (18–24) cohort enrolled in college. The earliest issues of college access focused on the historical exclusion of groups of people from higher education rather than substantially increasing the proportion of young adults with a college education.

In fact, our history of access mirrors our less frequently noted history of exclusion. Quite literally and with few exceptions, many colleges were closed to women, religious minorities (including Catholic and Jewish students), immigrants, and Blacks through much of the 19th and early 20th centuries. The systematic exclusion of religious minorities led to the establishment of church-sponsored Catholic colleges and a few institutions dedicated to the education of Jewish students. DePaul University in Chicago is now the largest Catholic university in the nation (National Center for Education Statistics, 2012), and it was founded near the turn of the 19th century when Catholic students were turned away from other institutions (DePaul University, 2012). Yeshiva University was similarly founded in response to systematic exclusion of Jewish students from most colleges and universities. In 2010, 263 Catholic and 37 Jewish institutions across the country opened their doors to a full array of students from a variety of backgrounds, including those historically excluded from higher education (National Center for Education Statistics, 2012).

Women constitute slightly more than 50% of the U.S. population, and yet, until the early part of the 19th century, they were not welcome into the classrooms of most of the nation's colleges. The earliest institutions to educate women were academies, typically the equivalent of secondary schools, and teaching seminaries, which trained unmarried women for roles as teachers (Thelin, 2004). During the first half of the 19th century, women's colleges developed rapidly. The founding of Mount Holyoke (1837) and Georgia Female College (Wesleyan College—1839) marked the beginning of a movement to establish full colleges for the education of women. In 1833, Oberlin College was the first in the nation to open as a coeducational institution, though it took eight years to graduate their first cohort of female students. Today, while there are fewer women's colleges now than there were 50 years ago, 60 women's colleges continue to operate in 24 states across the country.

The Servicemen's Readjustment Act of 1944

The return of military servicemen after World War II and the sweeping GI Bill is frequently credited with marking the shift from elite to mass access to higher education (Cohen & Kisker, 2010). As we look back, the passage of the GI Bill had a substantial impact on both near-term college enrollments and a more durable trend toward mass access to higher education, but it was not necessarily the intent of Congress to focus so much attention on postsecondary education. There were two problems Congress hoped to address. The first was to maintain a robust but fragile economy. The United States was still recovering from the Great Depression at the start of the Second World War, and the combination of removing military members from the civilian employment ranks and the economic activity generated from supplying the war effort helped place the U.S. economy on more level footing (Bowen, Kurzweil, & Tobin, 2005). Second, the experience of military servicemen returning after the First World War was a scar still fresh in the minds of many Americans. The country was not prepared to serve the needs of those returning veterans, and months of protests in Washington, D.C., underscored the inadequate response.

The education provisions of the Servicemen's Readjustment Act were just one of several key pieces designed to help recent veterans return to civilian life. Arguably, the unemployment support, medical insurance, and loan guarantees to purchase homes were at least as important, and many veterans took advantage of these provisions, but as Cohen and Kisker (2010) point out, nearly half of all veterans took advantage of the educational benefit. The popularity of that particular provision may have contributed to the sense of urgency and emphasis placed upon expanding the community college sector in the President's Commission on Higher Education convened in 1947.

Desegregation and Access for Black Students

The history of desegregation in the United States is embodied in the landmark decision in *Brown v. Board of Education* (1954), effectively reversing more than 50 years of "separate but equal" education for Black and White students. However, much of the battle was fought over access to higher education, beginning with some of the early litigation brought forth by the National Association for the Advancement of Colored People (NAACP). Many of these battles were fought over access to law schools—where judges could immediately recognize the fallacy inherent in the separate but equal doctrine. Slavery in the South and segregation and discrimination in the North resulted in the formation of small independent institutions to provide education to Black students. Cheyney (PA), Lincoln (PA), and Wilberforce (OH) were the first established colleges for Black students in the United States (Office for Civil Rights, 1991). The establishment of colleges for the education of Black students in the United States accelerated with the second Morrill Land-grant Act (1890) and the Supreme Court decision in *Plessy v. Ferguson* (1896). In 1977, the U.S. Supreme Court decision in *Adams v. Califano* intended to bring de facto segregation to an end in the Southern states, maintaining a dual system of higher education. It has, however, had the unintended effect of compelling Historically Black Colleges and Universities (HBCUs) to take affirmative steps to increase their enrollments of White students. Today, 99 HBCUs continue to serve more than 325,000 students per year (National Center for Education Statistics, 2012), the vast majority of whom are Black.

The most recent issue of race and college access has been that of affirmative action. In 1965, President Lyndon Johnson sign Executive Order 11246, declaring that employers must take affirmative action to ensure that applicants and employees are treated equally without regard to their race, color, religion, sex, or national origin. That executive order was issued during the Great Society days of the mid-1960s when equity and opportunity were at the forefront of the national public policy agenda. Affirmative action has been a lightning rod in college admissions for more than 30 years, and it is commonly viewed as providing disproportionate benefit to underrepresented minority, particularly Black, students. The initial challenge to affirmative action in admissions came in response to the admissions policy of the Medical School at the University of California at Davis (Ball, 2000). Alan Bakke claimed that he experienced discrimination for the color of his skin because spots were set aside in the admissions class for underrepresented and potentially less qualified students. The court struck down the policy but upheld the principle of affirmative action.

Similar challenges in the mid-1990s brought the question again to the U.S. Supreme Court. After California, Washington, and the ninth circuit states including Texas, Louisiana, and Mississippi eliminated the use of race in admissions, two cases were brought against the University of Michigan in Ann Arbor. The Court issued two separate decisions—the *Gratz v. Bollinger* case struck down the undergraduate approach to affirmative action, stating their point system for race amounted to a quota, which had been banned post-Bakke (Lewin, 2011). In the law school case (*Grutter v. Bollinger*), the Court upheld the principle on what appeared to be firmer footing than the 1978 decision. The question was settled federally, but critics of the policy began to challenge state constitutions, and within two years, voters in Michigan eliminated the use of race in admissions and hiring in higher education. At the time this book is being written, the U.S. Supreme Court has taken up another constitutional challenge to affirmative action in Texas (*Fisher v. University of Texas at Austin*).

What is commonly lost in the affirmative action conversation is that many groups benefit from one form of affirmative action or another in college admissions, but they receive less attention outside of admissions. For many years, women were the primary beneficiaries of affirmative action, particularly in an employment context. More recently, institutions that historically served a large proportion of female students are more affirmative in the steps they take to increase enrollment among men. At the heart of the issue—and the central tenet of the University of Michigan defense—is the issue of academic freedom. For many years, colleges and universities have celebrated their freedom to choose what they teach, how they teach it, and to whom they teach it. The courts have upheld the principle of academic freedom in a number of different ways, and it is critically important to the admissions decision-making process. As we discuss in the next chapter, the central role of the admissions professional is to craft a class that reflects the priorities of the institution. That will include some mix of academic achievement, athletic success, geographic diversity, talent in the visual or performing arts, and commitment to service, in addition to myriad other institutional priorities. As institutions, we make these calculated, affirmative decisions routinely, and race is only a piece of that puzzle.

More recent federal efforts have been made to make postsecondary education more readily available for Native American students and Hispanic students. The first Tribal Colleges (TCs) formed in the 1960s, in response to growing concerns over educational inequalities for underrepresented student groups in college (American Youth Policy Forum, 2001). They were small, rural, 2-year colleges that served the specific needs of Native students while maintaining the history, traditions, and customs of the tribal community (American Indian Higher Education Consortium, 2010). In 1978, President Jimmy Carter signed the Tribally Controlled Community College Assistance Act, formally codifying the Tribal College under Title III of the Higher Education Act. Today, the American Indian Higher Education Consortium (AIHEC) serves 37 tribal colleges in the United States and one in

Canada, enrolling more than 16,000 students each year (American Indian Higher Education Consortium, 2007).

The federal designation for Hispanic Serving Institutions (HSIs) operates differently than both HBCUs and TCs. According to the U.S. Department of Education, the definition of an HSI is any eligible institution with a full-time equivalent enrollment of 25% Hispanic students. Institutions must request the designation by submitting an assurance of eligibility when they apply for funding under Title V of the Higher Education Act for Developing Institutions (U.S. Department of Education, 2010). Today, the Hispanic Association of Colleges and Universities report membership of 234 colleges and universities with the HSI designation (Hispanic Association of Colleges and Universities, 2012).

One of the critical issues for an increasing number of Hispanic students, particularly those of recent immigrant families, is the eligibility of undocumented students for admission, in-state tuition, and financial aid. Federal policy has been the battleground for this issue for the past 15 years. In 1996, Congress passed the Illegal Immigration Reform and Immigrant Responsibility Act, effectively barring states from providing state benefits to undocumented residents not otherwise available to other U.S. citizens—in particular, in-state tuition (St. John, Daun-Barnett, & Moronski, 2012). Since that time, advocates have been proposing versions of the Development, Relief, and Education of Alien Minors (DREAM) Act at the federal and state levels to provide opportunities for access to postsecondary education for students who are undocumented but who have attended schools in the United States and are otherwise eligible for college. Immigration is the new frontier for college access, and the DREAM Act is one initiative in the ongoing access debate.

Access to What?

Educators and policy makers recognize that there is no single point of entry into U.S. higher education and, as such, that it is difficult to define access without a consideration of what one is able to access. In order to answer the question of what students have access to, we must consider for a moment the potential benefits of postsecondary education. From an economic perspective, access is defined in terms of wages and occupational prestige, where the benefits are primarily monetary and they accrue largely to the individual. The careers that require a college education tend, on average, to pay more and to be considered more prestigious. The relationship between education and labor market success has been well established for more than 60 years, and the critical question is whether the individual is better off as a result of postsecondary education than he or she would have been without it. We suspect the answer is yes in most cases, but with any investment, there is a level of risk. We recognize, however, that the benefits of postsecondary education—or education more broadly—may extend beyond the individual to society and that those benefits may be both economic and social in nature (Institute for Higher Education Policy, 1998). In this section, we consider critical points in the history of higher education that have shaped our thinking about what students are able to access today.

In the United States, we celebrate a large and highly differentiated system of 2-year and 4-year colleges, some of which are publicly subsidized, most of which are chartered as nonprofit corporations, and a number of which are for-profit corporations. We are home to the most selective and prestigious colleges in the world, and yet the majority of our institutions are nonselective, meaning that any high school graduate is likely to be admitted. Students are able to choose from religiously affiliated institutions, military academies, selective public research universities, and institutions tailored to specific careers or vocational paths. In fact, one of the strengths of the American model of higher education is that there is an institution for any student, regardless of individual interests or demonstrated capabilities. This sort of institutional diversity did not happen by accident, and while it is impossible to infer causal linkages between historical events and contemporary conditions, a number of events throughout our history have created conditions that define the current higher education context.

One of the unique and important features of our system is the distinction between public and private institutions. In truth, all postsecondary institutions are public by virtue of their state charter. But the 1819 case *Dartmouth College v. Woodward* called into question the extent to which the legislature could meddle in the affairs of an established college chartered by the state. *Dartmouth College v. Woodward* was brought by Dartmouth College against the state of New Hampshire when it attempted alter the institution's charter and exert some control over the college leadership. The Supreme Court, under Chief Justice John Marshall, ruled in favor of the college, establishing that the state could not alter the charter, as it was a contract between the state and the institution. As Thelin (2004) points out, the ruling worked to the benefit of all colleges and universities, and the public–private dichotomy was not a defining characteristic for another 50 years. The ruling did, however, create the conditions under which future institutions would be chartered by the respective states, and it is one of the factors that have resulted in the formal distinction between public and private institutions.

The Community College

It may not be an exaggeration to suggest that the most uniquely American postsecondary institution is the community college, and yet these institutions have only been in existence for little more than a century. Community colleges trace their roots to the junior college movement at the end of the 19th century (Cohen & Brawer, 2003). William Rainey Harper championed this distinction at the University of Chicago and, in 1896, Joliet Junior College was established to provide the first two years of higher education and provide a path to the University of Chicago for those students who demonstrated they were capable of more rigorous work. In many ways, the junior colleges served as filters for their 4-year counterparts, preventing less capable students from entering the baccalaureate institutions (Brint & Karabel, 1989). They were valued, however, for their connection with their more prestigious counterparts and particularly for their transfer function.

The roles and contributions of the community college were further solidified toward the end of the Second World War. The President's Commission on Higher Education (1947) laid out a federal blueprint for higher education that cast the community college in a prominent role, but it did not settle the question of whether these colleges should emphasize the liberal arts transfer curriculum or the alternative vocational pathways; in fact, it argued that both must be emphasized by community colleges.

The Great Society and Federal Financial Aid

Prior to the 1950s, higher education remained a relatively small industry for a privileged few. Enrollments declined during the Great Depression and remained flat throughout the Second World War. Even with a dispro-portionately large number of postsecondary institutions, colleges and universities served a small fraction of the potential college-going population. The Servicemen's Readjustment Act opened higher education to a group of students that would not have otherwise considered higher education—slightly older and with greater racial and class diversity than in the past. To put this into perspective, in 1945, 1.67 million of more than 139 million adults in the United States were enrolled in higher education; by 1975 the population grew to 215 million, and college enrollments skyrocketed to nearly 11.2 million, or more than 5% of the population (Cohen & Kisker, 2010).

The final significant event we discuss in the context of higher education is the passage of the Higher Education Act (HEA) of 1965—as part of Johnson's Great Society programs. HEA committed the federal government to a more formal role in higher education with grant programs to institutions for targeted development, student aid for low-income students, and student loans initiated as part of the earlier National Defense Education Act (NDEA). We spend more time discussing the federal role in financial aid as part of Chapter 5. The passage of HEA, much like the Elementary and Secondary Education Act (ESEA), is striking because the federal government has no formal role in education under the U.S. Constitution, and as such, the responsibility for education is left to the state. These two laws have cast the federal government as an important partner in both K12 and higher education. Today, the Pell Grant, for example, is the largest and most expensive need-based grant program in the nation, and the recent shift to direct lending from the federal government makes it the largest provider of student loans.

The Evolution of K12 Schools in the United States

Education has long been part of the fabric of the American way of life, but the early roots of schooling look very different from the contemporary K12 structures. As Diane Ravitch (1974) notes in her history of New York City schools, the establishment of public education was preceded by a patchwork of small religiously affiliated schools, private Latin grammar schools, and privately supported schools for the purposes of educating disadvantaged groups from freed slaves to poor immigrant youth. This patchwork dates back as early as 1636 and the Boston Latin Grammar School (Reese, 2005), founded during the same year as Harvard College. Ravitch (1974) points out that states throughout New England placed a high value on literacy in particular and viewed it as a key to active participation in civic society and American democracy. The Puritans in Massachusetts, for example, had established as early as 1642 that all children learn to read and that all towns with 100 or more households provide publicly supported primary and secondary schools. The state of Vermont established in 1777 that all counties should provide at least one publicly supported grammar school. In 1795, the New York State legislature allocated matching resources for the establishment of publicly funded schools, but as was the case in New York City, those funds were allocated to existing church-affiliated schools and the free African school (Ravitch, 1974).

The first publicly supported high school, according to Reese (2005), was the Boston English Classical School, founded in 1821. Ravitch (1974) explains that public schools were slow to evolve, at least in part, because education had been viewed as an activity associated with religions, and the denominational schools were both established and viewed as legitimate in the eyes of church members. She suggests that in New York City in particular, the first "great school war" was waged between the Catholic Church and advocates of public education. At this time, the distinction between private schools and free public education was more clearly established than it was in higher education, and as Michael Katz (1968) and others (Angus & Mirel, 1999) have noted, the debates over public support for education were hotly contested for much of the nation's early history. The primary focus of public education through the 18th and much of the 19th centuries was to teach students to read and write. Few of these students went on to "higher" schools and typically only those who would continue on to colleges or universities. Reese (2005) points out that even with the early roots of primary and secondary schools, formally structured public high schools would not emerge in full force until the 1880s.

Early Efforts to Align High Schools and Colleges

Throughout the 18th and 19th centuries, colleges and universities developed separately from primary and secondary schooling. At the turn of the 20th century, the Committee of Ten noted,

> The secondary schools of the United States, taken as a whole, do not exist for the purpose of preparing boys and girls for colleges. . . . Their main function is to prepare for the duties of life that small proportion of all the children in the country—a proportion small in number but very important to the welfare of the nation—who shows themselves able to profit by an education prolonged to the eighteenth year, and whose parents are able to support them while they remain so long in school.

The committee was formed by the National Education Association (NEA) and led by Charles Eliot, president of Harvard College, to examine the articulation of the programs of study in high school with the admissions requirements in college (National Education Association, 1894). To this point, each college required a battery of admissions tests for each prospective student, and the expectation was that each student would come to college with a basic familiarity with the classical academic disciplines. Most colleges tested students in the same common subjects, but they developed their own exams and set different thresholds for admission.

The 10-member committee focused on the following nine subjects common to many high schools of the day that fed students into colleges and most college admissions: (a) Latin; (b) Greek; (c) English; (d) modern languages; (e) mathematics; (f) physics, astronomy, and chemistry; (g) natural history; (h) history, civil government, and political economy; and (i) geography. A subcommittee was convened for each discipline to explore what should be taught, when it should begin, how many hours should be recommended, whether it should be differentiated by students, and how it should be taught (Leonard, 1953).

The Committee of Ten made two important contributions to our thinking about the alignment of high schools and colleges. First, it established the principle of uniformity, meaning that educators should develop a common set of standards for what constitutes high school level work and what is reasonable to expect of entering college students. The Committee took a modest first step by promoting the curricular paths identified above, but it opened the door for future conversations about how best to align these two systems. Second, it introduced the notion of elective courses. Eliot was an early advocate of allowing electives in the curriculum, but the recommendations on this point were modest.

Two years after the Committee of Ten report, the NEA convened a follow-up group to look specifically at college entrance requirements

(Wechsler, 2001). The Committee on College Entrance Requirements was far less widely regarded than the Committee of Ten, but it continued an important conversation about the development of a uniform standard for high schools and colleges. David Starr Jordan (1904) suggested colleges should adapt to the high school because schools are constrained by size and they serve a much larger population that has no intention to go to college. The University of Michigan, by 1870, was already wrestling with the issue of college admission and its relation to the high school curriculum and, under the leadership of President James Angell, created the first high school certification program in the country (Wechsler, 2001). Angell recognized that high schools offered a wide array of curricula even within the state and suggested that instead of requiring an admissions test—for which students may or may not be prepared—the university would accredit high schools. University examiners visited schools, examined the curriculum and, if qualified, granted formal accreditation by the University of Michigan, meaning that any student who completed the approved set of high school requirements would be admitted to the university without need for an entrance examination (Conley, 1995).

The North Central Association of Colleges and Secondary Schools, following the recommendations of the Committee on College Entrance Requirements, expanded upon the Michigan model, establishing standards for high school certification and college admission among all members of the association. New England colleges did not support the certification option, but they too felt the need for uniformity in their admissions requirements. Eliot supported greater uniformity but was not inclined toward the accreditation system. The Association of Colleges and Secondary Schools of the Middle Atlantic States met subsequent to the report on entrance requirements and suggested the creation of a joint board of examiners (Lazerson, 2001). In 1900 The College Board was formed under the leadership of Nicolas Murray Butler, president of Columbia University (Rudolph, 1962), and by 1901, the first round of exams were offered in the nine subject areas.

Both the accreditation system and the joint board of examiners were the result of a recognized need for uniformity in high school curricular requirements and college admissions standards, but the two offered different advantages. The accreditation system provided high schools with greater latitude to set their curriculum within certain parameters, if they saw themselves preparing students for college. Coordination within the region saved colleges both time and energy by eliminating the need for entrance exams. The College Board approach benefited colleges to a greater degree because their only substantive sacrifice was the content of the examinations. The College Board offered examinations in the nine core subjects, and each college chose which subjects to require and what score constituted acceptance to the institution (Hall, 1901). The challenge for proponents of a more "practical" curriculum was that The College Board approach did not leave open the door for alternative course work to count for college admission as easily as the accreditation system had.

The Comprehensive High School and the Development of AP Courses

The early roots of the American high school may be partly influenced by the work of the Committee of Ten, but as Angus and Mirel (1999) point out, the Cardinal Principles of Secondary Education, issued more than 20 years later, may have been more influential on the range of curricular offerings developed in public secondary schools. The principles established by the Commission on the Reorganization of Secondary Education represented a near-complete departure from the curricular emphasis of the 1894 report. Where the Committee of Ten articulated a series of course offerings recommended for all secondary students, irrespective of their future paths in life, the Cardinal Principles avoided prescribing curricular offerings and instead emphasized broader purposes including health, vocation, citizenship, and ethical character development (Commission on the Reorganization of Secondary Education, 1918). Instead of suggesting a more uniform curriculum for all, the Cardinal Principles allowed for schools to exercise greater discretion in terms of how they set out to achieve these broader principles.

The Comprehensive High School. The comprehensive high school has been considered perhaps the first uniquely American K12 educational institution (Conant, 1959; Krug, 1964; Wraga, 1994). It grew out of the progressive era and vocational education movements in the United States and took several decades to evolve. James Conant, former president of Harvard University, was an advocate of the comprehensive high school, and Wraga (1994) suggested that Conant's advocacy of the comprehensive school came just in time, as the comprehensive model would come under attack in subsequent efforts for reform. The comprehensive school remains the dominant secondary institution today, but many have called for strong efforts for reform, including the elimination of tracks (Oakes, 1992) and a more rigorous, uniform curriculum for all (American Diploma Project, 2002).

James Conant's comprehensive high school was an outgrowth of the vocational emphasis of the progressive period but might also be understood in the context of two important events that have shaped the relationship between high schools and colleges. The first was the creation of the Advanced Placement (AP) courses and examinations to eliminate overlap between the last two years of high school and the first two years of college. The AP program has become a signal of high school quality and an important benchmark in the college application process (Sadler, Sonnert, Tai, & Klopfenstein, 2010). Unfortunately, it has also given rise to greater disparities in educational offerings across schools and districts. The second was the proliferation of the comprehensive high school. In reality, the comprehensive school was an outgrowth of the earlier progressive era and the subsequent compromise among reformers and the fiscal realities of communities. The democratic ideal was to bring together courses spanning the range of human knowledge to expose students to as many curricular opportunities as possible, hoping that each student would find his or her set of interests while advancing toward a vocational path.

The 7-Year Plan and the Creation of AP. In 1951, educators at Harvard, Yale, and Princeton met with their preparatory school colleagues at Philips Exeter, Phillips Andover, and Lawrenceville to rethink the high-school-to-college transition (Blackmer et al., 1952). In their view, the overlapping curriculum from feeder schools to these elite private colleges led to two important problems, particularly for high achieving students: (a) waste for students exposed to the same material twice and (b) boredom for some students because the material did not adequately appeal to and challenge their intellects. They conducted interviews of former prep school students who enrolled at Harvard, Yale, and Princeton regarding their experiences in high school and college. Based upon this study, the committee proposed a 7-year plan to eliminate overlap for the best and brightest students. The cornerstone was the creation of a series of tests designed to place high-ability students into more advanced college coursework. Successful completion would place a high school student out of that requirement in college, thus eliminating as much as one year of college-level work. The "advanced placement" tests were later created by The College Board (Lazerson, 2001) and have become both a symbol of high school quality and of student academic preparation and achievement. The committee recommended that the AP tests be used solely for the placement of students into the appropriate level of college work (Blackmer et al., 1952), but today AP makes a significant difference, both in the college admission process and in terms of earning credit in high school for college level work. This is an important development because elite colleges demonstrated a stronger commitment to the rigorous academic core, which was less prominent in public comprehensive schools. If attending an elite college confers greater benefits and fewer public institutions provide the necessary preparation, then postsecondary access will be limited to certain groups, notably families with high socio-economic status who are able to pay for private secondary education.

P16 Alignment Today

Our current emphasis on aligning high schools and colleges stems from the early 1980s when considerable attention was paid to the perceived poor quality of the high school curriculum. The National Commission on Excellence in Education (1983) examined the state of education in the United States with particular attention toward the high school. Its members concluded that the high school curriculum was emblematic of a "rising tide of mediocrity" and that all students should have access to what they referred to as the "new basics," including four years of English; three years of math, social studies, and science; a half year in computer science; and coursework in a foreign language. The report focused on the expectations we have for students and the quality of teaching in schools and suggested we needed to expect more of both teachers and students.

One of the seminal works during that period was Powell, Farrar, and Cohen's (1985) *Shopping Mall High School*. They conducted a national study of high schools in the United States and found the curriculum of the comprehensive high school had become a collection of boutique courses, much like the small specialty stores one might find in a shopping mall, where all students could find something to their liking, irrespective of whether those courses prepared them for either career or college. The schools they observed were large, multifaceted institutions that lacked a coherent curricular plan that allowed many students to choose a path with low expectations and that left many students ill prepared for either college or the workforce.

Since the National Commission on Excellence in Education's *A Nation at Risk* in the early 1980s, state-level course requirement policies have changed dramatically. In 1980, 13 states had no formal high school graduation requirements, leaving those decisions to local districts (National Center for Education Statistics, 1996). By 1992, 41 states had either adopted minimum course requirements for high school graduation or had increased the numbers of credits required in the core subjects of English, math, science, social studies, and foreign languages (National Center for Education Statistics, 1996). In 2010, only five states maintained local control over the high school graduation requirement policies, and most states had raised their requirements over time (Cavell, Blank, Toye, & Williams, 2005; Council of Chief State School Officers, 2008).

In the past decade, states have shifted toward establishing minimum levels of rigor in math and science in addition to specifying the number of courses. In 1992, only three states required at least one science course with a laboratory component and none specified the highest level of math (National Center for Education Statistics, 1996). By 2004, 23 states required a biological science, physical science course, or both—and 17 states required at least Algebra I (seven of which were above that bar). The 2006 national commission to chart a course for the future of American higher education (U.S. Department of Education, 2006a) reinforced this linkage in its report to Secretary of Education Margaret Spellings. According to the commission,

. . . access to American higher education is unduly limited by the complex interplay of inadequate preparation, lack of information about college opportunities, and persistent financial barriers. Sub-standard high school preparation is compounded by poor alignment between high schools and colleges, which often creates an "expectations gap" between what colleges require and what high schools produce. (U.S. Department of Education, 2006b, p. 1)

Inadequate and substandard preparation suggests either that we have not made much progress since the early 1980s or that the standards have changed. The commission reinforces the growing belief that at least part of the problem is that students are not well informed—a consequence of the fact that high schools and colleges are not well aligned and the signals they send to students can be confusing or inconsistent.

Conclusion

The arguments for stronger alignment of K12 schools and institutions of higher education are appealing because they resonate with what students, parents, and educators feel. If we could simply compel high schools and colleges to work more seamlessly together, we could go a long way toward providing better information, clearer expectations, and stronger incentives to participate and succeed in college. However, we cannot forget that these two systems evolved in very different ways and for equally different purposes. The fact that societal expectations have converged does not compensate for the centuries of history that surround these systems. Perhaps the more important lesson from an alignment perspective is that both systems are incredibly heterogeneous and complex. In public primary and secondary education, schooling is organized by districts and schools, where within any given school students are grouped according to their ability and taught in differentiated ways—for some, this practice constitutes meeting students where they are and helping them to develop to the best of their potential and at their own pace, given their abilities and ambitions. To others, the practice of tracking students by ability serves to reproduce existing inequalities in society. In large urban districts, students are similarly sorted, though economies of scale have led to the sorting of ability by schools rather than by classes or building-level tracks. Instead of an honors track in a single comprehensive high school, large urban districts may have one or more magnet schools that test students for admission and another set of schools designated for vocational and technical programs. Institutional diversity can be found in distinctions between private schools—either religious or secular—and the growing selection of charter schools. The very best private schools are able to provide a level of education that exceeds what the average public school can offer, but they do so with considerable expense to families. Other private institutions, particularly those serving students in low-income communities and communities of color, may provide a similar level of education as their public peers but deliver it in ways that reflect the unique values informing its mission and vision. Advocates of charter schools emphasize the ability to experiment with alternative strategies to deliver education, but critics remind us that charters reallocate already scarce resources away from traditional public schools while many of those students will end up back at the public school.

In postsecondary education, students are similarly sorted, but that occurs more regularly across institutional sectors. Community colleges continue to serve vocational needs in line with the Career Technical Education (CTE) tracks in high school, but they also provide general education for transfer to 4-year institutions. Four-year colleges are sorted by prestige, which is a function of the proportion of applicants they admit, the academic profile of their incoming students, and the resources the institutions have at their disposal, including the quality of the faculty. Large research universities offer curricular programs in the professions (including engineering, pharmacy, and the health sciences) as well as the humanities and liberal arts. Small, private, liberal arts colleges provide an education reminiscent of the curriculum defended by the Yale faculty nearly 200 years ago—the courses are different, but the implied learning theory is the same. And the highly selective public flagship universities and elite private colleges continue to serve the very best-prepared students, with the clearest educational goals and the greatest advantages coming out of high school.

When we consider the high degree of institutional heterogeneity and diversity at both the secondary and postsecondary levels, we begin to see how difficult it is, in practice, to find a meaningful way to align systems. There is no simple way to identify a single standard in high school that will prepare students well for a single point of entry into college. When alignment occurs, it is most frequently between the colleges and their feeder schools. This has been the historic pattern, and it is difficult to imagine how this might change. In the absence of an alternative, we suggest that in order to improve access, we need to achieve the goals of alignment by empowering professionals operating at the intersection of the two systems to make the transition appear seamless. Admissions professionals play a key role in that intersection, though they can only be effective in partnership with school counselors working with students in the school setting, pre-college outreach service providers who are working directly with students in high-need and low-performing districts, and the growing network of independent consultants working to help students and families navigate the process and match with the best institutions they can at the price they can afford. When all of these groups work effectively together, we argue that we can make great strides toward achieving the goals of alignment, even in the absence of bringing the two systems more closely in line. The next chapter examines the roles each of these professionals play. We expect that stronger collaboration will result in better alignment from the perspective of students and their families—and that begins by developing a shared understanding of the roles of key partners.

3

UNDERSTANDING THE ROLES OF ADMISSIONS AND COLLEGE ACCESS PROFESSIONALS

College admissions professionals operate as part of a larger network of college access professionals. As such they should develop a clear sense of their roles in relation to the roles their counterparts play. We identify three key groups of college access professionals that work in complementary ways to admissions professionals—high school counselors, pre-college outreach providers, and independent consultants. All of these professionals understand the complexities of navigating the transition from high school to college, but they operate with different perspectives, roles, and responsibilities, while responding to different incentives and priorities. Frequently, they come from different backgrounds and experiences, and they leverage different assets and strengths to help students along the way. With some exceptions, these groups of professionals do not fully understand the roles and responsibilities of the others; they may make assumptions regarding how best to assist students through the transition; and at times, they may be distrustful of one another or at least ambivalent about the potential contributions of each. As a consequence, many college admissions professionals are underinformed about the roles and responsibilities of the others, which creates barriers preventing these groups from working effectively with their college access counterparts.

We believe admissions professionals, particularly those who spend a good deal of their time traveling and visiting schools, have an opportunity to help bridge the gaps in the network because they provide what the other professionals seek—seats for their students. School counselors, pre-college outreach providers, and, to a certain extent, independent consultants rely on admissions professionals for their knowledge and insights about the college choice, admissions, and decision processes. Whether they recognize it or not, admissions staff members also possess a key piece of information that students, parents, and other professionals need—knowledge about succeeding in college. Admissions professionals are situated on their respective campuses, they are a part of the institutional culture, and they are connected to many of the functions on campus responsible for students' success once they arrive. In years past, it may have been possible for admissions professionals to ignore what happens to students once they accept an offer and enroll at the institution, but increasingly admissions is viewed as part of a larger enrollment management apparatus in which these professionals are asked to think about how students transition into, through, and out of the institution. Many admissions professionals, particularly those more seasoned in the field, understand and appreciate that students and parents want this sort of information, but admissions staff only have direct contact with a small fraction of students at any given school, so the number of students who gain access to these insights is relatively few. For this reason, it is more important that admissions professionals view it as part of their professional responsibilities to develop a more thorough understanding of what it takes to succeed in college and to convey that information to school counselors, pre-college outreach providers, and independent consultants. We return to this issue in Chapter 8.

The remainder of this chapter describes the roles, responsibilities, and expectations of each of these four groups of professionals. We build from our earlier analogy in real estate and the incentives to which each group responds, and we speak more directly to the full range of roles, responsibilities, incentives, and pressures that influence and inform their work. We begin with admissions professionals, followed by school counselors because, when we think of who is responsible for helping students and their families navigate the college choice process, these are the two groups that immediately come to mind. We follow with a discussion of two additional professional groups: (a) pre-college outreach programs serving predominantly low-income, high-need, urban school districts with a large proportion of underrepresented minority students and (b) independent consultants who work most commonly with students at the other end of the income distribution—though the lines have been blurred between the two in recent years. Throughout, we infuse the voices of professionals in all four sectors to illuminate the roles and responsibilities they assume and more importantly, how they understand the roles of others. We believe the voices from the field add texture to our descriptions. In total, we have spoken to more than 25 professionals working across the four disciplines. We have spoken with professionals from a range of different institutional types and experiences—from urban and rural schools to community colleges and selective private postsecondary institutions. We do not suggest, however, that their experiences are representative in the sense that they generalize to all college access professionals or across all regions or every state—we will leave that to others to judge. Based upon our experience working with these professionals both locally and nationally, we are confident their voices represent the range of perspectives we have heard, though we acknowledge there may be others. As such, we see this as a starting point in the conversation among college admissions professionals and the array of college access professionals.

College Admissions Professionals

Admissions professionals operate at the intersection of high schools and colleges, and they serve both as promoters and as gatekeepers for their respective institutions. On the one hand, it is in the best interest of all colleges and universities if more high school graduates plan to attend college, so promoting the benefits of college is as valuable as touting the specific advantages of one's specific institution. On the other hand, the admissions staff is responsible for crafting the incoming class with a specific set of priorities in mind—ranging from a simple determination of one's opportunity to filling an honors program or admitting top artists, athletes, or children of alumni. No matter how we understand the role, the college admissions apparatus across the country serves as a great sorting mechanism for students, distributing opportunity throughout postsecondary education (Stewart, 1998).

Admissions professionals, unlike school counselors or other licensed professionals, do not have standardized licensure or specialized degree programs. Frequently, colleges and universities hire recent graduates or alumni, often based on personality, a love of the institution, or a more general commitment to undergraduate education. New admissions professionals spend a good deal of their time traveling throughout most of the fall semester, visiting schools and admissions fairs along the way. During the spring, they travel less, mostly to fairs, and focus on reading applications, making decisions, extending offers of admission, managing yield, and ultimately building the class for the subsequent fall. Similar to other new student affairs professionals, entry-level admissions staff experience high turnover rates as a consequence of long hours and extended travel, living out of rental cars, airports, and hotels for nearly a third of any given year (Holmes, Verrier, & Chisholm, 1983).

New admissions professionals are frequently hired for their enthusiasm for the institution and, in many cases, are only one step removed from their own undergraduate experience. The admissions professionals we spoke to had commonly served as tour guides or student ambassadors as undergraduate students and had established relationships either with the campus or external community. While there was no single academic path to admissions work, education, psychology, communication, or related social sciences were mentioned most frequently. Swann (1998) suggests that admissions offices also seek out math and statistics backgrounds for new counselors, but priority is typically given to those who are effective at speaking publicly to an audience. Admissions professionals who make the transition to middle management typically require a different skill set, with an emphasis on data analysis or integrative technologies, and frequently report earning a graduate degree in higher education administration, school counseling, school psychology, student affairs, or student personnel (Hodum & James, 2010).

In our conversations with admissions professionals, we found three groups of professionals: rookie road warriors, mid-career, and lifers. Rookies (first 3–4 years in the field) were typically right out of their undergraduate institution; they had no graduate degree and frequently expected to stay in admissions for only a few years. Mid-career professionals typically had 5–7 years of experience in admissions, may have been working on a graduate degree, and enjoyed their work but had considered career changes as years of travel had taken its toll. The "lifers," as Swann refers to them (Swann, 1998), had dedicated their careers to admissions and had experience ranging from 7–40 years in the field. When we asked about this distinction, one mid-career professional remarked:

> [W]e just hired two fresh (admissions counselors) out of college who literally are the workhorses who will jump on any opportunity needed, who are very driven. You see them walking down the halls and they are just full of confidence and dynamite and whatever else. And then I'm sitting back, having been there for a while and going through the motions of life and I'm just not so . . . I'm still excited but I'm not as excitable.

Admissions professionals are expected to answer hundreds of specific questions about their institutions, demonstrate a passing knowledge of every function and feature of their college or university, and to help students, parents, and other college access professionals understand and navigate the entire college going process. They serve variously as sales representatives, cheerleaders, party planners, talent evaluators, and ultimately gatekeepers to their institution. Several of the professionals we interviewed discussed the ways in which they learned to do their job, and most didn't start out with a formalized set of training. One road warrior noted that "there is no book. I just think it is common sense and also we've already been through the process ourselves in many different ways. . . ." Common sense is certainly helpful for any college admissions professional, but we have found that those who excel report some help along the way from strong mentors along their career and display a unique sense of personal agency and responsibility that frees them to take an active role seeking out the information they need to be successful in the field. One new admissions counselor noted,

> . . . I think teaching yourself is really important because that's the best way to absorb the knowledge. You can sit and listen to someone talk at you, which is how I learned about each of our programs for 8 hours a day for 2 days. I sat in my boss's office and he talked at me. He would get up every hour to go refill his coffee cup and it was horrible.

Admissions counselors reported to us that in most cases, they are largely self-taught either through formally structured experiences or informal interactions. One of the interviewed counselors talked about listening at college fairs her first year to representatives from other schools to see how they would answer specific questions. One rookie counselor reported spending the first several months on the job listening to telephone conversations, sitting in on information sessions and attending college fairs with senior staff. A few of the more senior professionals and lifers focused in their interviews on how they spend time mentoring rookies early on in the process. Those we spoke with at all levels agreed that most training occurred on the job and that senior staff were instrumental in orienting new staff to the work of the profession. The other form of on-the-job training reported frequently by admissions professionals was annual meetings of professional associations like the National Association of College Admissions Counselors (NACAC) and its state affiliates. These conferences and professional meetings generally provide meaningful opportunities for the transmission of valuable information from one generation of admissions professionals to the next and for establishing a social network for a professional community that can otherwise experience a good deal of isolation on the road and in their offices reviewing files.

Today, admissions professionals serve as the public voice for the college within the community, across secondary schools, and to prospective students (Swann & Henderson, 1998). Admissions counselors have evolved to be interpreters of the college for those visiting campus (Swann, 1998), and they are responsible for communicating and distilling the core values and beliefs of an institution for prospective students, families, and other educational professionals. They provide a human perspective and contact for those external to a complex and highly bureaucratic organization (Stevens, 2009). Several recent authors have examined the admissions field in such works as *The Gatekeepers* by Jacques Steinberg and *Creating a Class* by Mitchel L. Stevens. Both attempt to chronicle a typical admissions cycle to better define how and why decisions about applicants are made. Admissions offices tend to be secretive by their nature, sheltering their admissions process from public scrutiny. This tendency to obfuscate the process can lead outsiders to view the admissions process as a "black box," where it is unclear how the inputs of applications are transformed into the enrollments of a freshmen class (Willingham & Breland, 1982).

Institutional Marketing and Promotion

The office of admissions is frequently one component of a much larger enrollment management apparatus (Jump, 2004). Demographic declines of high school age cohorts in the 1970s forced colleges and universities to examine not only how they attract and enroll students but also how they maintain those enrollments to successful completion of a college degree. Some have suggested that the title of admissions "counselor" may be a bit of a misnomer, particularly given the emphasis on marketing and promotion in enrollment management. One midlevel professional notes,

> I really thought the term admissions counselor would mean "counseling," and while it does half of the time, the other half of my year is spent promoting my school. At times it's a little irritating to have such a focus on sales and enrollment numbers because it's not ultimately what I went to school for, but I understand that it's a necessary evil and appreciate its importance to the college.

This intensely competitive marketplace for top students has caused colleges and universities to focus on the profile of their incoming class and their reputations among peer institutions, which can at times come at the expense of helping students and families make informed choices about their future college and career opportunities. A number of admissions professionals continue to operate as counselors, helping students make informed choices, consonant with their own interests, aptitudes, and preferences, irrespective of whether the student will attend their institution, but it can be difficult to maintain this professional stance in the face of increasing pressure to grow the quality and size of the institution's enrollment.

The admissions professional's job at most moderately selective nonprofit colleges is cyclical in nature, repeating either by the semester or on a yearly basis. The seasons are broken down into travel (fall), review (winter), yield (spring), and reporting (summer). The first season is based around the necessary requirement for admissions counselors to get out "on the road" and meet with students at college fairs and high school visits. Travel season typically lasts from the middle of September to early November, but can last for most of the fall depending on the type of institution. During a typical travel season, admissions counselors visit local high schools in their service regions and travel from city to city, meeting with prospective students. This time is ostensibly intended to meet with prospective students in high schools and to cultivate relationships with school counselors and their secretaries (Lautz, Hawkins, & Perez, 2005). A mid-career professional described it this way:

> The travel stuff, depending on a counselor; some of them live for it, others could leave it at the door. Myself, I like to travel if when I'm going into a school or a college fair, the individuals there respect me for what I do. I do not like to be seen a sales shark. That's not who I am and I don't like being perceived that way. So travel for me is a toss-up. Of course I like traveling, getting out of the office, that's awesome, but when it comes down to it, I want to be respected for what I do and appreciated for what I do.

In any given visit, counselors may meet with a handful of students, but they will frequently spend time with the counseling staff, providing them with information and insights from the campus. These relationships are critical to help prepare school counselors for their role in the college choice process, and they have the potential to make school counselors into advocates for one's institution. Travel is a necessity of the job, but it can become wearying the longer a professional spends in the field. Travel is often a reason cited by mid-career professionals we spoke with as being a reason they would love to stay in higher education but were unsure about their future in admissions. The experience may be different at other types of institutions.

The second season consists of reading applications, reviewing, and making admissions decisions. Each professional staff member spends countless hours reviewing student applications, examining transcripts, perusing letters of recommendation, evaluating standardized test scores, and assessing resumes and essays. This season culminates in admissions decisions, committee or consultative deliberations over "marginal" students, and the extension of offers to the prospective incoming class. The third season is committed to managing yield. Admissions counselors focus on formalizing relationships to persuade students to visit campus and enroll at their school. The final season brings that cycle to a close with the reporting process when the professional staff reflects on the past year and evaluates the year's performance. A popular adage, as one mid-level professional noted, is "if you don't like what you are doing in admissions, wait two weeks and you will be doing something else."

NACAC gathers information annually about the admissions profession through their State of College Admissions report (Clinedinst, Hurley, & Hawkins, 2012). While much of the focus of the report is on the admissions process, demographics, and counseling, they devote the last chapter to the analysis of admissions counselors' roles and responsibilities. Consistently they find differences between the roles and responsibilities reported by professionals in public and private institutions, particularly when it comes to workload and preparation. They also find differences in the level of selectivity of an institution—most notably that admissions officers in public schools read almost 2.5 times the number of applications of their private school counterparts (Clinedinst, Hurley, & Hawkins, 2011; Clinedinst et al., 2012). Also, public schools were more likely to want their counselors to hold an advanced or graduate degree.

Relationship Development

Admissions professionals spend a considerable amount of time developing and maintaining relationships throughout the admissions cycle. While most admissions counselors work with students between 15 and 18 years old, some specific programs start working with students earlier in their academic career.

These relationships often start with a visit to campus, the student's high school, or at a college fair. The process of enrolling a student can be separate from enrolling a class during a given year, given that it may take two or three years of building a relationship with a student while maintaining focus on enrolling this year's class (Mahoney, 2001). As such, admissions professionals must take a longer view of the time they spend in schools and with students, particularly when speaking with younger students prior to the senior year. For students, this is a formative time, even though they are not actively engaged in the college choice process. They begin to form what marketing research refers to as a consideration set that will become more formalized once students begin to engage in the choice process in 10th or 11th grade (Dawes & Brown, 2005).

While many of these relationships develop between the student and the admissions professional indirectly through school counselors, it has become increasingly important to develop these relationships with the parents or guardians as well. Many of the professionals interviewed expressed that it is no longer a rarity to interact with parents early in the process. Regular and consistent interactions are easier for those who work in white-collar professions since they typically have a greater ability to call colleges or email during work hours. One mid-level professional noted that "developing relationships with parents is becoming an ever increasing part of the admissions professional's roles."

One of the most important relationships for admissions professionals is with the school counseling community. It can take several years of building these relationships before it is possible to understand or appreciate what motivates each school counselor and how to engage in meaningful interactions over a brief amount of time. But these relationships are crucial when determining the potential success of future students, and schools or programs with either higher than average counselor turnover or infrequent visits from admissions staff can be at a disadvantage. One admission professional remarked, "[T]hey know their students better than I do, they have been with them sometimes for 3–4 years. So it is important to get their perspective on if this student will be a good fit." This is especially true in areas considered to be feeder primary markets. In order for these relationships to work well, they must be mutually beneficial, and for school counselors the primary benefit is access to information. Admissions professionals know the application and decision processes, and they help school counselors understand the process so they can better serve their students.

Disseminating Information

For the most part, colleges and universities have separated their admissions and financial aid processes. Colleges make an effort to train and cross-train, but the populations who are employed in both have different skills. One professional noted,

Financial aid is a very touchy and complicated subject in a sense that everyone's situation is different. So once the student is starting explaining the situation, if I don't know . . . again I am not the type to mislead them into thinking that I know, just so that I can give them an answer. I want them to get the right service and the right answer. There is nothing worse than running around, "This person told me this, this person told me that." Hey listen, "I don't know, here is the contact I have. Here is somebody you can go speak to and this is somebody who can help you further."

Overall, admissions professionals are more knowledgeable about financial aid than other college access professionals, but they admit that they heavily rely on their own offices to handle that part of the enrollment process across all the institutional types. We discuss financial aid in greater detail in Chapter 5.

Admissions Professionals' Role in College Access

One of the more interesting points that were discussed in formal and informal interviews was the difference between the message that a college espouses from the top-level administrator and the message from the admissions professional in the field. Interviewees said things like "my dean would answer this different" or "my director would say" in regards to competition and ultimately helping a student make the best decision for their education. The counselors were overwhelmingly concerned with just getting a student to college; one professional commented, "I have no problem referring to another admission rep because it is also a fact that we all want them to go to college, [the] same goal." For those within a system like SUNY, admissions counselors have greater latitude, although they will still be expected to promote the system. Directors, deans, and other chief enrollment professionals are often concerned with the ways in which they are inherently better than their competition. One admissions counselor stated, "[I tell students] I will help you through this entire process, my school may or may not be for you, but if I help make the entire process easier for you then I've done my job." Most admissions professionals are aware of the competing pressures in making their class any given year, but they insulate prospective students and parents from the same message.

Admissions professionals continually strike a balance between serving as institutional marketers and advocates for college access. The counselors we spoke with were not explicit about this tension, but they clearly embrace both roles. Some of the admissions professionals in our interviews expressed a desire to be more of a counselor and less of a sales associate. They experience firsthand how little knowledge many students possess about the college choice process, and they want to help students make informed decisions—as any good counselor would do. But they recognize that their role as marketer forces them to focus more on what is best for the institution than for the prospective student. We recognize the existence of this dichotomy, but we think it has been framed inappropriately as a zero-sum game. In fact, we believe it is both in the student's and in the institution's best interests to provide more and better information to students and parents, even when that means diverting students to other institutions that may be a better fit.

School Counselors

School counselors operate in a highly structured and regulated work environment. They wear a number of hats within a given school, and they are increasingly asked to do more with less. The 21st-century school counselor is asked to perform a number of roles from individual personal counseling and career and postsecondary planning to academic scheduling and certification for graduation. According to the American School Counselor Association (ASCA),

> Professional school counselors are certified/licensed educators with a minimum of a master's degree in school counseling making them uniquely qualified to address all students' academic, personal/social and career development needs by designing, implementing, evaluating and enhancing a comprehensive school counseling program that promotes and enhances student success. (ASCA, 2013)

In addition to these broadly defined student-based responsibilities, school counselors are increasingly asked to assume leadership roles among the administrative staff, design curriculum, and manage public relations for the school. High school counselors have been asked to assume an increasing number and variety of responsibilities in schools, ranging from scheduling, testing, and discipline to behavior management, social work, mental health counseling, and college counseling, and each school has slightly different expectations (House & Martin, 1998). In this section, we highlight the role of the high school counselor in relation to the college choice process and the relationship with other college access professionals. It is important to recognize that college counseling is one piece of the school counselor's role, but it would be difficult to discuss the full range of roles and responsibilities in the space we have available. College counseling is a particularly important dimension of the high school counselor role because nearly 30% of high school counselors report spending the greatest portion of their time on college and career readiness (Clinedinst et al., 2012). One school counselor echoed this sentiment: "I would say when I am doing my seniors I will spend probably 60–70% of my day doing college admissions." We outline four key counselor roles that pertain directly to helping students manage

44

the transition from high school to college or career—student development, administrative support for the college-going process, college and career readiness counseling, and academic planning.

Student Development

School counselors spend a good portion of their time involved in the personal and social development of their students (Schimmel, 2008). Training for this facet of the job is the primary focus of the majority of the graduate school counselor education programs across the nation, and it is critical in terms of helping students make effective transitions to college or the workforce. It is also an extension of the mental health counseling model, which is prevalent among school counselor preparation programs. Personal counseling is often a time-consuming practice that seems to be more prevalent at the middle school level, where adolescent development is crucial. At the high school level, students need more academic counseling and support as they begin to focus on graduation and postsecondary education, but they continue to struggle with developmental milestones as they become increasingly autonomous and independent. Career development, which is a subset of personal counseling, is an overarching theme of any school counseling program because both school districts and parents want students to have a plan for life after high school. Developing this plan can be a challenge for school counselors because they face competing pressures to promote college for all while also recognizing that vocational pathways may be more appropriate for many students. In low-performing districts, this tension is magnified because many students are at risk of not completing high school at all. In these schools, counselors will spend much more time focusing on high school completion, even with district pressures to improve college-going rates.

Administrative Support for the College Choice Process

Counselors frequently manage multiple facets of the college choice process for their students, which can be incredibly time consuming. School counselors serving high proportions of low-income, first-generation, underrepresented minority students may spend a greater proportion of their time on these tasks because these students rely more heavily on counselors for this type of support than do their middle-class peers. The most time-consuming administrative responsibilities for school counselors in the college choice process are processing student transcript requests, completing student recommendations, administering college admissions test participation, and in many cases, assisting students with the college search and application. In a number of schools, we have also found counselors spend a good deal of time helping students and their families complete the Free Application for Federal Student Aid (FAFSA).

School counselors in affluent districts act as a resource for students and parents but traditionally have minimal involvement with searches and financial aid (Savitz-Romer, 2008). Quite often, these districts employ administrative staff to manage transcripts, SAT/ACT registrations, college applications, and programming for families on their role in the process. School counselors in first-ring urban suburbs and inner-city schools are frequently expected to provide more direct support for students filling out college applications and federal and state financial aid forms. As one public school counselor in a large urban district acknowledged, "I will sit on the computer with them and help them fill out the application. I would say 95% of my students I am doing that with them." The same counselor also said, ". . . kids will bring all their financial papers from their parents, they hand a folder to me and say, 'Here, can you help me do this?'" The degree to which counselors are involved directly in the administration of the college choice process depends largely upon whom they serve, and they do so in different ways. Counselors serving low-income families in high-need districts may assume more responsibility for college applications and the financial aid process, whereas those in more affluent districts will spend a greater proportion of their time providing students and families the information they need to navigate the process.

College and Career Readiness

In a report on the role of school counselors, the ASCA (2007) identifies 190 competencies for the profession, four of which pertain specifically to counselors' roles in the transition from high school to postsecondary education:

- Counselors expect that every student should graduate from high school and be prepared for employment or college and other postsecondary education.
- Counselors will have the knowledge to deliver principles of career planning and college admissions, including financial aid and athletic eligibility.
- Counselors will have the skills and abilities to develop strategies to implement individual student planning, such as strategies for appraisal, advisement, goal setting, decision making, social skills, transition, or postsecondary planning.
- Counselors will have the abilities and skills to help students learn the importance of college and other postsecondary education and help students navigate the college admissions process.

Clearly, school counselors are expected to help students plan and prepare for the possible transition from high school to college. However, it is also evident that college and career readiness plays a relatively minor role in the full set of expectations placed upon counselors. Only 5% of outcomes related to student standards reflected the importance of college counseling in their experience, and an even smaller proportion of measurable counselor competencies spoke directly to their ability to help students plan for post-secondary options.

Currently, unlike their private school counterparts, public school counselors are not accountable for postsecondary plans or participation. They will certify that a student has met all the state and local requirements for graduation, but they are not required to ensure that students have a plan after graduation, even though the ASCA does list that as a guideline national standard (ASCA, 2004). One of the critical, though less explicit, roles of school counselors is to create a college-going culture. A school counselor with fewer than 100 seniors who actively interacts with college admission personnel will find great satisfaction in reporting a high college-going rate to the district board of education, and more importantly, to the parents of these students. This high percentage of college-bound students indicates the school has a college-going culture, and parents are partners in helping their sons and daughters navigate the college choice process. In these environments, campus visits are encouraged and supported; regional information programs are provided; college representatives are invited guests at college night programs; college fairs include all the interested students from the high school; and a college and career center is maintained by the school counseling staff. It is likely that school counselors in these districts have developed professional relationships with the other college access professionals, but particularly with college admissions staff.

These districts are increasingly the exception rather than the rule. Too many counselors today are assigned many more students than they can reasonably serve through the college choice process. Estimates from 2011 suggest that the average student-to-counselor ratio in high schools is approximately 400:1, leaving very little time for counselors to meet all students' needs in the process (Clinedinst et al., 2012). Student-to-counselor ratios are not the only challenge. Most school counselors have not been formally trained in college counseling, at least through their graduate school counseling programs. Students and parents expect school counselors to be well versed in the college admissions process, but in truth they learn the process on the job as much as admissions counselors, and they depend on an apprenticeship relationship with more experienced colleagues (Matthay, 1992). With so many identified roles and competencies, it would be impossible for any single preparation program to train counselors in all aspects of their roles. One private high school counselor quipped, about the preparation for the role, that there is "0% percent formal training, 100% on the job training." This is a response we heard echoed throughout our conversations with school counselors.

Academic Planning

The academic planning role is an important part of assisting students in navigating the college and career planning process, and it begins for high school counselors the moment students enter ninth grade. Many school counselors dread the administrative dimensions of their job—particularly scheduling. Indeed, in some districts the school counselor is responsible for student schedules and the entire building master schedule. Student scheduling is a time-consuming (21.7%) part of a school counselor's job (Clinedinst et al., 2012), but it is the most tangible contribution many counselors make to helping students become academically prepared for college. In Chapter 4 of this text we discuss academic preparation in greater detail, but the role of the school counselor in this process cannot be overlooked or ignored. To the extent that school counselors function as gatekeepers, it happens through the academic planning process with students.

One of the very real challenges for school counselors is to help students develop an academic plan that will prepare them for life after high school. Some students will follow a path directly into the workforce, and their needs may be different than those who will go directly to college. For those students who plan to pursue a postsecondary education, each may face a different set of academic expectations. There are over 4,000 colleges in the United States and it would be difficult for any school counselor to know what each college expects. As a consequence, school counselors must rely on the relationships they develop with admissions professionals to know what colleges expect academically of their applicants. The most effective school counselors must be able to combine their training as counselors with an ability to effectively develop and sustain professional networks to access the information they need to help their students find the right academic path (Bridgeland & Bruce, 2011).

The school counselor is a vital link in the transition from high school to postsecondary education. The lack of a legislative mandate for school counselor positions in many states has made it difficult for districts to ensure that adequate support is available for students during these formative times. Career and college readiness is a feature of a school counselor's job that is fundamental to every student's achieving his or her potential and finding success. Ironically, as pressures to increase college-going rates among high school graduates rise, counselors are asked to assume more administrative responsibilities and are assigned many more students than they are able to serve well. Given the high student-to-counselor ratios today, schools will either need to double the number of school counselors placed in high schools or find alternative strategies to provide students and parents with the support they need to navigate the college choice process. This is where we believe pre-college outreach providers and independent consultants are poised to make important contributions for many students and their families.

Pre-College Outreach Providers

Unlike admissions professionals or school counselors, there is very little written to formalize the role pre-college outreach providers are expected to play. There are no national organizations representing their work, nor is there any formal certification, unless they come from other disciplines like school counseling or social work. The challenge, of course, is that there are a wide variety of models for these sorts of programs, ranging from the federally sponsored TRIO and GEAR UP programs to similar state-supported programs to smaller more targeted community based nonprofit organizations providing youth services. We talk about these programs in greater detail in Chapter 7. There are two key sources of information we draw upon in order to paint a portrait of the "typical" pre-college outreach provider. First, we examine calls for proposals from some of the major funding organizations for pre-college outreach. These calls typically provide some guidance regarding the expectations for the work of the program. Second, we draw upon our interviews with counselors and administrators in several pre-college outreach programs—all funded in different ways and with slightly different purposes. From these sources, we begin to build a profile of the pre-college outreach role.

Administrators

Pre-college outreach providers are, first and foremost, nonprofit managers. Most of the providers we spoke to did not define this as their primary role, but it clearly shapes how they work with students, schools, and other college access professionals. To a person, pre-college outreach providers were motivated to help students transition from high school to college. However, in order to work with students through these community- and university-based programs, all of these program staff assumed some responsibility for the management of the organization. The work of pre-college outreach providers is dictated by the regulations, terms, and conditions of those providing the resources (e.g. state or federal governments) and the approved grant application. The grant application serves as a contract and indicates what services will be provided to whom and in what ways. It also typically includes a set of intended outcomes that will determine whether the program has had its intended impacts. In our experience, these programs face a real crisis of purpose in many cases. On one hand, the staff want to serve those most in need who are willing to participate; on the other hand, high thresholds for performance create an incentive to cream only the top students who are already likely to succeed.

In Chapter 6 we talk about the importance of social capital and the value of a strong network, and many pre-college professionals report the importance of building and cultivating that network. Successful pre-college programs find ways to build those networks even when they are not always perceived as central to the process for many students. Admissions professionals know and come to appreciate the relationships they develop with school counselors because it may lead to increased enrollments from those schools. Equally school counselors recognize that admissions professionals provide knowledge and insight about a part of their role in which they are seldom trained. Those natural connections do not exist for pre-college outreach professionals, and as a result, some programs are more or less successful in developing their networks. Pre-college outreach providers are the one group of access professionals dedicated entirely to helping students navigate the transition from high school to college, but they depend upon counselors to attract students, and they rely on admissions professionals to create greater access to information for their students. As such, these professionals spend a good deal of time developing and managing relationships with schools and colleges.

The role very few pre-college programs are prepared to serve but that they are asked to play increasingly is that of data management and evaluation. These programs, like schools, are performance driven by funders and must report outputs and outcomes associated with their programs and activities. Depending upon the nature of the program, these organizations typically care about whether students are better informed about the college choice process, whether they are academically prepared to attend, and whether they attend college or apply for financial aid. As we discussed in the first chapter, understanding the work of college access professionals requires that one understands how incentives work. In this case, the primary incentive is to meet targeted benchmarks. If a grant calls for 80% of all participants to graduate from high school, then the program will find ways to improve that measure, which may mean serving different students. One of the program directors we spoke to pointed out candidly that they receive a good deal of pressure to serve more students in fewer schools (very high-need high schools), but they are resistant because they are unsure whether they can achieve their stated outcomes if they focus on one or two high-need schools.

Educators

If you ask pre-college outreach staff, they see themselves as educators, complementing the work of schools by helping students prepare for the academic rigors of both high school and college. A number of programs operate effectively as supplemental education services for many high-need, low-performing schools. Persistently low-achieving schools are required to provide supplemental education services to their students, and pre-college outreach programs that focus on academic preparation are attractive to schools because the resources come from the external funder. Only one of the programs we spoke to was designed in this way, but all of the others designed their programs to provide some form of academic support. Commonly, these programs provide afterschool tutoring, which is either structured specifically by subject or is done less formally to allow students the flexibility to do whatever work they bring. Tutors typically range from college work–study students to current or retired teachers. College admissions test preparation is another area frequently mentioned in our conversations with pre-college outreach programs. Some programs either offer their own internally developed version of an SAT or ACT preparation program, or they contract with one of the larger test preparation companies. The testing agencies make many of their test prep materials available online for anyone to access.

In our estimation, the most comprehensive and intensive intervention many of these organizations provide is the summer intensive program. Not all programs provide a robust summer experience, and not all students have access to them because they are expensive to provide, but they are typically the most educational feature of a given program. During a 4-, 5-, or 6-week period, students will spend each weekday (or week if the program is residential) taking academic courses, learning about college and careers, and engaging in co-curricular activities. In a few cases, these programs also teach courses like "Man Up" and "Social Graces" that are designed to help students recognize and understand social norms, conventions, and expectations that are likely to inform students' experiences when they go to college.

Social Workers/Counselors

Many pre-college outreach programs employ either social workers or licensed school counselors because they realize their students are likely to face an array of challenges that must be addressed before they are ready to think about college and careers. They also acknowledge that school counselors do not always have the time they need to work individually with students in the ways they might prefer. In most cases, counselors in these organizations focus on academic counseling related to the college choice process, but it is difficult for them to separate mental health counseling, career guidance, and postsecondary opportunities. Students must sort through their entire array of experiences to make informed choices about whether or where to go to college, and pre-college outreach programs must be prepared to assist along each of these dimensions.

Where pre-college outreach program providers resemble social workers most is in their role as advocates for students. More than a few of our interviewees indicated the important role they play connecting students and parents to the resources they need. One provider illustrated the importance of this role, saying that ". . . trying to move within that bureaucracy is really tricky . . . and having those relationships with the people in the administration building can be really helpful [for students]." Pre-college outreach providers advocate for students as they apply to particular colleges, but they may also play a similar role as students contend with financial aid eligibility. The Free Application for Federal Student Aid (FAFSA) can be a real obstacle for many families, and in high-need school districts there may be a higher proportion of students who experience more complicated living arrangements than fit traditional definitions. The result is either that students find it difficult to complete their FAFSA or they run into problems with verification once the college receives their application. Pre-college outreach providers spend a good deal of their time helping students sort through this process.

Community Organizers

Pre-college outreach programs funded by state or federal grants have experienced many cuts in funding over the past decade. As a consequence, these programs have been asked to do more with less, and they are frequently seeking alternative sources of support. In order to identify those new resources or alternative strategies for serving the needs of students, they develop close relationships with community partners, schools, and local funders. In the process, they become part of the fabric of the community and frequently participate in broader conversations around healthy communities, urban revitalization, and neighborhood and school reform. The relationships they develop through their community organizing work are critical for creating opportunities for students, but they come at a price. Most of these programs have relatively small administrative structures, and this part of their work pulls directors and others into more of an external role, spending less time with students. For those receiving federal and state grants, staff typically become part of larger networks of professionals who themselves are called on to advocate for continued support of their funding to their local and state political leadership. It is not uncommon for programs to participate in advocacy days at the state capitol to remind lawmakers of the important contributions they make in their respective communities.

Trainers

Finally, pre-college outreach providers experience relatively high turnover rates among staff and, as a result, are constantly in the mode of providing training to new staff. Many of these programs attract new college graduates and others with little prior work experience, which means they assume responsibility both for training them in the substance of the work they will do with students and for socializing them as new professionals. At the same time, these organizations need to continue providing professional development opportunities to stay abreast of changes in the college choice process.

We do not have any empirical data to suggest the sort of background a typical pre-college outreach provider has, but our targeted interviews found that recent graduates of school counseling programs, social workers, and graduates of higher education administration programs were more common than other pathways. Many of the program staff we interviewed were themselves former participants in similar outreach programs. As such, many of them understood the goals of the program and understood how and why it worked, but they required more formal training to provide the information and support students and families need to navigate the college choice process.

These are the roles typically articulated by those working in pre-college outreach programs, and some of their work is constrained by the expectations established in the call for proposals from the funders. For example, GEAR UP (Gaining Early Awareness and Readiness for Undergraduate Programs) is designed to engage middle school students from high-need schools to improve their knowledge about college, increase their chances for high school graduation, and apply to college. It does not set expectations for instructional support. Talent Search provides an even narrower scope of activities and students, focusing specifically on low-income students from low-achieving schools who have demonstrated some potential to succeed in college. The range of encouraged activities focuses narrowly on navigating the college choice process. While programs are welcome to do more, federal guidelines dictate a per-pupil funding amount that makes it difficult to provide much beyond what is minimally required.

Independent Educational Consultants

The history of independents is based in an arena of need and opportunity, and it is essentially a story of market demand. Students and parents recognize that school counselors have little time to spend assisting students through the college choice process. At the same time, they are aware that the choice of college may be the most important financial decision they make, save the purchase of a home. Families forced to choose between leaving the college choice process to chance or hiring an expert to assist them through the process are increasingly choosing the latter. This sentiment was much less an indictment of school counselors than it was a statement about the expanding complexity of the college admission process and parents and students wanting more information and service.

The drive of more affluent families to achieve an Ivy League or highly selective college education for their children led to the beginning of a cottage industry of individuals who would provide supportive services outside of the school setting for a fee. Many of the original independents were retired educators or professionals in the financial planning sector seeking to expand their businesses. There was no regulation or specific training for these individuals, and they essentially operated on a personal trust basis with little or no structure as to what they did with students and families.

The rise of independent consultants is similar to the growth of the tax preparation industry. Many families choose to file their taxes on their own, and they can do so with a range of electronic tools or they can submit a paper filing. Some families receive free assistance from the IRS or community-based initiatives like the Voluntary Income Tax Assistance program. Others will hire a tax accountant or bring their taxes to a retail outlet like H&R Block to complete their taxes. A similar array of options has become available to assist families as they navigate the college choice process over the past several decades.

Today, the majority of independent consultants operate in metropolitan areas, although demand is growing in smaller urban centers, rural communities, and online in the virtual environment. As the demand for independent services has increased, more people have entered the field, and it has become difficult to know whether they have the knowledge or training to serve families well. Many of these individuals saw an opportunity to make money on the college admission and financial aid process and after some minimal research advertised and opened a business. In the 1980s mothers and fathers who went through the process with their own children decided they liked the process enough that they opened a consulting business. Students who went through the process and graduated from an Ivy League university felt they had enough firsthand information to assist high school students in the obtaining admission. Technology companies saw a large market for providing information about individual colleges and everything from college searches to campus tours. Today, the only check on the industry is the market, and while it still works with only a small proportion of those planning on attending college, the presence of independent consultants appears to be growing. In recognition of the growing concern among families about paying for college, banks and other financially related organizations from certified planners to fund managers began to offer services to students and parents through an independent arm of their respective companies. All of these peripheral businesses created a flood of information that was carefully marketed but could be confusing and sometimes inaccurate. Self-regulation and ethical practice to organize and rein in this trend were obviously necessary for continued growth and accountability.

In 1976, the Independent Educational Consultants Association (IECA) was chartered by a group of individuals concerned with the growing lack of professionalism in the industry. Membership in IECA required professional and experiential credentials and an agreement to subscribe to an ethical set of standards developed by the membership. In 1997, the Higher Education Consultants Association (HECA) was formed, again by a group of consultants seeking to provide an ethically based professional organization for the growing number of individuals helping families specifically with the college admissions process. By 2012, HECA has grown from a beginning membership of 38 to well over 600 members, serving about 12,000 students. Both IECA and HECA are aligned with the Statement of Principles of Good

Practice of the National Association for College Admission Counseling (NACAC), which is the source of a professional code of conduct for over 13,000 high school and college professionals involved in the transition to postsecondary education across America.

Role of the Independent Educational Consultant

Although independent consultants can work with students at virtually any grade level, they typically begin working with families during the junior year of high school. A typical consulting relationship begins with an evaluative intake to get to know the student personally and academically. This is often followed by a career inventory or professional assessment of career goals and personal interests. Armed with a possible career direction (or lack of one), the independent consultant helps students perform a college search and create a cross-section list of schools that appear to fit their credentials and interests. Independent consultants will typically use a web-based tool to work with students through the college search process, and they will generate a consideration set for families. The list of institutions is later refined, but it serves as a starting point for families to begin to visit college campuses. After visits are completed, families weigh additional information about individual institutions to pare down a final choice set. The summer after the junior year is a fertile time for the student to write essays and begin applications that are often reviewed for content and clarity by the consultant.

At the start of the senior year, a student will hopefully be in a solid position to formalize his or her consideration set into a more parsimonious choice set, consider options like Early Action and Early Decision, and post applications, all under the watchful eye of the consultant. Once applications and transcripts have been sent (through the school counseling office), the student and family maintain contact with the consultant by discussing basic financial aid and scholarships and comparing aid award packages as they arrive. If multiple acceptances are received, consultants assist families with the final decision and will terminate the relationship once a final choice is made. Specialized work with athletes, artists, and special need students has come to define niche markets in the industry. Referrals to other providers involved in test preparation, essay assistance, financial aid planning and form submission help, and even personal etiquette training is becoming commonplace. The role of the consultant then resembles that of a general contractor who develops the overall plan and identifies the appropriate partners to assist with various features of the choice process, depending upon the desires of each family.

In 1979, the assembly of the National Association for College Admission Counseling (NACAC) extended voting membership status to "individuals who are employed by institutions, agencies or organizations which provide counseling, admission or financial aid services and who are in agreement with the purposes of NACAC" (NACAC, 1979). This endorsement, only three years after the chartering of IECA, provided much-needed support and an ethical base for the educational consultant profession. Today, independent consultants are a well-established part of the college choice process for a growing number of students and families, and they are a part of the reality for admissions professionals who are recruiting these students.

Although the path to acceptance of educational consultants has been a rocky road at times, their place in the continuum of college admission has gradually been accepted and appreciated by the other college access professionals. There still seem to be pockets of residual resentment by some school counselors who feel their jobs are threatened by educational consultants working outside of the school with their students, even though counseling loads in high schools are far too high to be sustainable without some external influence. The independent educational consultant is now providing a large share of these services to a multiplicity of students and families, and school counselors have embraced the reality that they can have consultants work in parallel to their programs in a much needed supportive role.

For a small but growing number of students, the independent consultant plays a critical role, shaping students' perceptions of institutional choices and their eventual choice of institution. Frequently, individual consultants will often do a "stop in" at a college, and professional organizations like HECA promote, organize, and coordinate multiple college tours for their membership. When independents attend professional conferences, they are welcomed at college tables and events. NACAC and their state and regional affiliates now have independent consultants involved in all phases of their organization and sitting on their governing boards of directors.

The independent consultant has and continues to evolve into an important player in the college admission process for thousands of students and families. From a modest beginning working with more affluent families in metropolitan areas, independent consultants continue to assume more and more of the share of college admission counseling across the country, entering even smaller markets. Although the industry is relatively unregulated, professional organizations like IECA and HECA have organized consultants into a cohesive, ethically based group that provides a variety of services to students, colleges, and high schools, as well as professional development for their members. In terms of other admission professionals, as a group, however, they currently interact most directly with some college admission personnel, relatively infrequently with school counselors, and virtually not at all with pre-college outreach workers.

Suggestions for Admissions Professionals

As we have described in the introduction to this volume, the work of admissions counselors is informed by the work of others engaged as college access professionals. Each of these professional groups plays a particular role in helping students navigate the transition from high school to college or career, and they are influenced by a different set of incentives and priorities. The role of the admissions professional is shaped by the competing pressures to promote their institution and to counsel students and parents as they attempt to navigate the college choice process. In our view, admissions professionals are engaged in symbiotic relationships with school counselors, pre-college outreach providers, and independent consultants. All three of these groups are committed to helping students navigate the transition from high school to college, and they all have access to students in different ways. As we have described, the most valuable time admissions professionals spend on the road is talking with their college access peers in schools and community-based organizations. The first recommendation we make to admissions professionals, particularly those early in their careers, is to spend some time in high schools to see what students experience on a daily basis and to observe how school counselors do their work and what challenges they face as they help students complete the college search. Most admissions staff members spend a good deal of time in schools, but they are typically there to speak, not to listen. We believe both are critically important, but the strength of the relationship one has with a school may depend more on whether the school counselors believe that you know them and what their school has to offer.

Along the same lines, we recommend that admissions staff identify the pre-college outreach providers in their service areas and spend time learning about the work they do and the challenges they face. These programs can be tremendously influential for low-income, first-generation, and underrepresented minority students, and they benefit when students and schools perceive that these programs provide opportunities to connect students with colleges. Frequently, these programs operate on college campuses, and they may have a contact with someone in the admissions office at their home institution, but may have fewer linkages to other colleges and universities.

We strongly encourage admissions professionals to help their college access partners understand the decision-making black box in admissions. Typically, when these exchanges take place, they are in the context of professional meetings or informal gatherings of school counselors and admissions professionals, and they operate at a superficial level. We have found a negative relationship between transparency and selectivity, which is consistent with the earlier works by Steinberg (2002) and Stevens (2009). Simply put, community colleges are much clearer about their admissions expectations than selective 4-year colleges and universities. We suggest that admissions professionals should consider bringing school counselors in during the application review process to participate in committee meetings and to observe how decisions are actually made when not all students will be admitted to an institution. We are less optimistic that opening the black box is all that significant, but we do suggest that opening access to this process can help to produce higher levels of trust and a stronger foundation upon which to build. We also suggest that these gestures should extend beyond feeder institutions to include counselors working at low-performing schools, where access to college remains an open question.

Finally, we suggest that admissions professionals embrace the growing independent consultant industry. This group of professionals serves a small but growing subset of the college-going population, and they can be advocates depending upon their knowledge of and experience with a given institution. We recognize that independent consultants represent a fairly recent and still underexamined phenomenon in college access, and it may not be as simple to systematically partner with members of the profession, but as it grows, the independent consultant network may grow more influential in terms of advocating on behalf of students. In some ways, independents are the closest corollary to the buyer's agent in real estate, but with less information and a higher level of commitment to the client.

4

ACADEMIC PREPARATION

Admissions professionals are expected to enroll the most academically capable class they can while also meeting headcount projections. This is true at community colleges in much the same way as it is among more selective public and private colleges. The simple reality is that better-prepared students are more likely to achieve some measure of success, no matter where they choose to enroll. It is no surprise, of course, that for most admissions offices, the quality of applicants' secondary school experience—as approximated by their grades, test scores, and the strength of their curriculum—is the primary factor in many institutional admissions decisions. The challenge facing most institutions in the United States is that the pool of potential high school graduates is shrinking while competition for more capable students is increasing. As a result, institutions need to figure out new strategies to enroll the targeted number of students while also maintaining their academic profile. Enrollment managers also recognize that the stakes are higher to retain a greater proportion of their students through degree completion and to increase their enrollments of transfer students who have demonstrated some aptitude for college level work and who do not count toward the institution's academic profile.

The first cut in most admissions processes considers whether students in the pool meet minimum academic guidelines; anyone below a certain threshold will be denied admission—among community colleges this threshold is typically set at whether the student has the opportunity to benefit and whether he or she has earned a high school diploma or its equivalency. At the same time, a number of offices establish a different threshold, above which students are automatically admitted. The percentages of applicants in each category may vary, but in any case, the majority of admissions decisions are made before any other factors are actually considered. The group sent to committee typically includes the remaining proportion of "average" students who are academically admissible but may demonstrate a weakness in their essays, recommendations, or extracurricular involvement, or may not meet one of an array of institutional priorities. Each institution has a fairly well-established sense of the range of academically prepared students they accept in a given year, based upon historical trends in student enrollment patterns. This sort of forecasting helps admissions professionals systematically sort through the applicant pool, make admissions decisions, and manage institutional yield. When done well, these algorithms include the likelihood that a student will be successful once he or she arrives.

In order to help new college admissions professionals better understand the issue of academic preparation, we begin by examining trends in the ways educators and policy makers approximate whether students are prepared for college. Next we consider existing research on policies and practices intended to improve students' preparation for college. The final section considers current approaches and promising practices for improving students' academic preparation for college while in high school. It is critical that admissions professionals have a clear understanding of the dimensions of academic preparation and that they can communicate those standards to their college access partners, particularly with respect to what those standards mean for admission to their respective institutions.

Current Trends in Academic Preparation

Over the past 30 years, the connection between the high school curriculum and college admissions has been at the top of the national education policy agenda. In 1983, The College Board issued a series of reports indicating the curriculum that students should complete in the core academic subjects in order to be college ready. In that same year, the National Commission on Excellence in Education (1983) issued its final report to the nation decrying the "rising tide of mediocrity" in high schools. That report called for high schools to adopt the New Basics curriculum—four years of English as well as three years of math, science, and social studies.

Since 1983, states have slowly adopted—and in a number of cases surpassed—the New Basics expectations. In 1980, 13 states had no formal high school graduation requirements, leaving those decisions to local districts; by 1992, 41 states had either adopted minimum course requirements for high school graduation or had increased the numbers of credits required in the core subjects of English, math, science, social studies, and foreign languages (National Center for Education Statistics, 1996). Fewer than half of all states have adopted the full complement of courses articulated in A Nation at Risk, but for 30 years, states have steadily moved in that direction. In the past decade, states have paid greater attention to the quality of those courses—the levels of rigor in math and science. In 1992, only three states required at least one science course with a laboratory component, and none specified the highest level of math required (National Center for Education Statistics, 1996). By 2008, 25 states required a biological science, physical science course, or both (Council of Chief State School Officers, 2008)—and 17 states required Algebra I or above (Daun-Barnett & St. John, 2012).

In addition to course requirements, states have sought to improve students' preparation for college and career in two ways—exit exams and subject specific content standards. In a post–No Child Left Behind period, all 50 states have some version of an exit exam—or series of examinations—to meet the expectations set forth in the No Child Left Behind Act. Here we draw the distinction between exit exams generally and those that students must pass in order to earn their high school diploma—mandatory exit exams. In 2008, 26 states had adopted a mandatory exit exam for high school completion—a policy most common in Southern states (Daun-Barnett & St. John, 2012). The tests are generally intended to assess the degree to which students demonstrate proficiency in the core subject areas. By extension, this is one of the mechanisms by which states hold schools, districts, and now teachers, accountable for student learning.

Courses and tests are meaningless metrics if they do not approximate some basic standard for learning. Admissions professionals typically think of this as high school quality. For any given applicant, admissions professionals assess the strength of their curriculum relative to what is available to that student and how likely students from those schools are to achieve success at the institution. Without a common set of content standards, "Math II" may mean something very different from one high school to the next. In fact, even a course as specific as "Chemistry" or "Algebra I" may vary by school, particularly if content standards are minimal or not formally established. In 2010, the National Governor's Association (NGA) and the Council of Chief State School Officers (CCSSO) partnered to develop the common core standards in English language arts (ELA) and math for Grades K–12, and those standards been adopted by 45 states and the District of Columbia (Common Core State Standards Initiative, 2010). According to policy makers, these standards should help to align course requirements with exit exams by standardizing what students should be expected to learn at each level and across the coursework.

In the transition from high school to college, we have two separate barometers that indicate, in different ways, whether or not students are leaving high school and applying to college with the tools necessary to succeed. The first and perhaps most obvious is the demand for remedial or developmental coursework in ELA, writing composition, or math. In a recent report from the U.S. Department of Education (Aud et al., 2011), nearly a third of all students entering postsecondary education for the first time in the fall of 2007–2008 took at least one remedial course. Those numbers are highest among community college students (42%), but even students beginning at research universities report remedial or developmental coursework (22%). Colleges point the finger at schools for failing to prepare students adequately for college-level work, but there are at least three other culprits. Secondary school educators argue that at least a portion of the responsibility belongs with colleges and universities because they are frequently unclear about academic requirements in their admissions process (Wellman & Vandal, 2011).

The second indicator of the gap between high school requirements and college expectations for academic preparation is whether or not students have access to different academic disciplines. Most students, parents, and counselors recognize the importance of being minimally prepared for college, but fewer understand that what it means to be "prepared" may depend entirely upon what field a student hopes to pursue. It can be complicated enough to keep track of the range of expectations across different types of colleges; it is far more difficult for students, counselors, or parents to keep track of differences by major and discipline. The reality is that many students have no real idea what major or discipline they hope to pursue in college.

The point is that at some institutions, the choice of academic discipline may mean more in terms of what is expected of students to be "college prepared" than any set of high school graduation requirements or formalized admissions expectations. It matters more what it will actually take to succeed in their chosen discipline. Many of the selective professional programs set higher academic standards for admission. In some cases, the more rigorous requirements are dictated by the academic rigor of the program. It would simply be too difficult to complete an engineering curriculum if a student finished his or her math sequence at geometry or Algebra II (which is possible in every state across the country). Similarly, it would be impossible for a student to enroll in a music program without ever having received prior training. Architecture, business management, and pharmacy are a few examples of professional programs that may have higher than average admissions requirements, which is both a function of the demands of the curriculum and the competition for scarce spaces.

This phenomenon is not limited to 4-year colleges and universities. Community colleges seldom talk about being selective in their admissions, but they frequently offer a number of programs that are more selective to pursue. Nursing is a common example. Today there is a national shortage of nurses, and colleges and universities struggle to meet the demand because they cannot hire an adequate number of nurse educators and field supervisors. As a result, community colleges may turn away as many as half or more of all the applicants from their nursing program, even if these students are admitted to the institution. Nursing is also unique relative to some other professional programs at community colleges because it is a heavily scientific curriculum, meaning that students should have completed more rigorous math and science courses than what is typically expected across the community college.

Existing Research on Strategies to Improve
Academic Preparation

In this section, we consider existing research on course requirement policies, mandatory exit exams, and remediation. All of these factors are situated squarely at the intersection of high schools and colleges and have an influence on the chances students will be academically prepared for college. We believe it is critical for admissions professionals to understand the broader forces shaping the educational experiences for the students they are likely to enroll. These differences may be particularly important for admissions professionals at institutions with a national or global student body because it helps admissions professionals account for variations in school quality and assess the overall academic profile of each individual student.

Course Taking and Mandatory Exit Exams

The research on course requirements is fairly consistent—more demanding requirements, on average, lead to increased course taking in the core academic subjects (Clune & White, 1992; Daun-Barnett, 2008; Sebring, 1987) and higher achievement and admissions test scores (Lee, Croninger, & Smith, 1997; Musoba, 2004; Schiller & Muller, 2003). Some research suggests that these relationships are complicated by the quality of teaching (Teitelbaum, 2003), class sizes (Finn, Gerber, & Wang, 2002), and the degree to which districts adopt state requirements (Sipple, Killeen, & Monk, 2004).

More recent research recognizes that while some of these relationships persist, there are unintended consequences or potential tradeoffs to these policies. For example, while higher math requirements are positively related to increased SAT scores and college enrollment rates, the opposite relationship exists with high school completion rates (Daun-Barnett & St. John, 2012; St. John & Musoba, 2006). Researchers found that in Chicago, the effects of adopting more rigorous requirements were modest—students may complete more lower-level courses in the core subjects, but their high school completion rates dropped, and their chances for attending college did not improve (Allensworth, Nomi, Montgomery, & Lee, 2009).

In nearly all cases, students are required to complete four years of English language arts and social studies. States typically require two or three years of math and the same in science, though the differences across these policies depend upon whether states require specific courses or leave those to the discretion of students and schools. Three years of math is different than suggesting that all students must complete Algebra I, geometry, and Algebra II. For some students, the two policies are one in the same—these are the courses they will complete. For others, particularly students who do not excel in math, they may find a combination of math courses that will earn them credit toward their diploma, irrespective of whether the courses challenge them and prepare them for college-level work.

Much of the data suggests that students are less likely to complete high school when subjected to mandatory exit exams, particularly among lower achieving students, females, and underrepresented minority students (Jacob, 2001; Ou, 2009; Reardon, Atteberry, Arshan, & Kurlaender, 2009; Warren, Jenkins, & Kulick, 2006). A number of these students will leave the traditional high school path and complete the GED.

Course Placement Tests and Remedial Coursework

Many colleges and universities administer placement tests to admitted students to ascertain placement in writing composition, mathematics, and in some cases, foreign language. For ELA and math, institutions typically use placement tests developed by one of the major testing agencies—ACT (COMPASS) or ETS (Accuplacer). Remedial and developmental education has been a contentious policy issue for two reasons. First, it appears that students are exposed to the same coursework twice, which is inefficient. This may be true for some students, particularly those recently out of high school where graduation requirements are high, but it does not apply equally well to nontraditional-age students who may never have been exposed to the same level of rigor. Developmental coursework actually represents the gap between what students are prepared to do in math and English language arts at the time they choose to enter postsecondary education and the standards a college or university establishes as the baseline for college-level work.

Second, while some of the early work on the relationship between remedial coursework and student outcomes found a positive effect of these courses (Bettinger & Long, 2005), more recent research suggests that remedial coursework is not effective—a small proportion of remedial students earn degrees and even when compared to similar nonremedial students, success rates are no different (Attewell, Lavin, Domina, & Levey, 2006; Bailey, 2009; Calcagno & Long, 2008; Levin & Calcagno, 2008; Martorell & McFarlin, 2007). In some cases—California State University (CSU) and City University of New York—systems have shifted the responsibility for remedial coursework away from the 4-year institutions to their community colleges (Academic Senate for California Community Colleges, 1995; Gumport & Bastedo, 2001). It may be more efficient to shift the burden of remediation to community colleges, but in the process, the policy may prevent some students from attending a 4-year institution.

Best Practices for Improving Academic Preparation

In this section, we turn our attention to the strategies employed by educators and policy makers to improve students' level of academic preparation as they graduate from high school. Perhaps the most important strategy to improve preparation is the comprehensive reform of schools—a topic well beyond the scope of this volume. We will, however, talk about school-based strategies including the Advancement Via Individual Determination (AVID), Talent Development through Johns Hopkins University, and College Summit, which typically involve some degree of collaboration between higher education and secondary schools. We leave community-based collaborative strategies to Chapter 7. Additionally, we discuss programs designed to provide opportunities for college-level learning in high school, including Advanced Placement programs, the International Baccalaureate (IB) curriculum, and college-based dual enrollment strategies.

School Reform Initiatives

High schools have been under close scrutiny for more than 30 years. Raising expectations for students has been a common strategy since *A Nation at Risk* and the publication of the *Shopping Mall High School*, but that approach assumes that students are not challenging themselves and are capable of completing more advanced coursework if required. To be sure, some students are capable of completing a more demanding curriculum, and course completion patterns bear that out. As Daun-Barnett and St. John (2012) illustrate, students are completing three additional core courses in their high school career by 2004 than they did more than a decade earlier. However, we also recognize that for many students, the problem runs deeper and may be systemic within schools and districts. We consider three particular school reform initiatives that have been tied closely to college participation—Advancement Via Individual Determination (AVID), Talent Development, and College Summit. Admissions professionals recognize that an important balance must be struck between the level of rigor of the curriculum students complete and their GPA as an indication of their performance in those classes.

AVID. More than 30 years ago, Mary Catherine Swanson, head of the English department for a high school in San Diego, created AVID as a new strategy to educate a changing population of students (Freedman, 2000). The district had been required by the federal courts to desegregate its urban schools, which meant a change in the demographics of a school that had a reputation for excellence. Swanson set out to raise academic expectations for a changing population of students who were being left behind by other educators. According to one evaluation of the program, "AVID is a college readiness program designed to increase the number of students who enroll in four-year colleges" (Tabor, 2011, p. 5). The program serves average students in middle school and high school who demonstrate their ability to benefit from the program with grades between 2.0—3.5 and some indication of basic proficiency in the core academic disciplines (Oswald, 2002). Swanson began with a single class of students in 1980 and now the AVID approach is being utilized in as many as 4,800 schools serving 425,000 students (AVID. org, 2012).

The program is structured around three pillars. First, each year they are enrolled in the program, AVID students participate in an elective class that is designed to help them develop academic success strategies, leadership skills, and the knowledge and awareness to navigate the college choice process. Second, the program provides professional development for teachers and administrators to learn about and integrate the AVID learning strategies into their classes and schools (Tabor, 2011). Third, the model assumes that a key to the success of AVID students is the academic support provided by program tutors. One of the challenges noted by evaluators is that schools find it difficult to identify an adequate number of tutors to maintain the 7:1 student-to-tutor ratio (Hines & Whitaker, 2005; Tabor, 2011).

The AVID program makes two important assumptions—all students can succeed at high rates, and schools should provide more support to help middle-performing students achieve at a higher level. Several small-scale evaluations have been conducted and made publicly available, and their findings are consistently positive—more students across all demographics achieve higher GPAs, more frequently complete advanced courses including AP and IB, and enroll in college after high school. Unfortunately, these evaluations are limited because they compare AVID students with non-AVID students—two groups that are different in important ways above and beyond participation in the program. This is not to suggest the program does not work—in fact, from an admissions standpoint, the program may indicate that these students are more likely to succeed precisely because they differ from their non-AVID peers. Participation in AVID is likely to indicate that students are actually better prepared for college than some of their other measures might suggest.

Talent Development.   While it is less explicitly linked to college access and participation, the Johns Hopkins University Talent Development program is a comprehensive school reform model intended to improve student outcomes critical to their chances for postsecondary participation. The program is based upon four pillars for school improvement: (a) team teaching and small learning communities; (b) specialized curriculum and coaching, which relies on highly qualified teachers and data-informed curriculum reform; (c) tiered student supports, including an early warning system to keep students on track; and (d) a climate conducive to academic success, inclusive of college and career readiness (Johns Hopkins University School of Education, 2012). The Talent Development model focuses on the ninth grade year as students transition from middle to high school.

Unlike other programs, Talent Development has been the subject of at least one rigorous impact evaluation conducted by Manpower Development

Research Council (MDRC) (Kemple, Herlihy, & Smith, 2005), which found that attendance rates increased, students earned more academic credits during their first year, and promotion rates improved from the first to second years. They also suggest that 11th-grade assessment scores improved among TD high schools and that a larger proportion of students graduated high school (Kemple et al., 2005). The success of TD depends upon the degree to which schools adopt the necessary structural changes. The ninth grade class is reorganized into a separate and distinct learning community, and the schedule is altered to accommodate block scheduling for math and English. The evaluation also found that schools were more likely to adopt the changes during the freshmen year than to continue that transformation in the upper grades, which has implications for the likelihood of long-term success. Researchers note that even with demonstrated success, many students in these low-performing schools continue to underperform, and the cost per student for the program is nearly $300. It is difficult to assess whether this total investment per school is worth the marginal gains achieved, but it does suggest improvements can be made in high schools.

College Summit.　　Unlike AVID or TD, College Summit was not developed as a comprehensive school reform strategy. In fact, it has little to do with the formal academic curriculum. Instead, it began as a simple idea from a social entrepreneur (Bornstein, 2004). J. B. Schramm and his colleagues saw a vast pool of untapped potential among low-income students attending some of the lowest-performing schools in the nation. College Summit began, as many of these programs do, as a tutoring program working weekly with school students. Schramm found that with such infrequent interaction, much of the progress was lost from one week to the next, so he decided to host a "summit" to bring high school seniors from many of these schools together for a 4-day intensive workshop on the college choice process. The model was designed to address three key barriers. First, College Summit recognizes that many capable students do not know how to navigate the college choice process and that they lack the guidance and support other students receive. Second, it recognizes that many of these students have not learned to communicate their strengths to an admissions committee. Third, the model assumes that the schools these students attend typically lack a college-going culture, meaning that few of their peers talk about college, and their counselors and teachers are not adequately prepared to provide the information and guidance they need.

Initially, the summit was utilized to influence the first two factors. A cohort of students would be sent from a given school, and they would all receive the intensive college choice training. Those entering seniors raise the bar for their peers by talking about life after high school, and they influenced others to engage earlier in the process. As students talk about the steps and demonstrate some success, those stories inspire others to consider postsecondary education. The model was expanded to provide training for teachers and counselors, and today the organization reports training 700 teachers to work with 25,000 students annually (College Summit, 2012). At the turn of the 21st century, College Summit sought to expand the model into schools and districts, and they developed their Senior Year Curriculum. The curriculum includes materials for both teachers and students and is designed to complement the summer summit. Throughout the evolution of the program, College Summit sought to connect summit graduates to their schools to create a network of influence on the college-going culture of the school, and it began to develop preview portfolios of hundreds of colleges and universities across the country to help students understand what is actually expected of these institutions in the admissions process. The program has also developed a web-based tool to help students manage their college application and choice process.

At the completion of this text, there were plans in place to conduct comprehensive evaluations of the College Summit efforts in Chicago and across California. The only evaluation report currently available for the program suggests positive impacts as it looks at aggregate changes over time, but participation rates varied dramatically across schools, and there were no meaningful comparison groups—participating schools were screened simply for the availability of data (Ironbridge Systems, Inc., 2010). Like many evaluations of this type, the findings are subject to the effects of other factors not accounted for in the analysis.

All of these programs offer great potential in terms of helping more students plan for college, navigate the choice process, and enroll in postsecondary education. Though different in a number of ways, all three programs are designed to influence the structure and function of schools to better prepare students for college. They make different assumptions about what students need and how best to provide it, but they all address some of the potential barriers students face. All three are explicit in their attempts to change the culture of the respective schools. AVID does so by changing expectations for students and providing additional supports to ensure their success; TD changes the structure and function of the school by creating small learning communities and implementing block scheduling; and College Summit focuses on empowering students to influence one another by helping them master the college choice process. Each of these programs acknowledges that, while the outcomes are strong and positive, many students continue to fall through the cracks. The programs may help admissions professionals identify a greater proportion of what Schramm identifies as the 180,000 capable low-income students that do not otherwise attend college, but they are unlikely to affect the much larger proportion of low-income students that are already well behind what might be considered college or career ready.

College-Level Learning in High School

While many students are underprepared to enter college and require remedial coursework upon admission, some students simply have not been given
access to a full complement of rigorous courses to challenge them through
their entire high school career. For more than 60 years, educators have
looked for ways to more efficiently and seamlessly provide students with
the most challenging curriculum they are able to complete as a way to prepare for college-level work, and perhaps earn college credit along the way. In
this section, we explore the three most common strategies for allowing students to complete college-level work while in high school—Advanced Placement (AP), International Baccalaureate (IB), and dual enrollment. There are
variations on these themes, but for sake of space, we focus on the most
common models today.

The range of dual enrollment strategies—variously known as college-
level learning in high school (CLLHS), concurrent enrollment, and credit-
based transition programs—are designed to provide college-level learning
opportunities for high school students. The Advanced Placement (AP), International Baccalaureate (IB), and the College Level Examination Program
(CLEP) have served the needs of high-achieving high school students for
more than 40 years. Dual enrollment programs, largely provided by community colleges, are small in comparison to the AP program, but they serve as
many as 1.2 million students at approximately 11,000 high schools (NCES,
2005). Johnstone and Del Genio (2001) identify three forms of college-level
learning in high school (CLLHS) including exam-based (AP, IB, and CLEP),
school-based (college courses taught in high schools either by high school
teachers or college instructors), and college-based (students attend college
level classes on college campuses, frequently with college students) programs. They suggest that each type of program has its advantages but can
be limited in important ways.

Advanced Placement (AP).   The AP program is the largest and most widely
regarded strategy to provide high school students the opportunity to complete college-level work before they enter college (The College Board, 2003).
Advanced Placement was launched as a pilot study in 1952 among small
elite preparatory academies and several Ivy League colleges. The purpose of
the program was to eliminate duplication in coursework between the senior
year of high school and the freshmen year of college (Johanek, 2001). In
the era following World War II, there was growing concern that a sizable
number of high school students were not sufficiently challenged at the end of
their high school careers and that they could be better served by completing
college-level work prior to high school graduation. The administration of
the program was assumed by The College Board in 1956 and, as Figure 4.1
shows, served a modest number of high schools. In 1955, only 104 schools

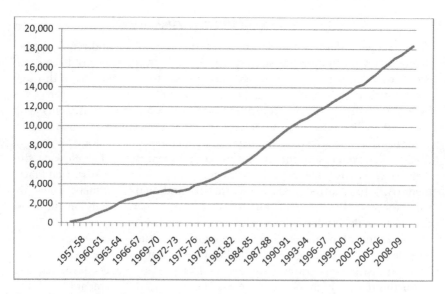

Figure 4.1 Number of Schools Participating in AP Program, 1956–present
Source: The College Board (2011a). AP Data 2011. Retrieved April 30, 2012 from http://media.
collegeboard.com/digitalServices/pdf/research/AP-Annual-Participation-2011.pdf

across the nation administered AP courses for slightly more than 1,200 students. Since that time, the AP program has grown almost every year from its modest beginning to serving more than 18,000 schools, with 1.97 million students taking 3.7 million AP exams.

AP is widely regarded by colleges and universities because it is offered in the school building and the credit is granted based upon scores on an externally validated exam. Test-based strategies generally favor students who are better test takers. Today, completion of AP courses alone is a less effective predictor of success during the first year of college because a growing percentage of students do not take the exams. Enrollment in AP courses is typically considered in the admissions process, irrespective of whether or not a student earns credit for that course.

The College Board developed a comprehensive training program for teachers of AP courses that encouraged teachers to participate in a range of professional development activities including workshops, exam reading, the summer institute, or the annual AP conference (Geiser & Santelices, 2004; Klopfenstein, 2004; The College Board, 2003). Admissions offices note that completion of AP courses can have a positive effect on admissions decisions (Clinedinst, Hurley, & Hawkins, 2011). The AP program has grown in popularity over the past 30 years in large part because so much attention has been paid to the important relationship between the strength of a student's academic curriculum and his or her chances for success in college (Adelman,

1999, 2004). In 2006, Exxon Mobile partnered with the Bill and Melinda Gates Foundation and the Dell Foundation to create incentives for states to expand their AP participation rates (National Math and Science Initiative, 2008). The initiative came on the heels of a national report on the growing need for improvements in science and math education (Committee on Prospering in the Global Economy of the 21st Century & Committee on Science Engineering and Public Policy, 2007).

International Baccalaureate.   The International Baccalaureate (IB) curriculum is an alternative to the AP curriculum that has been around for more than 40 years but that has not gained the same notoriety as AP. The International Baccalaureate Organization (IBO) (2012a) was founded in 1968 in Switzerland, and its early schools were private international schools. The program has expanded worldwide, and an increasing number of schools adopting the curriculum are public, state-supported institutions. The IBO has established a comprehensive curricular program for students from ages 3–19 divided into three sections—the primary years, the middle years, and the diploma program. Typically, in admissions, we recognize the 2-year IB diploma program, but some students may participate in the IB curriculum for their entire schooling career. Currently, 3,395 schools across 141 countries offer the IB curriculum; 680 of those schools operate in the United States.

The IB diploma curriculum differs dramatically from the AP program. The only commonality is that both challenge students with rigorous course content aligned with the expectations of postsecondary education. Where AP offers 31 college-level courses in math, science, foreign language, literature, history, politics, and the study of societies, these courses are not linked together formally as a comprehensive curriculum. The IB program is designed, first and foremost, as a comprehensive curriculum designed to prepare students for lifelong learning in a 21st-century global society (International Baccalaureate Organization, 2012a). To complete the 2-year diploma, students are required to complete six courses—a combination of languages, social studies, mathematics, experimental sciences, and the arts. In addition to those required courses, students are required to complete a course in the theory of knowledge, write an extended essay, and complete requirements in creativity, action, and service. In order to earn the diploma designation, students must successfully pass written examinations in each course and score at least 24 points (out of 45). Like AP, examinees are graded by external IB evaluators (International Baccalaureate Organization, 2012b).

IB was not initially designed to create the sorts of efficiencies for high-achieving students that were a focal point for the AP, but it is one of the many ways colleges and universities can, and have, considered them. Because IBO operates in so many countries, it has paid a great deal of attention to how the IB curriculum aligns with the postsecondary expectations in each place. The United States is arguably the most difficult to manage in terms of alignment because we have no national standards for college admission and each institution makes its own admissions decisions. IBO indicates a variety of ways colleges and universities in the United States recognize the IB diploma. For most institutions, they view IB courses as comparable to AP and they will offer credit on a course-by-course basis, typically if a student has achieved a minimum score (4–6) (International Baccalaureate Organization, 2012c). Additionally, some schools choose to grant IB diploma recipients second-year student status, or they provide early decision or additional "points" in the admissions decision. In a few cases, institutions provide targeted scholarships for IB diploma students and may allow students to place out of certain courses or gain admission to honors programs.

The IB is a strong, well-respected academic program, but it does have its critics. In particular, there is a small but vocal opposition for philosophical and ideological reasons. The IB curriculum was framed in terms of international standards, consistent largely with the values espoused by the United Nations and, by extension, the documents and treaties supported by the organization. Critics argue, that the "universal" values of the UN and the IBO are inconsistent with many of the core values of the United States and should not be taught to students in the United States (Quist, 2007). Critics also argue that comparably rigorous curricular options are available in existing public schools and that subscribing to the IBO model undermines local control because it cedes curricular decision making to an international organization (Darst Williams, 2008). Others argue the cost is prohibitive to scaling IB to reach a substantial proportion of students. In addition to fees for courses and examinations, schools are charged an estimated $10,000 annually (Lewin, 2010; Mathews, 2010). Our experience suggests that students who complete the IB diploma have completed a demanding college preparatory curriculum and are well prepared for college-level work. The IB is currently available to a small subset of the high school population and, given the cost of participation, it is likely to signal a high-quality curriculum in affluent, highly resourced school districts and private schools.

Dual Enrollment. The work of Johnstone and Del Genio points to the central limitation of the literature in this area. While a fair amount has been written exploring the nature and scope of dual enrollment strategies in high school, very few studies examine the impact of these programs on student outcomes. NCES (2005) provides estimates, for example, of how many students enroll in AP and other school- and college-based dual enrollment programs in a given year, and The College Board and the International Baccalaureate programs can identify the numbers of students completing these advanced courses and earning college-level credit among all high school students, but these sources do not attempt to address whether students are better off as a result of the programs. Johnstone and Del Genio (2001) recognize the political realities of dual CLLHS and the potential implications for students, schools, colleges, and policy makers, and they suggest the impact of the program can be understood and evaluated in a number of ways.

Bailey and Mechur Karp (2003) conducted an extensive review of the literature on credit-based transition programs, defined as "[any program that] encourages and allows high school students to take college courses and to earn college credit while still in high school" (p. vii). They reviewed 45 publications examining credit-based transition programs and concluded that little is known about ". . . the overall characteristics and effects of these programs." (p. 21). They suggest that few of these studies examine the effects of dual enrollment on student outcomes. In a few cases, researchers explore the relationship between participation in the program and college enrollment, course grades, school attendance, and high school completion. However, very few of these studies control for prior achievement, personal characteristics, or other potentially influential factors. Their typology of programs mirrors Johnstone and Del Genio (2001) with two important differences. First, Bailey and Mechur Karp recognize that dual enrollment is growing as an option for middle- and lower-achieving high school students. They acknowledge that, in most cases, these programs continue to enroll high-achieving students and suggest future research examine outcomes for lower-achieving students. The second difference they report is a growing trend toward the creation of early and middle college high schools, which in many cases appeal to a broader array of students. They hypothesize that the range of credit-based transition programs hold some potential to promote college access and success among a wider range of students, but their findings suggest that potential has not yet been realized in a systemic way.

Smith Morest and Mechur Karp (2006) report on their field study of colleges offering dual enrollment programs and emphasize the potential for dual enrollment programs at community colleges to expand credit opportunities to low- and middle-achieving students. Despite this expectation, they found that among the 15 sites in their study, most participating students were high achievers in high school. They conclude that a number of important questions remain, including what proportion of participants successfully earn college credits, whether they apply to degree programs, and whether it is plausible to reduce cost by eliminating course overlap. They are especially weary of the claims that these credit-based programs can or do serve the needs of middle- and low-achieving students, and their field research suggests that has not been the case. Given their findings, it may be important to ask whether the program discussed in this study expands opportunity to lower- and middle-achieving students.

Most recently, Swanson (2008) utilized the National Education Longitudinal Study (Swanson 2008) to examine the relationship between dual enrollment in high school and both student persistence and degree completion in college. Her findings suggest that a modest relationship exists, particularly among students who have established some degree of academic momentum (completed 20 credits or more by the end of the first year in college). Unlike many of the studies reviewed by Bailey and Mechur Karp (2003), Swanson employed a number of controls for students' background, including demographic characteristics, family background, and high school achievement.

The research on dual enrollment is relatively thin, but from an admissions perspective, it may be best to think about these programs in terms of transfer articulation. In most cases, dual enrolled students will generate a college transcript for successful completion of one or more of these courses. Those transcripts are frequently indistinguishable from any other college transcript, except for the fact that these students will apply to the institution as a first-time student and not as a transfer. In most cases, one of two sets of policies will inform how admissions staff deals with dual-enrolled credits, across the spectrum of credit-based transition programs. Many institutions will accept the credit, consistent with their treatment of courses from the same institutions for transfers, but there are no guarantees that an institution outside the one granting the credit will actually accept it toward a degree program. Other institutions view dual enrollment programs with suspicion. The two public flagship institutions in Michigan—the University of Michigan and Michigan State—have both implemented "double-dipping" policies. Simply put, they have said that they will not count any course for college credit that was simultaneously counted for high school credit. They acknowledge that the courses are taken into account as part of the admission process, but no other credit is granted.

Suggestions for Admissions Professionals

If there is one lesson to take from all of this, it is that students, parents, and counselors need to know what it takes to be academically prepared for college, and admissions professionals should be prepared to answer this question in a more thorough and comprehensive way. In order to answer this question, admissions professionals must understand the educational context from which their applicants are coming, they should be familiar with the range of strategies currently being employed to improve academic outcomes for high school students, and they should be familiar with the sorts of initiatives being employed by schools to improve students' chances for postsecondary success while in high school. That answer should also include a frank discussion of what academic preparedness means at their campus and how the expectations may differ across disciplines.

The application review process is mysterious to those outside of it, and the academic criteria used by colleges are the most important ingredients in that black box. Perhaps more than anything, admissions professionals need to help students understand the complexities of identifying academic preparation. It is not simply a list of courses, or a GPA or test score. It is also the degree to which students have challenged themselves to the most demanding curriculum available and the extent to which students are adequately prepared to place into college-level work when they arrive on campus. Students in low-performing districts, in particular, need to understand that passing a course is not sufficient to demonstrate mastery of a subject and that remediation is a possibility for students who either did not challenge themselves or attended schools where few advanced options were available. Ultimately, admissions professionals understand that academic preparation is the single most important factor in the process, and they are responsible for helping others understand what it means at their respective institutions and how that level of preparation can be achieved.

One of the ways admissions professionals attempt to influence students' academic preparation for college is to present to high school sophomores and juniors on the academic expectations of their institutions. We believe the more important conversations are between admissions counselors and the school counseling staff, including middle school counselors when possible. Academic preparation has to begin earlier in the student's career—much of the groundwork has already been laid by the sophomore or junior year. School counselors in high-need high schools also require clearer explanations from admissions offices regarding the admissible range of grades and test scores for students as well as special admittance programs. Admissions professionals can spend more time helping school counselors in these lower-performing schools to understand what pathways might exist for their students, which might include transfer articulation pathways through partnering community colleges.

Our final recommendation to admissions professionals is to share data with the schools about actual enrollments and eventual success rates of their students. Most schools do not know where their students go once they leave high school. They typically track college applications through the school counselors, but there is a lot of time between graduation and fall enrollment. School counselors would like to know whether their students actually enroll, whether they require remedial coursework once they arrive, and whether or not they are successful earning a degree or transferring to another institution. This information is available and can be summarized and reported back to school counselors. It can also be used to initiate a conversation about what it would take to improve upon those success rates within a given school.

5

PAYING FOR COLLEGE

College admissions professionals are not financial aid counselors. They are, however, the first line of contact with most students and their families, and as it turns out, paying for college is at the top of their list of questions. It may not be the first one they ask, but it will certainly make a difference in the choices they make about whether to apply and where to attend. In fact, the issue of college affordability may be the distinguishing factor between the role of admissions professionals as marketers and that of advocates for access. Institutional pressures to enroll the right class of students at the right numbers and with the right profile create a powerful disincentive for transparency. As marketers, admissions staff attempts to enroll each student at the highest price they are willing and able to pay, meaning they will vary the tuition discount for each student, depending upon their relative priority and their likelihood of attendance. Stated differently, colleges do not want to tell families how they discount tuition because net price is one of the powerful marketing tools they employ to yield enrollments. These are strong motivating forces that we will not attempt to minimize in this chapter. Recall that we believe college admissions professionals must play both the marketing and the access roles well. Instead, we use this chapter to help admissions professionals understand affordability and financial aid from the perspective of the students.

It is important to understand that paying for college is an important issue for every family, not simply low-income families. On this point, we should recognize that students' decisions to attend one institution over another will be affected by both their willingness to pay and their ability to pay their portion of the cost of attendance. Willingness to pay is affected by the experience individuals have with an institution and is informed by their perception of the quality of the education they will likely receive. From an economic perspective, families are rational actors in their college choice decisions, and the amount they are willing to spend is affected by their projections of the relative value of the credential once they earn their degree. They may pay more if they perceive the quality to be worth the investment, but they must first be convinced of the value before they will choose to spend more for the education.

76

In this chapter, we believe the balance can be struck by first understanding the issue of college affordability for low-income students. For families with the economic means to send their children to college, the current process of tuition discounting may work reasonably well. We know that many students and their parents overestimate the cost of college, and those gaps grow among low-income, first-generation and underrepresented students (antonio & Bersola, 2004). The problem of perception is that the sticker price for a college education is a much stronger signal to students than are the range of subsidies available to help cover the cost. Simply put, it is easier for families to find sticker prices than it is to calculate their own net price.

Affordability is a critical issue for middle-class families as well—although for them the question is more a matter of choice. As such, we believe discussions of affordability must be a part of how admissions professionals engage with students and their professional counterparts in schools and community organizations. We also recognize, however, that admissions professionals are frequently removed from the financial aid packaging process, meaning that, on average, they know less about how to pay for college and frequently rely on their own experiences. This chapter should help new admissions professionals understand what parents and students know about the cost of college and how they are affected by price, what the trends have been over time for both prices and financial aid, and what strategies have been employed to help more students and parents find the right mix of information and financial support to make college achievable.

The Rising Costs of Higher Education

Basic laws of supply and demand suggest that as the price of a product rises, the demand for that product declines, all else being equal. Markets are more complex than this, but, if these principles held for postsecondary education, we should reasonably expect declining participation rates. After all, costs rose by 2–3% above the rate of inflation for much of the 20th century (Ehrenberg, 2007) and nearly 5% above inflation through the first decade of the 21st century (Baum & Ma, 2012). Figure 5.1 provides an illustration. Over 30 years, postsecondary prices have risen fairly consistently at rates above inflation for community colleges, 4-year public institutions, and private not-for-profit colleges. If the price of tuition and fees had only risen at the rate of inflation, the trend lines would have remained flat at 100 or equivalent to prices paid in 1982. The trends suggest that by 2012, the price of college is nearly three times as high as it was in 1982 after adjusting for inflation (Consumer Price Index), depending upon the sector.

Of course, we know that all else is not equal, and the cost of college has risen considerably during a time when the value of a college degree has also risen in terms of labor market returns. Economists have posited a number

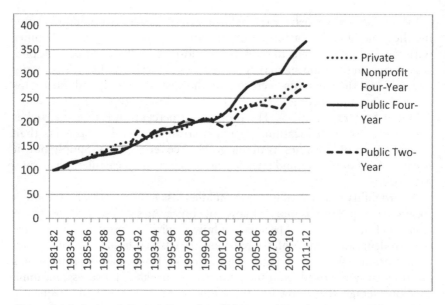

Figure 5.1 Inflation Adjusted Growth in Tuition and Fees by Sector, 1982–2012

of explanations for the rising price of higher education, from the rising cost of technology to the growing costs of healthcare and energy to the wasteful spending of colleges and universities. A few argue that college prices have been driven up by the increasing availability of federal student aid (Curs, Singell, & Waddell, 2007), while others suggest the culprit is our ever-increasing pursuit of prestige vis-à-vis institutional rankings and the success of individual academic programs (Ehrenberg, 2002). Others have suggested that colleges spend vastly different amounts on the education they provide relative to the amount of revenue they are able to generate (Bowen & Carnegie Council on Policy Studies in Higher Education, 1977). Finally, some argue that while costs in higher education have risen dramatically, they are similar to other industries that rely on highly skilled workers—suggesting that cost of college is partly influenced by our own successes preparing future generations of college-educated talent and accelerating the advancement of technologies. The reasons for these increases are complex, and this chapter is not intended to answer the question of what drives up the cost of college. For those interested, we suggest the recent work of Archibald and Feldman (2010). Our takeaway is that college access professionals should recognize that rising cost is a concern to students and parents and that colleges and universities have a responsibility to help students and parents understand tuition and fees and the array of aid programs available to help them pay for their education.

Tuition and fees vary considerably by institution and type, and while costs have risen dramatically, most students continue to attend relatively affordable institutions or receive subsidies to attend more expensive alternatives. The third section moves us closer to understanding the net price of college by examining the range of federal aid programs, a sample of model state financial aid programs, the increasingly popular place-based tuition guarantee programs, and the growing array of strategies to help more students take steps to understand price and apply for aid. We conclude this chapter by considering what students and their parents need to know about the cost of college and the price they are likely to pay.

Making the Investment in Higher Education

When students are asked to estimate the costs of tuition and fees for college, they commonly overestimate price. Some research suggests that students' knowledge of price improves over their high school career (Bell, Rowan-Kenyon, & Perna, 2009), but they remain underinformed by the time they must make decisions about whether or where to attend college. Avery and Kane (2004) report similar findings on students' knowledge of price, but they also find that students overestimate available aid, meaning that their estimates of net cost should suggest that the benefits of college participation outweigh the costs. Dynarski and Scott-Clayton (2006) argue that part of the information problem is a consequence of a complex financial aid application. The Free Application for Federal Student Aid (FAFSA) is longer than many tax forms—it includes questions not asked by the IRS, and it is not transparent enough for individuals to estimate their eligibility from prior years' taxes. Dynarski and Scott-Clayton (2006) suggest that a simpler form would allow families to consider costs much earlier in the college choice process while sacrificing very little in terms of accuracy.

Policy makers have made some improvements. In 2011, all colleges and universities were required to make a net price calculator available on their websites so that students could more closely approximate their own cost if they chose to attend the institution. Unfortunately, the price of postsecondary education is far more complicated, and these tools, for all their virtues, are likely to fall well short for most students and their families. Institutions are also likely to develop these tools in different ways, making it difficult to compare anticipated net price from one institution to the next. The challenge for admissions professionals is that the sticker price is not a good reflection of the actual price students will pay. We know a good deal more about the variety of subsidies and aid programs for students, but educators, policy makers, and community leaders have not been clear about how they will apply to particular students. In fact, most students will be affected by three separate subsidies above and beyond those that affect sticker price—federal financial aid, state grant programs, and tuition discounting practiced by institutions. It is also possible that a growing number of students will have access to local and community-based subsidies to help offset the cost of college. As a result, it has become very difficult for us to help students and their families estimate their net cost, which is partly what they need to make an informed decision about whether or where to attend college.

Nationwide, student loan debt has exceeded $1 trillion and has now surpassed credit card debt (Chu, 2009). Higher education bears some responsibility for this growing debt crisis, which begins by helping students and families understand this debt earlier in the college choice process and finding ways to manage that debt more responsibly. It might also mean that we need to think differently about how we package students' financial aid or how we collect information about the range of debt students may assume during this time period, including credit card debt and direct-to-consumer loans students access on the private loan market that are not always reported to their respective financial aid offices. We believe that in more cases than not, the debt students assume will be worth it over the long run, but that may not be true for all students.

Understanding the Price of College

When we talk with high school students, sticker price is nearly always the first question on their minds. Unfortunately, when students talk with us about paying for college, we hear fewer questions of how to afford it and more statements of fact that they cannot afford it. Instead of asking how much college costs or whether it is expensive, students will declare something like, "I heard college costs $40,000 a year" or "There is no way my family could afford to send me there." It is not difficult to understand why students believe college is so expensive. A growing number of colleges in the United States charge more than what many families make in a given year— a perception that can create the impression that all colleges are unaffordable. In 2011, 123 colleges and universities posted tuition and fees above $50,000—up from only 58 institutions in 2009 (Ellis, 2011b). The media reports these stories and adds fuel to the fire by implying that these exceptions are in some way indicative of the larger pattern across all of higher education; while these are important institutions in the United States, they represent only 2% of all colleges and universities. The simple truth is that most students pay nowhere near $50,000 per year. What is typically lost in this conversation is that many students attending those very expensive institutions pay some amount less than the sticker price as well—and increasingly, many of these institutions are replacing loans with grants for students below some income threshold.

Each year, The College Board conducts two surveys for their *Trends in Higher Education* series—*Trends in College Pricing* and *Trends in Student Aid*. The college pricing survey summarizes the results of their Annual Survey of Colleges. Figure 5.2 illustrates why it is so difficult to communicate to students and their parents what college will actually cost. The graph shows five separate cost categories across four simple categories of institutional tuition rates—community colleges, public in-state, public out-of-state, and private not-for-profit colleges. The first cost listed for each type of institution is the average tuition and fees for full time attendance, and it shows that sticker prices vary dramatically. Community colleges remain a bargain at less than $3,000 per year, and half of all undergraduates today are enrolled in public 2-year colleges (National Center for Education Statistics, 2011b). It is not shown here, but a number of community colleges also publish out-of-state or out-of-district rates that are higher, though not as high as the in-state public rates. The graph in Figure 5.2 illustrates clearly, with tuition and fees alone, the average prices by sector range from $2,963 to $28,500, which means that the private not-for-profit price is set at roughly 10 times the price of the community college.

The College Board budget reports both tuition and fees and then separate living expenses. When living expenses are included, the initial sticker price for students rises to between $15,000 (community college) and $43,000 (private not-for-profit), on average. Typically, we do not include the costs of living in our estimates because students will live somewhere whether they are in college or not, and if you look closely at institutional estimates, living

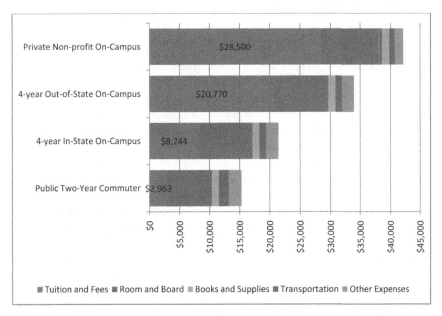

Figure 5.2 Average Estimated Undergraduate Budgets, 2011–2012
Source: The College Board. (2012a). *Trends in College Pricing* Washington, DC: author.

expenses do not vary nearly as much as tuition and fees. While it might not be the first thing a 4-year admissions professional considers, economists remind us that one of the greatest expenses for students is the opportunity costs associated with forgone wages they would have earned if they had chosen to work rather than attend college. Assuming a minimum wage of approximately $8/hour, an average college student is passing up on $16,000 per year for a chance to earn substantially more per year over a few less years. The challenge, of course, is that most students have no idea how much they may actually earn after college.

We suggest that sticker price and the range of potential costs associated with college attendance is a good place to start the conversation with students and their parents. Prices have risen dramatically, but most students attend institutions that are less expensive than those most commonly discussed in the media. Parents and students need to understand the differences in price, but we recognize that for some, even prices on the lower end of the range are simply too high for their families to afford. For these families, we are even more concerned with helping them understand the price they will actually pay for that education, which is almost always likely to be some amount less. In order to help students and families develop a better understanding of their net price, we must consider how federal, state, and institutional aid impact the bottom line and develop simpler, more transparent ways of communicating that to students and their families through our college access professional partners.

Net Price and Trends in Student Aid

If we as a society expect students and their families to make informed choices about whether or where to attend college, then we must empower them with the best and most targeted information to approximate their net price. Specifically, the process begins by educating the public about what they are likely to pay given their institutional preferences, family income, state and local place of residence, and academic profile of their students. We know, for example, that there are four key factors when considering net price: institutional sticker price, federal aid, state and local scholarship programs, and tuition discounting or institutional aid. Of these, sticker price is the most powerful signal because it is relatively simple to find and is the same for everyone. After that, the picture becomes blurry. Federal aid, for example, is mostly distributed according to financial need. The criteria for state scholarships vary between need-based and merit- or non-need-based aid, and in most states there are multiple programs. Colleges and universities routinely offer scholarships in the form of tuition discounting, but that money is intended to improve yield in targeted ways. If we want to help students and parents understand what they will pay for college, then we need to begin by explaining financial aid at each level. In each of the sections that follow, we provide pertinent background and context, discuss the main features of aid programs at those levels, and when available, consider what research tells us about the effects of each on students' access to college. Once we do that, we turn our attention to helping families better estimate their own net price.

Sources of Federal Support

The federal government has provided support to higher education for nearly as long as we have had a national government. During the 18th and 19th centuries, the federal government allocated land for the purposes of expanding higher education first through the Northwest Ordinance and again through the Land Grant Act of 1862. More formalized financial support for higher education began effectively during the 20th century, first in terms of support for federal research and development conducted on college campuses and then eventually through the direct allocation of resources to students for undergraduate education. Much of the early federally sponsored research was conducted on behalf of the Department of Defense, but during the middle part of the 20th century, the National Science Foundation (NSF) and the National Institutes of Health were created and funded to support campus-based research. Currently, the federal government spends an estimated $34 billion dollars conducting university-based research (Matthews, 2012). Much of this money is spent on biomedical research, basic and applied scientific research, the social sciences, and defense. R&D spending has a direct effect on colleges and universities but only an indirect effect on students—particularly graduate students who receive support to pursue their degrees.

The first large-scale federal student aid program was the Servicemen's Readjustment Act—popularly known as the GI Bill. In 1944, Congress passed legislation to provide services and support to accommodate servicemen returning from the Second World War—the tuition benefit was one of several features, including subsidies for purchasing a home. The GI Bill has gone through several iterations since its inception and continues to serve the educational and career needs of veterans returning from active duty. Evidence from studies of the various iterations of the GI Bill suggest that the education benefit has had an appreciable effect on the enrollment of men in postsecondary education, especially following a military conflict (Stanley, 2003). In 2012, GIs who served a minimum of 36 months active duty were eligible for 100% of tuition and fees at an in-state public 2- or 4-year college or an amount not to exceed $19,000 to selected private colleges (U.S. Department of Veterans Affairs, 2012). The benefits are granted proportionate to the amount of time served and the nature of the serviceman's discharge.

In this section, we focus on federal support through Title IV of the Higher Education Act (HEA) that helps students and their families pay for the cost of college. Federal aid to students assumes four basic forms: need-based grant aid, need-based (subsidized) and non-need-based (unsubsidized) loans, federal work–study, and tax credits. We do not discuss tax credits in detail, but we mention them here because they are intended to help families defray part of the cost of college. These programs operate through the tax code and are separate from the programs articulated as part of HEA.

Federal Grant Aid

The largest, most visible federal student aid program is the Pell Grant, named after Senator Claiborne Pell, who served as Senate Education Chairman when the program was conceived (a summary of federal programs is available in Table 5.1). However, the first federal grant program for students was the Educational Opportunity Grant (EOG) as part of the 1965 Higher Education Act (Curs et al., 2007). The act allowed for financial aid to flow directly to postsecondary institutions based upon the numbers of low-income students they served. That aid was administered to students by the participating college. By the first reauthorization of HEA (1972), the institutional aid program became known as the Federal Supplemental Educational Opportunity Grant (SEOG), and Congress created the Basic Educational Opportunity Grant (BEOG), which allocated grant dollars directly to students based upon their expected family contribution (EFC) (for more information about how EFC is calculated, see Baum [2004]), where a zero EFC will qualify students for the maximum award.

The SEOG program continues to flow directly to participating postsecondary institutions and must be awarded to students of exceptionally high need, beginning with those that have a zero expected family contribution (EFC). In order to participate in the programs, institutions must provide a 25% match of the federal funds. In 2010, the program was appropriated $757 million, meaning that slightly less than $1 billion in need-based aid flowed through colleges and universities to high-need students (National Association of Student Financial Aid Administrators, 2011).

The 1972, amendments to the HEA ushered in a new era of federal student aid. Instead of filtering money to students through institutions, the BEOG was a portable grant that followed high-need students to whatever eligible institution they chose to attend. The federal Pell Grant has been the single largest means-tested financial aid program in the country, and in recent years the program has grown substantially both in terms of total appropriations and the size of maximum awards. In 2001, the program award $9.9 billion in student aid, with a maximum grant of $3,750 (Curs et al., 2007). In fiscal year 2011, Congress appropriated more than $41 billion for Pell Grants, with a maximum award of $5,550 (U.S. Department of Education, 2012a).

In 2006, two additional grant programs were added to supplement Pell Grants. The American Competitiveness Grant (ACG) is an incentive grant to

Table 5.1 Federal Student Aid Programs, FY 2011–2012

Grants

Program	Eligibility	Annual Awards
Pell Grant	Undergraduate students with demonstrated financial need	Up to $5,550 (max. for 2011–2012).
Federal Supplemental Educational Opportunity Grant (FSEOG)	Undergraduates with exceptional financial need. Pell eligibility a priority, but based on availability at postsecondary institution	$100–$4,000.
Teacher Education Assistance for College and Higher Education Grant (TEACH)	Any level of student completing coursework necessary to teach in primary or secondary education. Must teach in area of teacher shortage and serve children in low-income families.	Up to $4,000 annually for up to 4 years. Graduate students also eligible for up to $8,000 total.
Iraq and Afghanistan Service Grant	Non-Pell-eligible undergraduate students whose parent or guardian died as a result of military service in Iraq or Afghanistan. Students must be either under age 24 at time of death or enrolled in college at the time.	Up to $5,550 (max. for 2011–2012).
Federal Work–Study	Both undergraduate and graduate students eligible. Based on financial need and level of available funds at the school.	No minimum or maximum.

Loans

Federal Perkins Loans	Undergraduate and graduate students with demonstrated financial need. Depends upon availability of funds at institution.	UG: Up to $5,500. Grad: Up to $8,000.
William D. Ford Direct Loans	Undergraduate students with demonstrated financial need; must be at least half time.	$3,500–$5,500 depending upon year in school.
Direct Subsidized Loans	Undergraduate students with financial need; must be at least half time.	$3,500–$5,500 depending on year in school.
Direct Unsubsidized Loans	Undergraduate students enrolled at least half-time and no financial need necessary.	$5,500–$12,500 (less subsidized loans) depending on year in school and dependent status.
Direct PLUS Loans	Graduate students or parents of dependent undergraduate students to help pay for college. Must have strong credit history.	Cost of attendance less any other financial aid received.
Direct Consolidation Loans	Borrowers with multiple federal student loans.	No minimum or maximum.

entice low-income students to complete a more rigorous curriculum in high school. Pell-eligible students who completed the approved college preparatory curriculum in their state were eligible for a supplemental award during their first two years. Students who continued into approved science, technology, engineering, math (STEM), or foreign languages were eligible for the national Science and Mathematics Access to Retain Talent (SMART) Grants beginning during their third year in school. These programs represented a first attempt by the federal government to tie academic merit to financial aid, though they were eliminated prior to the 2011–12 academic year.

The State Student Incentive Grant (SSIG) completed the triumvirate of means-tested federal financial aid programs. The SSIG was established in the 1972 amendments to HEA and offered funding to states for the first time in 1974. The SSIG amendment was an attempt to foster a collaborative funding mechanism between states and the federal government (Lee, 1980). The federal block grant requires a 50% match from the state and is to be administered to students with demonstrated need. Prior to 1974, 38 states or territories offered some form of means-tested student aid, and by 1978 all 56 had a program in place. In 1998, the program was renamed the Leveraging Educational Assistance Partnership (LEAP). By 2010, LEAP was funded at a level of $165 million, though it was not included in the 2011 budget and thus was also eliminated.

These programs, taken as a collective, were designed to leverage federal dollars to encourage states and institutions to focus their financial aid efforts on low-income students. Unfortunately, FSEOG and the LEAP (when it was funded) were modest relative to the Pell Grant, and the latter has been defunded, thus removing the incentive for states to maintain need-based aid programs. Most of the state-level programs developed to take advantage of SSIG and LEAP are now well established and have not been threatened with elimination, but higher education spending has been cut substantially throughout the first decade of the 21st century and if the trends continue, these programs may be at risk as well. One of the challenges for all of these programs is that evidence of effectiveness of federal need-based programs is mixed. Researchers have found it difficult to isolate the effects of Pell Grants from other aid programs, but in general, the conclusions have suggested that most students' enrollment decisions are not influenced by changes in price, though it may affect their choice of institution (Curs et al., 2007).

Student Loans

During the early years of federal student aid, grants were the primary federal mechanism to influence postsecondary opportunities. As Figure 5.3 illustrates, federal spending on grants outpaced loans through 1980. Since that time, spending on loans has grown at a much greater rate. In 2011, spending on federal loan programs—primarily the subsidized and unsubsidized

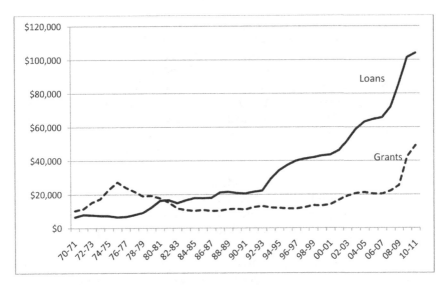

Figure 5.3 Shift in Federal Aid From Grants to Loans (in Millions), 1971–2011
Source: The College Board. (2012b). *Trends in Student Aid* Washington, DC: author.

Stafford loans—was nearly double the federal investment in grants. Advocates for increasing college access have been critical of this shift, which corresponded with growing concerns for middle-class families' ability to pay for college (Hearn, 2001). Today, student loans are a critical source of support for many students and their families who could simply not afford to attend college without them. However, continued reliance on loans has exposed a growing number of students to high levels of student debt, including both federal loans and education loans originated on the private markets. The two largest federal loan programs are the subsidized and unsubsidized Stafford loans through the direct lending. The subsidized loans are means-tested, and eligibility is determined by a student's demonstrated need through the FAFSA.

Eligible students will qualify for up to $3,500 per year in 2012 for their first two years, and that amount increases gradually to $5,500 in subsequent years (see Table 5.1). Dependent students may qualify for no more than $23,000 in subsidized loans and $31,000 total loans during their undergraduate careers. These loan caps have not risen to keep pace with rising college prices. Federally subsidized loans carry two principal benefits for students. First, the interest rate is low and set by legislation, meaning that students can expect their interest rates will not change over time. Second, the interest for these loans is paid by the federal government during the time students are enrolled in school. Students only begin to accrue interest six months after they are no longer enrolled in any postsecondary education.

The unsubsidized loan program has become the largest federal loan program. The difference is that students begin to accrue interest from the moment the loan is originated and are required to pay on the loan immediately. Students are not required to demonstrate financial need for this program, and the loan amounts are more generous, meaning that in 2012, students could borrow up to $12,500 per year. In 2011, the federal government shifted away from private lenders for federal loans to direct lending, meaning that the federal government is the lender for these loans. The change was made to eliminate the cost of subsidies provided to banks and state guaranty agencies that were providing or securing many of these loans. To this point the shift has not impacted availability of student loans for students, although it has resulted in the consolidation of programs. In 2010 and 2011, the Perkins loan program, which was federally supported but provided through the colleges and universities, was not funded, and the fate of the program is currently being debated among policy makers (Nelson, 2011).

The PLUS loans are available to parents of dependent students or to independent graduate or professional students. The interest rates are lower than what is available on the private loan market, and the award limits are equivalent to the cost of attendance less any other aid received. However, unlike other programs, the awards depend upon the credit worthiness of those applying for the loans. And like the unsubsidized programs, interest accrues from the moment the loan is originated and repayment begins immediately.

The growth of the student loan market is a double-edged sword. On the one hand, these loan programs coupled with the availability of funds through the private loan markets have made college possible for many—particularly among middle-income families—at both the undergraduate and graduate levels. On the other hand, average student loan debt is on the rise, which may constrain student opportunities when they leave college. In 2011, average debt among all borrowers exceeded $25,000 (Ellis, 2011a), and these estimates do not include credit card debt that has also been on the rise. According to estimates, college students carry an average of more than $3,100 in credit card debt, up nearly $1,000 in five years (Chu, 2009).

One of the promising student loan developments in recent years has been the introduction and expansion of the income-based repayment (IBR) option. Students now have an option under the direct loan program to pay back their loans according to their ability to pay. If they leave school (graduate or not), and their family income is sufficiently low as calculated by the federal government, they will pay a portion of their loan, commensurate with their ability to pay. If at the end of 20 years, they have not been able to pay all or a portion of their loans, the debt will be forgiven, assuming they have been current on payments throughout that time (Federal Student Aid, 2012). In exchange, students will extend the amount of time required to pay their loans and will accrue more interest along the way. IBR is not an entirely new idea, but it is a relatively recent development in the United States. A similar model has been employed in Australia for many years. The advantage of this option is that it removes some of the risk for prospective students who may otherwise question whether the investment is worth the benefit. The program also provides a safeguard against dramatic declines in labor market opportunities, as has been the case during the recession of the late 2000s. Federal Student Aid also offers a 10-year loan repayment option for borrowers who go into public service and continue payments throughout that time.

Additional Federal Programs

Need-based grants and loans are the two most important federal contributions to making college affordable for a broader cross-section of students, but there are at least two additional federal strategies worth mentioning— federal work–study (FWS) and tax credits. FWS is means-tested, like the other federal programs, and it is offered by the institution. The Student Aid Report (SAR) indicates whether a student qualifies for FWS given his or her expected family contribution (EFC). There are two key differences with FWS. First, the awards tend to account for a modest portion of the total aid package. Students may qualify for more FWS than an institution is willing to offer in their aid package, and there are no guarantees a student will be able to find a job on campus that accepts FWS. Institutions must provide as much as 50% of the salary students earn—except for those activities deemed community service, where the federal contribution may be 100% (U.S. Department of Education, 2012b).

Tax credits are another form of subsidy intended to provide an incentive to middle-class families to invest in higher education. Currently, three federal tax credits are available to students and families—the Hope, Lifetime Learning, and American Opportunity Tax Credits (AOTC). The first two programs are treated as tax expenditures, meaning that the credit reduces a filer's federal income tax liability. Families that earn too little money to owe federal tax do not benefit from these credits. The AOTC has been structured as a partially refundable tax expenditure, meaning that low-income filers can claim a refund of up to 40% of the credit (up to a maximum of $1,000). The AOTC was introduced as one of many stimulus programs in 2009, and it has increased the proportion of tax credit benefits going to families with incomes below $25,000 (Baum & Payea, 2012).

State Aid Programs

The federal government helps to maintain affordability for many students and provides the lion's share of financial aid to students, but the single largest supporter of higher education is the state. Typically, states provide support for higher education in two ways—direct appropriations to public colleges and universities and grant aid to students. Appropriations have the effect of keeping public tuition and fees low, relative to private higher education. These subsidies typically take the form of per-pupil allocations or separate capital expenditures. Figure 5.4 illustrates how public subsidies for higher education have changed over time.

The trends suggest that since 1995, state appropriations have fluctuated but grew in current dollars through much of the first part of the 2000s. In 1995, states provided direct support to public higher education of $42.8 billion and that number has grown to more than $72 billion in 2011. That sounds like a substantial increase in state funding, but there are two additional facts to consider. First, if states had simply maintained their support for higher education to reflect inflation as indicated by the Consumer Price Index (CPI), states would be funding appropriations to public institutions at almost $30 billion above current levels—assuming enrollments remained the same. The second factor to consider is enrollment growth over time. According to the National Center for Education Statistics (NCES, 2011b), higher education enrolled 14.8 million students in 1999, and 10 years later, enrollments had grown to over 20.4 million. The quick summary is that state appropriations have not kept pace with either inflation or increased enrollments.

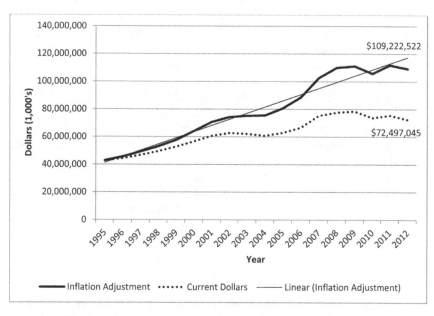

Figure 5.4 Total State Appropriations to Higher Education Current and Constant Dollars, 1995–2012

Colleges and universities will be quick to tell you that they have increased spending on financial aid for students as they raise their sticker prices. However, as The College Board (Baum & Payea, 2012) summarizes, institutional subsidies have not kept pace with the rising sticker prices. Now we turn our attention to state financial aid programs—and in particular, signature aid programs. In some states, these programs provide substantial funding to students, relative to their public tuition rates—New York and Minnesota are two that come to mind. Other states have not adequately kept pace with financial aid at the state level, including Michigan, which recently eliminated its signature merit grant program. Most states offer an array of financial aid programs, but their signature programs tend to be the largest and reflect the values of state policy makers most closely.

Signature financial aid programs tend to be the third largest subsidy to higher education, behind state appropriations and capital expenditures. Even though each of these programs is unique, we have found there to be three general types of signature programs—need-based, merit-based, and hybrid programs. We review examples of each here—the New York State Tuition Assistance Program (TAP) (need), the Georgia HOPE (merit), and the Indiana 21st Century Scholars (hybrid). In truth we could have chosen a variety of different states as exemplars. The Cal Grant is perhaps the largest need-based program outside of the Pell Grant; the Florida Bright Futures is an interesting and complex merit-based program that defines merit in a variety of ways; and both Tennessee and West Virginia maintain interesting hybrid programs. We chose these programs for two reasons. First, we are familiar with these programs from personal and professional experience, and in that sense, they serve as convenient illustrations. Second, with the exception of TAP, there is a fair amount written about these programs.

The New York State Tuition Assistance Program (TAP)

The Tuition Assistance Program in New York State is one of the oldest and largest state-sponsored need-based financial aid programs in the nation. TAP was an outgrowth of the Scholar Incentive Program (SIP). The 1961 program was unique among state scholarships because there were no limits on the size of the awards or the number of awards granted. The granting of awards was based upon state net taxable income, and all eligible students received the award (New York State Higher Education Services Corporation, 2012). The SIP award could be used in conjunction with the Regents Scholarship or other programs so long as financial assistance did not exceed the cost of attendance.

New York is known for its means-tested TAP program, but its earliest predecessor was a merit award—which is still in existence. The Regents College Scholarship was designed to encourage academically talented students to consider attending college—a real concern at a time when a substantial proportion of the high school graduate population did not choose to attend college. By the 1970s, state leaders were more concerned about the chances for low-income students to attend college and less so about the fate of academically talented students, so in 1974, the New York State legislature reduced Regents program funding and established TAP as an extension of SIP (New York State Higher Education Services Corporation, 2012).

TAP is the second largest need-based program in the country (behind the Cal Grant), and yet it has received little attention among researchers. Unlike HOPE and the 21st Century Scholars, we found no published studies of the effects of the program on college enrollment. The TAP program and its predecessor (SIP) were both launched before research in financial aid programs was common. What is clear, however, is that the awards have always been generous relative to the cost of public higher education. In fact, TAP may have been set at a higher than expected maximum award because the state is home to so many private not-for-profit colleges. TAP-eligible students may use that money at any public or private institution in the state. To place the size and scope of TAP in perspective, the program cost the state $78.8 million in 1974 and served more than 235,000 students; in 2010, the state spent $898 million to provide support to more than 330,000 full-time equivalent (FTE) students (National Association of State Student Grant and Aid Programs, 2011).

TAP is among the most generous need-based state grant programs in the country for two reasons. First, the maximum award is set at $5,000, which is nearly equal to the maximum Pell Grant ($5,550). Second, and perhaps more importantly, the State University of New York (SUNY) and its sister system in New York City (CUNY) have maintained a commitment to relatively low tuition rates. In 2012, SUNY tuition and fees averaged approximately $7,172, and CUNY was slightly less. Low-income students in New York are eligible to receive enough combined federal and state need-based aid to cover the cost of tuition, fees, and a portion of their living expenses and books.

Georgia HOPE Scholarship

In 1992, Governor Zell Miller signed legislation to create a state lottery with the proceeds going to support education. The HOPE scholarship was one of several programs targeted for funding from the state lottery. Beginning in 1993, graduates of Georgia high schools that had earned a 3.0 GPA were eligible for free tuition to a public 2- or 4-year college in the state. In order to maintain the award throughout their college careers, students were required to maintain a 3.0 college GPA. Initially, the program set an income threshold of $66,000, which was eliminated entirely by their third year of the program.

One of the early concerns raised by critics of the program was that the program was disproportionately advantageous to middle- and upper-income families because federal aid reduced students' financial need. Since that time, the program has been modified to allow low-income families to receive some benefit from the program beyond what is covered by Pell Grants.

The Georgia HOPE is the model merit aid program in the United States that has been emulated by a number of other states. In 1993, Arkansas was the only other state with a signature merit aid program; within the next decade, more than a dozen states had large-scale merit aid programs, and most of the 14 were in Southern states (Cornwell & Mustard, 2004). None of the other programs have gained the notoriety of the Georgia HOPE. The program was both an inspiration and namesake to the eventual federal HOPE education tax credit. One of the virtues of the HOPE scholarship program is that eligibility criteria are simple and straightforward. If students complete the required courses in high school, graduate, earn a 3.0 GPA, and gain admission to a public college or university in the state, they are eligible to receive full support for tuition and fees. There is little guesswork among students, families, or educators regarding whether students are eligible.

The effects of the program on access to college are generally mixed. On one hand, Georgia increased the proportion of high school graduates that enrolled in college, compared to other states in the region (Cornwell & Mustard, 2004; Dynarski, 2003). On the other hand, it appeared to have a disproportionate impact on White students relative to their Black counterparts, having the effect of widening the gap in college participation rates by race (Dynarski, 2003). Unfortunately, two-thirds of HOPE recipients lose eligibility during their first year in college due to the GPA requirement, and reentry into the program is possible but not common. The estimated benefits are modest when compared to the size and cost of the program. At its peak, the HOPE scholarship enrolled more than 256,000 students at a price of more than $747 million to the state (Georgia Student Finance Commission, 2012). Those numbers have declined in recent years, largely as a consequence of changes made to the program.

While Georgia HOPE has been the model for nearly 20 years, the program faces enormous challenges. When it began, the lottery provided funding to four initiatives, but in 2012, the cost of HOPE exceeded the revenues. In 2012, policy makers in Georgia were reconsidering the viability of the scholarship, particularly in light of the financial pressures to grow enrollments. In 2013, students will be required to earn a higher GPA (3.7) to qualify for the full tuition guarantee—this program will be called the Zell Miller Scholarship. The original HOPE will continue to require the 3.0 GPA, but it will only cover 90% of tuition at a public institution (University System of Georgia, 2012). Neither scholarship program will include fees or books.

Indiana 21st Century Scholars (TFCS) Program

The 21st Century Scholars program is different from both TAP and HOPE and, in some ways, combines elements of the two. First, it is not the signature need-based aid program—that distinction belongs to the Frank O'Bannon Scholarship (St. John, Daun-Barnett, Fisher, Lee, & Williams, 2008). Second, it is a need-based program in the sense that students must qualify for free or reduced-cost lunch while in the eighth grade. The program also establishes merit criteria, though the standards are more permissive than the Georgia program. Initially, any eligible student maintaining a 2.0 GPA (on a 4.0 scale) was eligible. In 2007, the state added the requirement that students must also complete the Core 40 (college preparatory) high school curriculum for the graduating class of 2011 (Indiana Commission for Higher Education, 2011).

The distinctive feature of the scholarship is the administration of the college pledge. Middle school students who are eligible for free or reduced-cost lunch are asked to sign a pledge indicating that if they meet the academic standards and maintain certain behavioral standards, they are guaranteed that Indiana will cover the cost of tuition and fees to a public 2- or 4-year institution (St. John, Musoba, & Simmons, 2003). A portion of the aid can also be applied to private tuition and fees. The award itself is modest—in fact, the O'Bannon Scholarship covers most of the costs for these students and many other students. What the O'Bannon does not cover, the 21st Century Scholars program does. And like other initiatives, TFCS is last dollar, meaning that all other forms of aid are taken into account first. But unlike other programs in Indiana, this is the only program that guarantees the price for students will be zero.

Initially, far fewer students signed the pledge than were eligible. Estimates suggest that only a third of eligible students signed the pledge, meaning the program has served anywhere between 4,000–10,000 students (where TAP and HOPE served many more students). Even though the state established 14 regional centers around the state to help scholars take advantage of the guarantee, there were no systematic efforts to maintain student knowledge of and enthusiasm for the program through their high school years. The results of evaluation studies suggest that for those students who participated, the program was successful. Scholars were more likely to complete demanding courses in high school, go to college, apply for financial aid, attend college in state, and demonstrate success in college (St. John et al., 2008).

Institutional Aid Strategies

The third layer of financial aid is developed at the institutional level. While it is beyond the scope of this chapter to examine the range of tuition-discounting strategies or rationales employed by colleges and universities, it is important to recognize that institutions utilize an array of tools to attract and retain students, including need-based aid, race-specific scholarships, academic merit awards to attract high-achieving students (e.g. honors), and awards for talents in noncurricular domains (e.g. athletics and the arts). In short, tuition discounting is a complex process, and as much as we would like to see a simpler, more transparent alternative, we understand there are good reasons why that will never be the case.

Instead of delving deeply into tuition discounting in general, we focus our attention on the subset of institutional strategies designed specifically to address financial need. A number of institutions around the country have begun to take clear steps to eliminate cost as a barrier for low-income students. Princeton and Harvard were two of the early adopters of these institution-specific programs. In both cases, the colleges have chosen to replace loans with institutional grants to cover the expected family contribution for families below a certain income threshold (Avery et al., 2006; Princeton University, 2001). These institutions have set the income criteria near the median family income in the United States—$40,000–$42,000 at the time these first programs were initiated at the end of the 1990s. Generally, these early efforts appear to have expanded access in targeted ways for low-income students. In the case of the Harvard program, the elimination of cost for low-income families increased the applicant pool of eligible students. The result was an increase in applications and a comparable yield for low-income enrollees (Avery et al., 2006). In their investigation of a private university in the Northeast, Linsenmeier, Rosen, and Rouse (2002) found the program did not have a significant effect overall, but it appeared to be beneficial in terms of enrolling low-income underrepresented minority students.

A number of selective private colleges and public flagship institutions around the country have followed suit. Unfortunately, the reason many of these institutions are able to make a guarantee of this nature work is that comparatively few low-income students will gain admission to their institutions—they are far too selective, meaning that many of these low income students will not meet the academic threshold for admission. When we look at the Harvard model or any of the others, they have not substantially changed the socio-economic mix of students—rather, they have inspired a few more to consider these institutions, and for a handful of students, they have made a substantial difference (Avery et al., 2006). These institutions also have other advantages—they tend to be very expensive overall (like the institutions in the over $50,000 club described earlier), and they manage larger than average endowments.

A number of public flagship institutions have followed a similar course. The University of Virginia launched AccessUVA in 2004 to provide access to a high-quality education for all students who are prepared to take advantage. They have guaranteed that they will meet 100% of financial need for all students whose family incomes are below 200% of the federal poverty rate—approximately $75,000 at the time the program was initiated (University of Virginia, 2011). The University of North Carolina at Chapel Hill has made a similar commitment to low-income students through its Carolina Covenant. Any academically eligible student admitted to the institution with family income below 200% of poverty level is eligible. The one difference may be that work–study is a part of the package to help low-income families earn a Carolina degree debt free (University of North Carolina at Chapel Hill, 2012). Neither of these programs have been evaluated to the extent of the private versions discussed earlier, but both report serving a sizable number of students who, at very least, would have assumed greater levels of debt to take advantage of their educational opportunities.

Flagship public universities are not quite as selective as their Ivy League counterparts, but they tend to be the most selective institutions in the public systems, and their students are more advantaged than those attending the other public universities in the state. The point is that most institutions, public or private, cannot afford to make this sort of need-based guarantee because they serve a greater proportion of low-income students, and they lack other forms of revenue (like endowments) to offset tuition and fees they will no longer collect. These programs are more or less plausible depending upon both the selectivity of the institution and the actual cost of the program for the institution. In the case of North Carolina, the program is much less expensive because the state already maintains a fairly generous need-based grant program and has continued its commitment to relatively low tuition— at the time of writing this book, North Carolina may be the one state that has maintained a low tuition/high aid approach to funding public higher education. Ultimately, we suspect that programs like these may inspire some students to achieve more in high school, and they may also influence some schools to ramp up their efforts to prepare more of their students for college, but given the economics, most institutions will not be able to provide this sort of guarantee. We have found, however, that a new class of tuition guarantees has emerged that is similar to the institutional approaches but has the advantage of bringing new sources of revenue to the table—place-based tuition guarantees.

The Kalamazoo Promise and the Potential of Place

In 2005, the city of Kalamazoo, Michigan, announced, under the leadership of the superintendent of public schools Janice Brown, that beginning with the senior class, it will guarantee the cost of tuition and fees for any graduate of Kalamazoo Public Schools (KPS) who attends a public college or university in the state (Miller-Adams, 2008). The requirement was simple—gain admission and maintain degree eligibility—and any student would attend college free of charge. The only caveat was that the award was scaled according to the amount of time a student attended school in the district—65% for a minimum of four years, including graduating from high school; up to 100% for those in the district the entire time (Miron & Cullen, 2007). The Kalamazoo Promise represents a new breed of tuition guarantee programs, and for as many as have tried, it has been difficult to emulate (Daun-Barnett, 2011).

The Kalamazoo Promise was, first and foremost, an economic development strategy—or rather part of a larger regional economic development plan (Kitchens, Gross, & Smith, 2008). The city, like many in the Great Lakes region, was part of the rust belt of declining urban centers and was in search of ways to connect to an evolving knowledge economy. They surmised that the best way to attract knowledge employers was to invest in the college-educated talent required to fill those jobs. Because economic development was at the forefront of the agenda (and the reason anonymous donors were willing to pay the bill), it did not matter which students took advantage of the tuition guarantee—it could be low-income students, but the program would be equally successful if it brought more middle- and upper-income families back to the district. The strategy has been so successful in terms of both economic and educational outcomes that other communities—from Denver and Pittsburgh to El Dorado, Arkansas, and Syracuse, New York— have lined up to try and replicate their success.

The piece that few have been able to replicate is the first dollar guarantee. In financial aid, we observe a general race for the last dollar, meaning that a provider will meet any remaining need after all other sources of support are taken into account. Postsecondary institutions typically operate in this manner by virtue of the fact that they administer and package financial aid for students. Last dollar scholarships are more efficient because funds are not provided to students who are able to meet their cost through other subsidies. Last dollar programs can be confusing to students because no matter how many sources of financial aid they are able to obtain, they only receive enough to cover their basic tuition, fees, and general cost of attendance. First dollar is truly unique. The private anonymous donors in Kalamazoo simply write a check for the full amount of tuition and fees for every student (scaled to eligibility) no matter what additional sources of aid students bring to the table. For low-income students, that means any need-based award they receive from Pell Grants can be applied to housing or other educational expenses.

Last dollar initiatives tend to be more complicated to communicate than the Kalamazoo version. In many cases, there will be some students who do not receive the full benefit or who will pay something, meaning the program is a generous scholarship program rather than a tuition guarantee. Consider a recent place-based scholarship program in Buffalo, New York. Community leaders have partnered with Say Yes to Education to provide a place-based scholarship to all students who graduate high school in Buffalo

Public Schools or their partnering charter high schools (Say Yes to Education, 2012). The scholarship is a last dollar guarantee of tuition at a public institution or a participating private college scaled to the amount of time a student attends an eligible school in Buffalo. However, it does not include the cost of fees, which make up a quarter of the student bill for local 4-year public institutions, excluding room and board. For low-income students, the distinction is not important. They will qualify for enough aid from Pell Grants and TAP to cover tuition and fees plus some of their additional expenses. For high-income families (where EFC exceeds cost of attendance), it will mean a scholarship that will help them cover a good portion of their cost. For lower-middle-income families, some will still be required to meet all or a portion of their expected family contribution. The challenge is that students and their families will find it difficult to assess what they will qualify for under this program.

The second limitation is related. If the signal is not clear to students and families, particularly to those outside of the district but considering a move, it is unclear what amount they will receive or ultimately whether the move will be worth it. In short, it will be limited in terms of local economic development. This is not to say that the benefit will not be worth the potential cost of moving or the risk of a lower-quality education than they might receive in other places but that the program is too difficult to assess for families to make that decision. Under those conditions, it may be equally difficult to convince private donors to invest the money when the potential payoff for them is viewed, at least in part, as growing the human capital potential of the metropolitan center in a regional economy.

Conclusion

Paying for college is one of the most important investments families make, and it is the question of every parent when visiting campus or engaging with admissions counselors elsewhere. Millions have figured out how to pay the bill, but as costs rise, low-income students will continue to select themselves out of college attendance. That is a loss for colleges looking to fill enrollments, and it is a problem for a society that is calling for a more educated workforce in a knowledge-producing economy. If we hope to achieve any of the goals national leaders have set for education, then we must figure out how best to make college accessible for low-income, first-generation, and underrepresented minority students who are most susceptible to increasing prices.

As we have indicated throughout this chapter, there are some tremendous opportunities to help students and their families pay for the cost of college, but it has become an increasingly complicated landscape that is even more confusing for those not working within higher education. The complexity of the system underscores the need for admissions professionals to work even more closely with their financial aid colleagues, and we find that in an era of enrollment management, this linkage happens with greater regularity. It should also mean that admissions professionals spend more time understanding the financial aid side of enrollment management and communicate that complexity to school counselors, pre-college outreach providers, and independent consultants, none of whom have access to information about financial aid quite like admissions professionals do.

For admissions professionals, it means that they must understand and be able to communicate the complexity of the financial aid system to students and parents in a way that is accessible and honest—from the range of federal and state programs to the priorities of non-need-based aid at the institutional level. Helping families understand that tuition varies according to one's ability to pay is a good place to start. Net cost calculators may help as well, but it depends upon how these tools are built. The federal government has established some guidelines, but campuses have some discretion. We believe the most important role admissions professionals can play with regard to the issue of paying for college is to educate their school counselor, pre-college outreach, and independent consultant colleagues on how financial aid works at their respective institutions so they can help more students and parents make sense of the complex financial aid environment.

6

CONNECTING STUDENTS AND PARENTS TO THE RIGHT INFORMATION

The great irony of the information age is that while information has never been so easily accessible to all people, the sheer volume of information available makes utilizing that information increasingly difficult. The Internet has opened up new possibilities for us to think about how best to help students and families plan, prepare, and apply to college, but we should be cautious not to assume that these changes will actually make the process simpler or more democratically accessible. This may be one of the more important quandaries for admissions professionals. We have increasingly pushed the college choice and application process online, which is convenient for many families; it may even be more efficient for admissions offices. From the perspective of first-generation, low-income, and underrepresented minority students, though, moving these processes to the Internet has made going to college more complicated, not less.

Understanding Social and Cultural Capital

Information is a powerful tool that has never been so democratically accessible and yet so difficult to utilize. In this chapter we consider the likely sources of college-related information—including the array of individuals who influence students on the path to college—and we examine how that information is distributed to students and parents. A few observations are important as we begin this chapter. First, there is no lack of information in this area. Cottage industries were built around helping students and their families navigate the complexity of the college choice process. Today, the Web has become the definitive source of information—a simple Google search for the term "going to college" yields more than 12 million hits, making it nearly impossible to sort through all that is available.

Second, everyone is concerned about access to information, but for different reasons. Many of our programmatic efforts attempt to provide low-income, first-generation, and underrepresented minority students with the information they need to plan, prepare for, attend, and succeed in college. Most families recognize the value of college but have no idea what to ask or where to begin. Our experience suggests that for any program or information session we host about navigating the college-going process, many, if not most, of the participants are the families you would not expect to need it—upper-middle-class, college-educated parents, and their students who attend affluent suburban schools or private preparatory academies. These families understand the value of college and can speak to the experience, but they know full well that the process has changed considerably and the stakes are much higher than they were a generation ago. They also appreciate that college is the most important investment they will make in their children's futures, and it is not an investment one leaves to chance—hence the growth of the independent consultant market.

Third, even with the best, most accurate and reliable information, students and their families continue to need guidance and support as they make their way through the process. We liken this to the evolution of WebMD, the comprehensive medical web portal. Today more than ever, people have been empowered with accurate and reliable information to diagnose and treat potential maladies. However, making that information available to all has not eliminated the need for doctors—quite the contrary. We suspect (though cannot prove) that WebMD has never cured anyone, though it has certainly changed the nature of the conversation between patients and their doctors. This is precisely why we believe it is so important that we catalyze a much larger network of college access professionals with expertise in these areas. New and better information will not eliminate the need for guidance and support, but it may change the conversations we have with students and parents about going to college—including how best to employ this new set of college access tools.

In this section we consider two questions: (a) What information do students and their families need to navigate the college choice process, and (b) How is that information accessed and distributed? The answers to the first question are in many ways intuitive, but they are rooted in different theories and it is important to consider each. In our examination of the second question, we focus on the importance of cultural and social capital—two sociological theories that explain in very practical ways how families, communities, social networks, and institutions serve to distribute information to students in different ways and for a variety of purposes.

What Information Do Students and Parents Need?

The answer to this question is largely a matter of perspective and is shaped by one's experience. Economists, for example, assume that students are rational actors who make decisions by weighing the costs and benefits and who will continue to invest in education until the anticipated benefits no longer outweigh the costs. Implicit in much of the research on college choice is that students possess all the information they need, and will make a rational choice about the greatest level of benefit based on the cost to attend coupled with the opportunity cost of leaving the labor market for an extended period (Niu & Tienda, 2010). From this perspective, the two most important pieces of information are the price of college and the benefits of attendance (for example, estimated wages). Embedded in the issue of price is the quality of the investment, either in terms of the institution selected or the major chosen. Even if we assume that students or their parents are rational economic actors, research has recognized that their rationality is bounded by the nature and extent of the knowledge they possess and their own unique circumstances (Perna, 2006; Plank & Jordan, 2001). The rising price of college is only one of several prominent barriers for students. For example, many students leave high school inadequately prepared for postsecondary education, and some proportion of them could have taken a more rigorous path through high school. For others, the process of achieving success in school, identifying future career plans, identifying appropriate college options, and completing the requisite applications is overwhelming and may serve as a barrier to college opportunity. We examine each of these pieces of information below.

The Price of College

Students and parents are not well informed about the cost of college. Researchers at Stanford University, for example, report findings from a multistate study indicating that both groups overestimate the cost of college and those differences are exacerbated for low-income families and for first-generation and underrepresented minority students (antonio & Bersola, 2004; Kirst & Venezia, 2004). The cost of college is a real and growing concern for many families, as an increasing proportion of students are leaving college with debt, and the amount of loans they assume have grown. Nationwide, student loan debt has exceeded credit card debt for the first time, climbing to over $1 trillion (Mitchell & Jackson-Randall, 2012). At the same time, the average loan debt per student has surpassed $25,000. The College Board reminds us that while the price colleges charge has risen much faster than inflation, net cost, or the amount students actually pay, remains much more reasonable. Unfortunately, this message has been difficult to convey because financial aid programs are complicated and institutions are wary about sharing their tuition discounting practices—as we discussed in the previous chapter.

Research has shown that in general, students are responsive to the price of higher education. Leslie and Brinkman (1987) found, consistent with demand theory, that enrollments were inversely related to the prices charged to students (tuition or net cost), that student aid had a positive impact on enrollment, and that enrollment decisions were positively associated with the tuition prices charged by competitors. Their findings confirm what one might expect—enrollment probabilities fall as prices go up. Additionally, they find that lower-income, older, and community college students are generally more responsive to price and that upper division students are less responsive to fluctuations in tuition and net price. What is interesting in all of this literature is that, while studies have fairly consistently shown these relationships, in practice, as tuitions have risen nationally, so have overall enrollments. It may mean that while students are sensitive to prices, they are choosing from a variety of different alternatives including different institution options.

Heller (1997) conducted a follow-up and expanded upon Leslie and Brinkman's research by summarizing the important advances of price response theory, particularly in the context of various forms of student aid, across different sectors of higher education, and among different groups of students. Heller warned that while the relationship between tuition and enrollment remained consistent, financial aid in its various forms did not act as a simple reduction in the price of college. Tuition, in his review, played a more prominent role in enrollment decisions than any form of student aid. The reason is simple—sticker price acts as a much clearer signal regarding price than any form of tuition discount because we (in higher education) tell people the sticker price up front. We tend to be less forthright about how we discount tuition in postsecondary education, which leaves families uncertain about their net price. As such, at least part of the problem with these economic approaches is that families never have as much information as they need to make informed decisions until very late in the process when they receive financial aid offers from institutions.

Economists and education researchers have examined the extent to which information influences the postsecondary choices students make, and their findings suggest that access to information is important but may not result in the "rational" decisions economic models suggest. Long (2004) notes that students and families overestimate the cost of college and know very little about financial aid. Avery and Kane (2004) conclude, in their examination of the Boston COACH program, that students overestimated the cost of college, but they also overestimated the economic benefits of earning their degrees. Bell, Rowan-Kenyon, and Perna (2009) found that 11th-grade students were better informed about the college choice process than 9th-grade students but continue to demonstrate gaps in their knowledge regarding the cost of college and programs designed to help students pay for college. All of these analyses suggest that information may be one of the challenges students face in their college choice process.

Academic Expectations

While college affordability is one of the critical barriers to postsecondary opportunity, it is not the only area where students lack necessary information. The work of the Stanford Bridge project underscores that students underestimate the academic expectations for postsecondary preparation (antonio & Bersola, 2004). In the absence of high expectations and clear guidance from parents, teachers, or counselors, students will complete only what is minimally expected to graduate from high school, which is typically insufficient to begin college-level work. Admissions professionals bear some responsibility for the lack of guidance students appear to have regarding what academic paths align with postsecondary expectations—in part because our threshold in the admissions process is fluid. The larger problem is more directly rooted in the existing chasm between high school graduation requirements and college admissions expectations, which we discussed in some detail in Chapter 3.

Admissions professionals find it difficult to answer a direct question about the admissions requirements to enter their institution (or any other for that matter) for good reasons. First, every institution has a slightly different set of standards. Even community colleges within the same state system will set different cut scores on placement tests in math and writing, and the differences are more dramatic across institutional sectors. Placement tests have not been formally aligned with state content standards, and, in many cases, tests are not particularly well aligned with the content taught at the postsecondary institution. The second problem we face in terms of clarifying academic expectations for college is that demonstrated academic success is only one of several priorities admissions professionals weigh as they decide whom to admit. As soon as we attempt to explain that the academic profile for men is lower than that for women or that test scores for musicians are lower than for those admitted to engineering, we are confronted with looks of either frustration or confusion. The third reality facing admissions professionals is that the profile of any given applicant pool may fluctuate—either in predictable ways relative to demographic shifts or more idiosyncratic responses to societal conditions like labor market opportunities. It may be more appropriate for students to think about their high school academic experience relative to their intended majors in school, but that will require a fundamental shift in how we prepare students for career exploration.

Navigating the Process

Hossler, Schmit, and Vesper (1999) suggest that information is not perfectly and uniformly available to students and their families. They recognize that students have access to different types of information, and their understanding of that information is situated in the places they live and attend school. In their three-stage model, Hossler et al. (1999) suggest that different forms of information should be brought to bear at different stages in the process. During the early predisposition phase, information is used to influence students' aspirations and plans for college, whereas the further along students progress, the more instrumental knowledge about the college search, application, and choice process grows in importance. For a more comprehensive treatment of the college choice process, see Hossler et al. (1999).

The piece of information that is most analogous to purchasing a home, as we described in the first chapter, is how to navigate the college application and decision-making process. In many cases, students will only run this gauntlet once, maybe twice, during their lifetimes, and they seldom receive advance training on how and when to begin the process. Parents may face these issues several times depending upon the number of children they have and their ability to be involved, but they will by no means be experts in the process. Admissions professionals must take the lead to help their college access partners in schools, pre-college outreach programs, and independent consultancies to understand how and why it changes so they can guide their students and families.

These changes generally fall into two categories—those decisions made by institutions to make the process simpler for admissions professionals and external forces that impose changes upon institutions. The cost of managing the college application review process is substantial, and institutions are constantly searching for ways to simplify the workflow and process decisions more efficiently and effectively. One example has been the movement toward the use of electronic transcript services. For many years, colleges have experimented with electronic application systems, which moves institutions a step closer to a full electronic review, but several pieces of the application (including transcripts and letters of recommendation) have been slower to move into the digital space—an issue we address in greater detail in Chapter 8.

The potential benefits for colleges may come at the expense of schools. For one, these systems assume that school-based student information systems are accurate and reliable and that they were set up for the purpose of extracting data in this way. In many cases, this transition has been difficult for schools, and it costs them time and resources to participate effectively. But it also does something else that schools do not always appreciate—it reduces the transcript to its essential data elements for the purpose of comparing students on common metrics. In the process, it strips the school's identity from the document, and it removes any benefit or advantage a school may wish to convey through that document. Every school, like every college, wants to portray their students in the best possible light, and this process is antithetical to the goal of the schools. The burden of processing transcripts typically falls to the school counseling staff and any new process, even a more efficient one, only complicates their work. In this case, for example, not all colleges will accept electronic transcripts in XML format so they may either continue paper documents or send PDF images. The result is that counselors will no longer have a single routine procedure for processing transcripts—a considerable burden for professionals with little discretionary time during a given school day.

In other cases, external forces influence the application process. For example, many different strategies have been considered and tested to simplify the college application process for students. The logic is simple. Students may fill out as many as 10 or more applications, and each of these forms is essentially the same. That is to say 95% of the information any college or university needs is identical to virtually every other institution. The Common Application (referred to as Common App) is one very popular example of a national effort to ease the application process by standardizing the form for all participating colleges and universities so that students only complete the majority of the process once. Of course, if a student applies to some institutions that participate in Common App and others that do not, the process remains duplicative. The state of North Carolina was unique in its ability to move all of its electronic college applications into a comprehensive web portal (Tillery & English, 2009)—a story we discuss in greater detail in Chapter 8. They made this move at a time when institutions were still beginning their online presence, but none since then have had such universal success statewide. In this case, the move toward the portal was championed by the North Carolina State University System, and private colleges voluntarily participated.

Irrespective of why the system changes over time, we can rest assured that it will continue to change, and the only professionals who will be able to keep pace are those in admissions offices across the country and independent consultants who are hired for their expertise in this arena. School counselors need to keep current with these changes, but they consistently lack the time necessary. Pre-college outreach professionals have the time to spend with students and families, but they are not as well connected to admissions professionals within these systems. Even the programs sponsored by colleges and universities find it difficult to connect their professionals to the admissions counselors on their own campuses.

How Do Students and Parents Access the Information They Need?

In the previous section, we examined the types of information students and families need to access in order to successfully transition from high school to college. Now we turn our attention to the ways in which information is transmitted to students and their families. Sociologists have spent a great deal of time examining the flow of information to students in the broader context of social stratification and inequality. As discussed earlier, economists recognize the value of information in the cost benefit analysis, but they largely assume that information is readily available, even while recognizing that information asymmetries are common problems in all sorts of investment decisions. Sociologists recognize that the flow of information is essential to providing postsecondary opportunities and not all students have the same access to the information, support, and guidance they need to make informed choices along the way. Theories of both cultural and social capital have been used to articulate the noneconomic, but very real, value of the context within which a student is raised and the networks of relationships to which they have access.

Cultural Capital

We spend a good deal of time in schools and among educators and policy makers who voice the opinion that what we really need is to create a college-going culture for students in schools and at home. What they mean by "culture" is seldom articulated, but they are convinced that culture is a critical dimension of the college choice process. Culture is a complex phenomenon that cannot be easily distilled or manufactured, but we develop a better sense of its influence by recognizing the values students possess that might reasonably be linked to one's culture. A number of researchers, theorists, and educators, beginning with Pierre Bourdieu, have examined how culture is transmitted from one generation to the next and how that "capital" serves to maintain one's relative position in the social hierarchy.

Building upon the work of Bourdieu and applying it specifically to the college choice process, McDonough states that "cultural capital is that property that middle and upper income families transmit to their offspring which substitutes for or supplements the transmission of economic capital as a means of maintaining class status and privilege across generation" (McDonough, 1997, p. 8). To the extent that this particular form of cultural capital has value in terms of college participation, McDonough has captured it quite right. We prefer to think of cultural capital, however, in more generic terms so as to recognize that all individuals possess some form of cultural capital that has more or less value depending upon the context to which it is applied. As Perna and Titus (2005) note, "[C]ultural capital refers to the system of attributes, such as language skills, cultural knowledge, and mannerisms, that is derived in part from one's parents and that defines an individual's class status" (p. 488).

We are all influenced by the values, knowledge, and experiences of our families, our religious institutions, and our communities and schools. All of these structures shape the way we view the world and our perception of our place within it; and this form of capital certainly informs the value we place on education and the degree to which we move from compulsory education through high school into the elective world of postsecondary education. From this perspective, it should be clear why we pay so much attention to first-generation, low-income, and underrepresented minority students in the college choice process. These are the groups of students least likely to have the direct influences of families, friends, and neighbors who have experienced postsecondary education. Most of our intervention efforts assume

107

that students come with a deficit in terms of cultural capital, or at the very least this particular form of it. Tierney and colleagues (2005) have advocated on behalf of a cultural integrity framework that assumes all cultural contexts have value and that intervention strategies should seek to leverage those strengths rather than to fill existing gaps. Our challenge then is twofold: Can college access professionals recognize the value in other forms of cultural capital, and can outreach efforts serve as a surrogate for the forms of capital that will help to prepare students for the next steps into postsecondary education?

Social Capital—Mobilizing Social Networks for the Flow of Information

If information and support are the currency exchanged from one generation to the next when it comes to college participation, then social capital provides the vehicle by which it flows. The strength of one's network is very much related to the sorts of opportunities they have at their disposal. How often have we heard the aphorism "It is not what you know, it is who you know?" We generally recognize the truth in this statement or lament the fact when things don't quite go our way. For those of us who exchange social capital as currency, we know it is a bit more complicated, but, all things being equal, relationships have value. And we should be clear, if college admissions professionals know anything, it is the value of a robust network of peers, colleagues, and professional acquaintances. The concept of social capital was formally articulated by both Pierre Bourdieu and James Coleman, and each reflects a slightly different orientation to the construct (Dika & Singh, 2002).

Dika and Singh (2002) note that while the concept has come to include both the transmission of social norms and access to institutional resources, "Bourdieu [saw] social capital as a tool of reproduction for the dominant class, whereas Coleman [viewed] it as (positive) social control, where trust, information channels, and norms are characteristics of the community" (p. 34). This is an important distinction, given our work of increasing access to college for a greater proportion of students, because we recognize that while social capital has been used to maintain class privilege, it may be one of the critical remedies educators employ to level the playing field today. Lin (2001) summarizes, "[S]ocial capital consists of resources embedded in social relations and social structures, which can be mobilized when an actor wishes to increase the likelihood of success in a purposive action" (p. 24). Anyone who has ever recommended a friend or a family member for an opportunity understands intuitively how social capital operates. They also appreciate that the value of the exchange is beneficial both to the recipient of knowledge or contacts and to those in the exchange.

If we shift our conversation for a moment to the more specific purpose of the book, we recognize that the relationships admissions professionals have with school counselors, pre-college outreach providers, and independent consultants operate in much the same way. As Farmer-Hinton and Adams (2006) note, "[S]ocial capital refers to social relationships from which an individual is potentially able to derive institutional support, particularly support that includes the delivery of knowledge-based resources, for example, guidance for college admission or job advancement" (p. 119). Each of the professional groups we have identified has a form of capital that has value within the network and can be exchanged to the benefit of the work they do. Admissions professionals offer knowledge about the admissions process to those who serve students and insight into what it takes for students to succeed once they arrive on campus. The other three parties offer prospective students to meet admissions targets—whether that means simply filling a class or identifying students from particular target populations like athletes, honors, or underrepresented minority students. All parties stand to benefit from the exchange, and we have not even discussed students, who we believe will be the ultimate beneficiaries of a strong social network.

The question with which we must contend is whether we can effectively supplement or substitute social capital or plug students into these existing networks where the benefits operate in much the same way. In this section, we consider what we know about several of the important sources of social capital in the lives of traditional age high school graduates and college participants—parents, counselors, teachers, and peers. Each of these groups has an influence on the lives of individual students, and they are all part of social networks of one form or another. As Perna and Titus (2005) note, "[T]he amount of social capital to which an individual may gain access through social networks and relationships depends on the size of the networks as well as the amount of economic, cultural and social capital that individuals in the network possess" (p. 488). The value of these different forms of capital depends upon the context, the members of the network, and the particular situations for which the network is being activated. After we consider what we know about the roles of these major groups, we turn our attention to several programs designed, at least in part, to plug students into a larger social network and, by extension, provide them access to the forms of social capital most likely to have value in the college choice process.

Parents

There is little argument that parents are the single most important source of both cultural and social capital in the lives of high school students. They are at the center of the social network, and they are in the best position to connect their children to the resources available through that network. Coleman's (1988) articulation of social capital has positioned parents and family structures as the exclusive source of social capital, but the research employing his theory does not account for the differences in resources available across different networks. Even if we assume that all parents have a great deal to offer their children, which we believe is an important place to start, it should be equally clear that they do not all offer the same benefits or in the same quantities.

Unfortunately, conversations about the role of parents commonly devolve into either criticisms of parents who appear to be disengaged from the college choice process or frustrations over the helicopter tendencies of parents thought to be overly involved in the postsecondary experiences of their sons and daughters. Both extremes surely exist and create problems for a number of students, but our emphasis on the extremes detracts our attention from what we think is essential to understanding parents—that all parents want what is best for their sons and daughters—which is why legacy applicants are so important to admissions professionals. These parents want to provide their sons and daughters every advantage they enjoyed and that includes attending the same college. All college admissions professionals must assume this fact to be true, even in the face of evidence to the contrary, if they hope to empower a greater proportion of students to pursue a postsecondary education and to succeed along the way.

Research documenting the important role of parents in their sons' and daughters' academic careers is substantial (Dika & Singh, 2002; Kim & Schneider, 2005; McNeal, 1999) and consistently supports the notion that the involvement of parents is positively associated with educational success throughout schooling and into the transition from high school to college. Researchers have found, however, that the concept is difficult to operationalize, and as such, the specific mechanisms by which it works or the causal implications are limited. When social capital has been translated into specific measures, the focus has been on the structural features of the family (presence of one or more parents, number of siblings, level of education of parents) (Dika & Singh, 2002) and the engagement of parents in three separate activities—conversations with their children, engagement with teachers, and the extent to which they monitor students' behaviors (McNeal, 1999). Researchers are less clear about whether these measures accurately capture some latent concept like social capital or whether they really measure differences by income or level of education that are also related to the chances students will attend college.

One of the key criticisms of existing research in this area is that researchers have typically employed a very narrow definition of the term "parent," and in doing so, they underestimate the potential influences of guardians or extended family who may have a similar influence on students. As we broaden the definition of parents, we come to recognize that an array of influential adults may be able to provide similar benefits to students, which is important as we consider the roles of counselors, teachers, and peers. This is a logical and important first step as we broaden the social network to be inclusive of college access professionals, teachers, and peers. We argue that it is useful to keep parents (broadly defined) at the center of the social network. Equally, we believe that if those relationships between students and their parents are paramount, then any effort to substitute or enhance the social capital by schools or other programs must connect parents to the same sets of relationships and access to information and support. They will continue to be a key in the long-term success of their children, and they need to have the tools to provide support beyond the time most of our college access professionals work with them.

Counselors

School counselors are the natural extension of school-based social capital or institutional agents (Farmer-Hinton & Adams, 2006; Stanton-Salazar & Dornbusch, 1995). Stanton-Salazar and Dornbusch surmise,

> Success within the educational system for working-class and minority youths, is dependent on the formation of genuinely supportive relationships with institutional agents . . . who have the capacity and commitment to transmit directly or to negotiate the transition of institutional resources and opportunities. (p. 117)

We have spent a good deal of time up to this point discussing the role of counselors, and it is clear they are a critical piece of the social network supporting students as they engage in the college choice process. School counselors play a critical role in the lives of many students, but as McDonough (2005) points out, increasing their capacity to provide more college counseling is limited by several factors: (a) the high national student-to-counselor ratio of 457:1 (American School Counselor Association, 2010) is nearly twice the recommended average of 250:1, (b) debates over whether providing support for college and career readiness is counseling or an extension of the marketing function of colleges and universities (McDonough, 2005), and (c) increasing administrative responsibilities placed upon counselors (House & Martin, 1998).

According to the National Office for School Counselor Advocacy (NOSCA) (2011), counselors are cognizant of the dilemma they face. On one hand, they recognize the centrality of their role in the college choice process, and yet few report that their schools are committed to this part of their work. We suggest this may be related to the expanding role of counselors as senior building-level leaders and the fact that they continue to assume new responsibilities without eliminating any others. To compensate for their lack of time to dedicate to working with students individually on the college choice process, many counselors either turn to other modes of delivery (e.g. classroom visits and group sessions) or partnering with outside agencies, paraprofessionals, or even peer leaders. All of these approaches hold some promise, but all of them remind us that counselors may need to think differently about how they achieve their goals in terms of helping their students plan and prepare for life after high school.

Teachers

In this volume we have not cast teachers as college access professionals, but, as we remind students in classrooms consistently, there is no more important relationship—from a college-going perspective—than the one between students and their teachers. We have not included them as part of the college access network for two reasons. First of all, while they are critical to helping students become effective students, they are not typically connected to the social network that helps students find the information and support they need to attend college. As Croninger and Lee (2001) note, "[S]tudents' relationships with their teachers represent a potentially valuable resource that can help students resolve problems and succeed at school" (p. 549–550). Teachers are also among the most college-educated individuals many students will meet during their secondary schooling, but they typically do not have the time to commit to engaging students in conversations about college and career plans. The accountability movement has placed teachers and schools under closer scrutiny, leaving little time for engagement beyond the core academic curriculum. We do, however, believe that even in an informal way, teachers remain critical sources of information and support for students considering college.

Research on teachers suggests that their most direct influence is on students at risk of dropping out. As Croninger and Lee (2001) note,

> [W]hen adolescents trust their teachers and informally receive guidance from teachers, they are more likely to persist to graduation. Although teacher-based forms of social capital are generally more beneficial for all students, those who benefit most are students most at risk of dropping out of high school. (p. 568)

Teachers are clearly influential for high school students, but it seems unlikely that they can be given the space in the school day to engage students in the college choice process. Our hope is that more teachers can be empowered to share their postsecondary experiences with their students as a way to celebrate and promote college going as part of the school culture.

Peers

Educators recognize the important influence peers have on one another. Hossler et al. (1999) recognized that as students move through the college choice process, peer influences grow in importance as students turn to one another for access to information and support. Others recognize, of course, that peer influence is a double-edged sword (The Center for Higher Education Policy Analysis, 2005). Middle- and upper-middle-class peers, for example, may expand the size and scope of one's social network. In these cases, peers may be similarly engaged in the college choice process and can provide both information and support to one another as they learn to navigate the choice process. Sokatch (2006) found that friends' plans for college is the strongest predictor of 4-year college enrollment among low-income, urban minority students, meaning that if students' friends plan to attend college, they are more likely to do so as well. Fletcher and Tienda (2008) have found that the size of one's peer network, as defined by the number of students from one's school attending the same college, has a positive effect on students' early measures of college achievement.

Hossler et al. (1999) indicate that peers grow more influential in the college choice process as they progress from the search to the choice phase of the college choice process, and the effects are lasting. Holland (2011) found, in her retrospective account of students who have successfully transitioned to college, that the effects of peers were critical in the choices they made regarding students' educational plans and their experiences. A summary of existing literature drafted by The Center for Higher Education Policy Analysis (CHEPA) (2005) suggests that programs designed to facilitate peer influence on the college choice process should include creating a clear identity for the group and scheduling regular and sustained meetings, with a focus on academic preparation over socialization.

Conclusion

In this chapter we addressed the possible sources of social capital as a way to identify the nature and scope of the potential social network that may be activated to the benefit of students. In the next chapter, we turn our attention to some examples of some of the initiatives designed to maximize social capital and increase college access among low-income, first-generation, and underrepresented minority students. These programs are just a few examples of the initiatives many of our pre-college outreach providers manage on a regular basis. We should be clear that while social capital formation is almost always a critical feature of these programs, they tend to be much more comprehensive, particularly with respect to providing tutoring support or test preparation. We do not intend for this discussion to be comprehensive, but it provides a flavor of the ways in which programs attempt to build a scaffold of social capital for students and their families.

College admissions professionals should recognize the value of social capital in the work they do. In fact, their ability to do much of their work is predicated on the strength of their social/professional network. We are suggesting nothing short of plugging admissions professionals more regularly into the network that supports students who might otherwise be at risk of not attending college. By extension, we believe that by plugging school counselors in high-need districts and pre-college outreach providers into the same network that typically comprises mostly feeder relationships, we will create a more robust network for low-income, first-generation, and underrepresented minority students.

7

PRE-COLLEGE OUTREACH PROGRAMS AND STRATEGIES

In Chapter 3, we discussed the roles of each of the four groups of college access professionals and the ways they engage with students and interact with one another. In this chapter, we discuss two separate developments in college access work that have implications for the work of college admissions professionals. The first part discusses the array of pre-college outreach programs designed to help students and their parents navigate the college choice process. This section provides a more complete picture of the work of pre-college outreach providers. We examine what is known about the federal TRIO and GEAR UP programs and consider the range of other state, local, and privately funded pre-college outreach initiatives. Despite the fact that many of these programs have been around for more than 20 years, school counselors, admissions professionals, and independent consultants report that they know very little about what these programs do or how they work with students. The second section considers the growth of paraprofessional staff to help more students transition from high school to college. We focus specifically on two strategies—the National College Advising Corps and AmeriCorps programs—to illustrate how volunteers and "nominally compensated staff" are providing some of these college access services in both community-based organizations (CBOs) and schools alike. We also recognize that many of these programs utilize federal work–study students, college student volunteers, participants in service learning courses, and occasionally retired professionals. While we do not discuss the latter in much depth, they represent important sources of staff support for many of these programs and schools. Increasingly, these paraprofessionals assist students in the transition from high school to college, and they constitute an important new connection for admissions professionals.

Pre-College Outreach Programs

One of the alarming realities facing public high schools in the United States is that, despite growing expectations for students to attend college, counselors have been asked to assume greater administrative responsibilities in addition to their traditional roles dealing with scheduling, testing, and student conduct. The American School Counselor Association (ASCA) and the National Association of College Admissions Counselors (NACAC) both advocate for a student-to-counselor ratio of 250:1 (American School Counselor Association, 2010; McDonough, 2005) yet the actual numbers remain substantially higher at 457:1 (The College Board, 2012). Recent trends suggest those numbers have improved slightly, but with added responsibilities, it is unlikely that counselors alone will be able to meet the college-advising needs of all of their high school students.

Pre-college outreach programs have the potential to fill some of that gap, but as Perna and Swail (2001) note, as little as 10% of the eligible student population is served by these programs. In Chapter 4, we discussed three established pre-college intervention programs (AVID, Talent Development, and College Summit) serving a large population of students. Although somewhat more familiar and systemic in nature compared to many of the programs described in this chapter, it is important to recognize that these privately funded initiatives on the national level are still classified as pre-college outreach efforts. In truth, it is difficult to estimate the reach of all of these programs for two reasons. First, there are many federal, state, and locally sponsored programs funded both by tax dollars and private resources, and there is no conclusive source of data on all of these initiatives. As such, it is likely that a larger proportion of students have access to some form of pre-college outreach program. However, the numbers reported by many of the existing programs overestimate services because they do not account for the intensity of their interventions when they report their figures. Stated more bluntly, many of these programs report "touches," meaning any student they have engaged at any time and for any level of intervention.

A number of researchers have written about pre-college outreach programs, although few have conducted comprehensive evaluations of these programs. Gullatt and Jun (2003) discuss three common types of programs— informational outreach, career-based outreach, and academic support—and establish 10 principles for promising programs. Researchers at the University of Southern California (Tierney et al., 2005) edited a volume dedicated to the topic and asked researchers to respond to nine separate elements of effective outreach, including academic preparation and work with families, peers, counselors, and mentors. The responses from experts in the field suggest that each of the components has an impact on college access, but little existing work has tested the effects of these programs empirically and rigorously. Below we describe the federal outreach programs for which there is a good deal of information and some indication of potential impact, followed by examples of state and federal programs that provide a taste of the range of initiatives available to students.

Federal Programs

In 2012, approximately 14.5 million students were enrolled in public high schools across the United States, and an additional 1.3 million attended private schools (National Center for Education Statistics, 2011a). More than 80% of these students plan to attend college—most of them a 4-year degree program—and yet a smaller proportion will successfully make that transition. Estimates suggest that 70% of ninth-grade students will finish high school in four years (Greene & Forster, 2003; Heckman & LaFontaine, 2010; Swanson & Chaplin, 2003). In 2012, 3.4 million students graduated from high school in the United States. Research suggests that as many as 75% of high school graduates will enroll in a postsecondary institution within several years of graduation (Ingels et al., 2002), but success rates are modest. Approximately 50% of students enrolled in a 4-year institution will earn a degree within six years, and only 30% of community college enrollees will earn an associate's degree in three years (National Center for Higher Education Management Systems, 2010). The latter is particularly concerning for college access professionals because community colleges enroll as many as 50% of all undergraduate students in the United States.

There are a number of obstacles along the path to the degree, including the level of academic preparation students receive prior to college, the rising cost of college, and information and support to navigate the college choice process, which affect students in different ways along the path. Where the federal government has attempted to improve academic preparation through school reform and college affordability through Title IV (HEA) financial aid programs, they have invested in the TRIO and Gaining Early Awareness and Readiness for Undergraduate Programs (GEAR UP) programs to provide students with the knowledge and support they need to transition from high school to college. Table 7.1 shows that between GEAR UP and the high school–based TRIO programs, programs sponsored by the federal government serve more than 1.3 million students at a total cost of more than $860 million (in 2011). To put that number into perspective, just under 10% of all high school students (Grades 9–12) in the United States are served by one or more of these programs. With the possible exception of the Upward Bound Veterans program, each of the federal programs is designed to serve low-income, first-generation, and underrepresented minority students, frequently attending high-need or failing schools and more often located in metropolitan centers. These programs are similar to the extent that they address the informational needs of students transitioning from high school to college. However, as the table suggests, programs vary dramatically in terms of the resources dedicated per student, which has an effect on the intensity of the intervention. Below, we discuss what is known about several of the major federal programs.

117

Table 7.1 Federal Investment in Pre-College Outreach Programs

	Funded Programs	Students	Budget (FY 2011)	Funding per Participant
Educational Opportunity Centers (EOC)	128	192,196	$46,676,723	$248
GEAR UP	211	748,000	$323,212,000	$432
Talent Search	461	319,678	$138,658,540	$434
Upward Bound	951	64,262	$305,387,247	$4,752
Upward Bound (MS)	131	6,992	$33,812,442	$4,836
Upward Bound (Vet)	47	5,780	$13,180,173	$2,280
	1,929	1,336,908	$860,927,125	

Gaining Early Awareness and Readiness for Undergraduate Programs (GEAR UP). GEAR UP serves more than half of all students participating in federal pre-college outreach programs, and their total appropriation of $323 million was the highest total among all programs. GEAR UP was the most recent edition to the federal access programs, and it operates independently from TRIO. According to the 1998 amendments to the Higher Education Act (HEA), the purposes of the program were twofold: (a) to address existing inequities in educational opportunity for low-income students and (b) to increase U.S. global competitiveness, recognizing the important link between postsecondary education and the demands of a 21st-century knowledge economy. The funds are allocated in one of two ways—to state agencies or to partnerships of local school districts, colleges, and CBOs (U.S. Department of Education, 2012c). Approximately two-thirds of the $323 million funds locally based partnerships, and the remainder is distributed directly to states. Grants are awarded on 6-year cycles to high-need districts serving populations that are more than 50% low income as approximated by free- or reduced-lunch eligibility.

Two features distinguish GEAR UP from its more established TRIO peers. First, programs are required to begin working with students no later than seventh grade and must follow entire cohorts of students through the end of high school. Second, the work of local initiatives must be school-based and include all students in designated grade levels across participating schools (U.S. Department of Education, 2003). The school-based model allows programs to provide a more consistent service to all students, integrated into the school day and the school curriculum. Per-pupil expenditures are modest for the GEAR UP program, but the grant requires partners to match federal support dollar for dollar in either cash or in-kind support. State awards are expected to provide 50% of their award in scholarships for low-income students, and the remainder of the funds should be used to improve college readiness and academic preparation.

An early formative evaluation of GEAR UP found that local agency-based programs offered three basic types of services—tutoring or mentoring, college planning and readiness, and staff professional development. Because these programs operated within schools, tutoring and mentoring was a primary focus of the early funded projects. Some of the GEAR UP programs offered summer experiences, which are the most intensive form of the treatment students receive. However, these summer programs are expensive to operate, and GEAR UP has established a cap of no more than $800 per student, making the summer difficult to provide without alternative sources of support.

Upward Bound (UB) Standard Program. The Upward Bound Standard program is the oldest of the federal pre-college outreach initiatives, and it predates the Higher Education Act (HEA) by a year. President Lyndon B. Johnson included it as part of the 1964 Economic Opportunity Act to assist students from disadvantaged backgrounds to attend college (McElroy & Armesto, 1998). The original program was designed to serve high school students ages 13–19 who came from low-income backgrounds and who had received "inadequate secondary school preparation" (Seftor, Mamun, & Schirm, 2009, p. xiii). We list both the UB Math and Science and the UB Veterans programs in Table 7.1, but we do not discuss them here. Because Upward Bound was founded specifically to improve the academic preparedness of low-income students for life after college, most programs focus on providing supplementary instruction and after school tutoring services in addition to counseling support and intensive summer bridge experiences. As Table 7.1 shows, Upward Bound is second only to GEAR UP in terms of resources, but it serves a much smaller number of students—spending $4,752 per student compared to only $432 in GEAR UP.

Upward Bound differs from GEAR UP in at least three important ways that affect the cost of the program. First and foremost, the focus is academic instruction, which is expensive to provide at the level of intensive academic support many of these students require to prepare for postsecondary education. Second, the program targets students rather than schools, meaning it does not serve the entire population of students in a given school. There are economies of scale to be achieved when all of the work of a program occurs in a single building rather than spread across several schools. Recent revisions to the call for proposals has placed greater emphasis on serving students from the persistently lowest-achieving schools, defined by the state as a failing school in need of corrective action and falling within the bottom 5% of Title I schools in the state, but they are not expected to serve all students in each of the participating schools. Third, the summer bridge program is expected to last for six weeks and is both the most intensive piece of the intervention and also the most costly to provide.

Two-thirds of all enrolled students must meet two criteria: (a) They must come from low-income families, defined as those who fall below 150% of poverty—approximately $34,575 for a family of four in the contiguous 48 states, and (b) they must be the first in their family to attend college (U.S. Department of Education, 2011c). Exceptions can be made to serve students outside of these two criteria, but those decisions need to be justified. The program has been evaluated a number of times across its nearly 50-year history, and the most recent findings indicate that the impact of the program is mixed. Researchers found no overall effect on postsecondary enrollment rates or choices of institution, no effect on financial aid application patterns or Pell Grant receipt, and no effect on degree attainment beyond certificates (Seftor et al., 2009). They did find, however, that UB participants were more likely than comparison group students to earn a certificate. Additionally, for the lowest-achieving group of students served and for those who remain in the program for the longest period of time, UB appears to have an effect on both college enrollment and degree completion. The limitations of the program may be, at least in part, attributable to federal requirements. UB programs are expected to achieve very high success rates among students at greatest risk for not attending college, which can serve as an incentive for programs to focus on the most capable students from those high-need schools. Doing so helps to achieve the aggregated outcomes but might actually suggest that the program has no effect because these students were already more likely to overcome their circumstances. And as Seftor et al. (2009) point out, it is possible that students who are in the "control" group have access to programs like UB that provide similar benefits. When that is the case, any estimates of outcomes for those students will have the effect of underestimating the effects of the program under investigation on student outcomes.

Talent Search Program.   Talent Search was launched under the 1965 Higher Education Act (HEA) and was the second of the original three TRIO programs (with Student Support Services, which works with students enrolled in college). According to the U.S. Department of Education (2011b), Talent Search is intended to "provide academic, career, and financial counseling to its participants and encourages them to graduate from high school and continue on to and complete their postsecondary education" (n.p.). Talent Search is funded at a per-student level more similar to that of GEAR UP than Upward Bound, meaning it cannot provide the same intensity of intervention as is expected in the family of Upward Bound programs.

In order for Talent Search to achieve its goals, it must operate like GEAR UP, but with an emphasis on high schools rather than middle schools. There is an important difference, however. As discussed earlier, GEAR UP programs are designed to serve entire school populations; Talent Search programs are not. The program is designed specifically to address students' level of access to the information they need to navigate the college choice process, from the courses to take in high school to the college search to the completion of the college application process and the FAFSA. These programs are intended to serve students who have academic potential for college but who do not have access to the right information. While all programs differ in terms of the services they provide and the students they serve, few are able to offer intensive academic support or comprehensive summer immersion experiences (both of which are central to UB Standard and the Math/Science and Veterans programs).

A 2006 evaluation conducted for the U.S. Department of Education examined records of Talent Search programs across three states (Florida, Indiana, and Texas), and their findings suggest that the program offers promise. Two basic findings were consistent across the states. First, participating students were more likely to apply for financial aid than students from similar backgrounds (Constantine, Seftor, Martin, Silva, & Myers, 2006). Second, TS students were more likely to enroll in postsecondary education than their comparison group—more of which were likely to enroll in community colleges than 4-year institutions. The evaluation reports mixed findings on the relationship between program participation and high school completion, with notable gains in Florida and Texas but not in Indiana. Students in these investigations are never randomly assigned, and there are limitations to the extent to which researchers are able to attribute differences to the impact of the programs, but the findings are suggestive.

State-Sponsored Programs

In 1992, the U.S. Congress created the National Early Intervention Scholarship Partnership (NEISP) program as part of the reauthorization of the Higher Education Act (HEA). The legislation provided grants to states that were willing to establish or maintain need-based aid programs and to provide an array of pre-collegiate services including counseling, mentoring, academic support, and dropout prevention for students, as well as separate information and support for parents. By 1998, nine states had received funding through a competitive process to create state pre-college outreach programs (U.S. Department of Education, 1998).[1] The program was eliminated in favor of what became the GEAR UP initiative in 1998 (Perna & Swail, 2001).

In a 2003 review of state-sponsored pre-college outreach programs, Cunningham, Redmond, and Merisotis (2003) highlighted 17 initiatives across 12 states—all of which were either very well established or had been formally evaluated.[2] These programs varied from extensions of the GEAR UP program in Washington state to comprehensive scholarship programs like the

21st Century Scholars program in Indiana and the Higher Learning Access Program (OHLAP) in Oklahoma. In New York, two programs received additional support through NEISP—the Science and Technology Entry Program (STEP) and the Liberty Partnership Program. These programs vary in terms of the programmatic focus, the students eligible for services, where they are located in the community, and the degree to which they are integrated into broader state college access strategies. The 2003 report is as close to a comprehensive report as exists today. Others have highlighted specific programs like those serving Hispanic/Latino students (Gandara, 2002) or specifically high achieving underrepresented minority (URM) students (Gandara & Maxwell-Jolly, 1999). In this section, we discuss two state-sponsored programs—21st Century Scholars (Indiana) and the Science and Technology Entry Program (STEP—New York). In the next section, we discuss examples of two locally developed programs. Often it is difficult to differentiate because no matter the source of funding, all of these programs operate locally and adapt to the existing challenges and opportunities present in their communities.

Indiana 21st Century Scholars. The Indiana approach is unlike any other pre-college outreach strategy. In fact, the Scholars program is best known as a need/merit hybrid scholarship program (we discussed the scholarship in Chapter 5). Low-income students (those who have qualified for the federal free lunch program) sign a pledge in middle school indicating that they will do their part to prepare for college and stay out of trouble in exchange for free tuition and fees when they graduate high school. In addition to the scholarship, the state has established as many as 14 regional service centers to provide programming and support services to students and their parents as they navigate the college choice process (St. John, Musoba, Simmons, & Chung, 2002).[3] Many of these centers are located on or near college campuses, but they are not community located in the same ways as other programs. They provide similar forms of outreach programming as the other programs, but their service areas are more broadly defined. Evaluations conducted to date focus on the scholarship program and its connection to the advanced high school curriculum (Core 40) and not on the efforts of these regional service centers (St. John et al., 2008; St. John et al., 2012).

The Indiana model is driven by the scholarship first and foremost, and as such, the outreach programming has received less attention and fewer resources. It becomes difficult to coordinate programming and support activities when the centers are so far removed from most schools in their regions. As such, this program requires additional attention at the local level to ensure that students receive the support and encouragement they need to take advantage of the 21st Century Scholars program.

New York STEP Program. The Science and Technology Entry Program (STEP) is one of the signature programs for the K16 Initiatives and Access

Programs through the New York State Education Department (NYSED) (New York State Education Department, 2011). The program was initiated through legislation in 1986, predating NEISP by six years, and was designed to serve high science- and math-capable students from low-income backgrounds beginning as early as seventh grade and extending through high school graduation. In 2000, more than 5,400 students were served across 40 programs in the state, and by 2012, those numbers exceeded 8,500 students across 60 programs.

The program was designed to target two key problems in New York— the shortage of students entering the science, technology, engineering, and math (STEM) disciplines, and licensed professions (e.g. law and accounting), and the particular lack of students of color in those fields. It is designed for students who, by virtue of the focus on math and science, tend to perform relatively well in school though they may not have the same opportunities as students in other schools. As such, these students are more likely to attend college even before they set foot in a STEP program. Not surprisingly, 97% of program participants graduate from high school, and most go on to college—findings that are in stark contrast to other students attending the same schools. In addition to the general STEP program, the state also sponsors a medical STEP program for those aspiring to the health-related professions. The two key components of the STEP program are (a) the academic support through either an after school curricular component or individual tutoring and (b) the summer 4–6 week intensive program. In New York, preparation for Regents exams is a critical component of these programs, but they also focus on helping students navigate the college choice process. In most cases, these programs do not offer scholarships, but they do provide guidance and support for students applying for financial aid.

Locally Initiated Programs

St. Clair County Know How 2 Go. No single program operates in isolation and, in many ways, they are all frequently influenced by local, state, and national initiatives. Such was the case in St. Clair County, Michigan, as the county created a regional initiative to improve postsecondary access for students in its service region. The St. Clair conversation, like many across the state of Michigan, began with the announcement of the Kalamazoo Promise. Community foundations and other local leaders across the state began conversations about the plausibility of replicating Kalamazoo, and many of them developed creative—and less costly—strategies to promote college access. St. Clair was one of the early adopters, and their efforts were supported by three key factors—the federal College Access Challenge Grant (CACG) to states; the National Know How 2 Go campaign sponsored by the Lumina Foundation for Education, the American Council on Education, and the Ad Council; and the formation of the Michigan College Access Network (MCAN).

St. Clair began its work prior to all of these initiatives, but each contributed to its ability to maintain and grow its initiatives. CACG created the conditions for a statewide college access agenda and provided the initial seed money to begin MCAN. The network grew its sources of funding and, within a year, was providing grants to communities for the purpose of expanding their college access efforts. Know How 2 Go provided a framework and a brand to a community that found one of its primary challenges was convincing students and their families of the importance of going to college. Within two years, it was a model for other communities. The work in St. Clair has been achieved with four broad priorities (St. Clair County Community Foundation, 2010). First, St. Clair officials adapted the national social marketing campaign from Know How 2 Go to address what they recognized as apathy about college participation across the community. Second, they hired a staff member to work in the highest-need school in the county to help students navigate the college choice process. Third, St. Clair emulated a very successful strategy of helping to connect low-income students with a state-legislated program designed to provide tuition support to students whose parents had been on Medicare for a period of time while the students were in school. The Tuition Incentive Program (TIP) had been underutilized in Michigan largely because few families or schools were aware of its existence or how to help students apply. Finally, the Regional Education Service Agency (RESA) committed space and staff time to the creation of a county-wide college access center and a parent coordinator to help parents understand the college choice process and to support their students as they make the transition. These locally developed programs are different in important ways from more conventional programs. In fact, they frequently reflect an array of separate initiatives brought together under a larger umbrella. In the St. Clair program, the umbrella was provided by the RESA, and it brought a number of partners together with independent resources and strategies that collectively help to improve students' opportunities for success.

The Neighborhood Academic Initiative. Many locally developed programs operate in large urban areas where poverty rates are high and student achievement is low. The Neighborhood Academic Initiative (NAI) in Los Angeles is one such program. In 1990, the University of Southern California developed a pre-college outreach program and an incentive grant to prepare more students from the local South Los Angeles community to attend USC for college. NAI was designed to serve students beginning in seventh grade. In order to participate, the parents of students were required to be involved. Students attended classes at USC for two hours each day before school began and were expected to attend the Saturday enrichment academy (Tierney & Jun, 2001). According to Tierney and Jun (2001), a cultural integrity framework suggests that "academic success hinges on the ability of a program such as NAI to meet students' localized needs by affirming the cultural contexts in which they exist rather than ignoring or rejecting them" (p. 214). The idea that cultural background is an asset rather than a liability is critical to understanding how NAI works with students in the LA community.

An early study of the impact of the program followed the first cohort of seventh-grade students through high school graduation and into college. Of the original group, a third of the 40 students left the program; the remaining students finished the program and completed high school. Six of 10 graduates went on to a 4-year college—in comparison to peers at the same schools, 60% is a very high rate of 4-year enrollment. However, even with this high level of intervention for a sustained period of time, fewer than 50% of the original program participants attended a 4-year institution, and very few were able to take advantage of free tuition at USC.

College Success Center at Bennett High School. One of the persistent limitations frequently pointed out by critics of pre-college outreach programs is that they serve a very small portion of the larger student population. Most of these programs are also designed in ways that encourage programs to select students most likely to demonstrate success, at least within very high-need schools. Most directors express frustration about this dilemma but must make recruitment and enrollment decisions based upon their grant-specified targets and ensure they can demonstrate the expected levels of success. As a result most programs are relatively small—from a local STEP program of 50 students to a federally sponsored Talent Search program serving 650 students—and few are large enough to serve a single school in a comprehensive way.

In 2010, local community leadership in the city of Buffalo was funded under the federal Promise Neighborhood Initiative (U.S. Department of Education, 2011d) to provide comprehensive birth to career support services to a single neighborhood. Within the neighborhood was one of the highest-need and persistently low-performing high schools in the district. The College Success Center was created for that high school with three goals in mind—(a) free counselors from the administrative burden of the college choice process so they could spend more time counseling students, (b) serve as a conduit between the school and community to bring additional college access initiatives to bear for students, and (c) serve the college choice needs of an entire school population. Faculty and graduate students staff the center, and AmeriCorps VISTA volunteer members work within the school schedule to help students plan, prepare, and enroll in college. The program brings additional adults into the building who can provide support to counselors, teachers, and administrators already asked to do much more with less. The program has not yet been formally evaluated, but early indications suggest that more students have received support to apply for college than in years past.

The Growth of Paraprofessional Staff

When we asked counselors at one local college preparatory academy about their use of paraprofessional staff to support their college access activities, we received a blank stare, as though the idea had no relevance for their work. In fact, at this particular school, additional support may not have been necessary—they had five full-time counselors to work with 850 high school men. We received mixed responses when we spoke with college access professionals about the use of paraprofessional staff. First, like our colleague at the private boys' academy, some simply had no experience with it. In this section, we discuss the rise of paraprofessionals as an indication of things to come. For admissions offices, this is actually standard practice. Current undergraduate students serve in a part-time capacity as ambassadors, tour guides, and shadow hosts; these offices routinely sponsor interns, and in many cases, they rely on alums to recruit in geographic areas beyond the traditional markets of the school.

Pre-college outreach programs rely more heavily on paraprofessionals than other college access professional groups, mostly out of budgetary necessity. They frequently employ college students as tutors and mentors and they may also utilize service organizations like AmeriCorps (discussed later in the chapter) to maximize their service capacity, given declining resources. What we are most interested in is the growth of a sector of service-related activities designed to supplement the work of educators who operate at the nexus of high schools and colleges. We begin by discussing the more contentious strategy employed in education today—Teach for America (TFA). TFA, for better or worse, set the stage for paraprofessionals to supplement the work of educators in some of the highest-need districts in the country.

Teach For America (TFA)

Teach for America was a modest proposal in a 1989 undergraduate thesis at Princeton University, written by Wendy Kopp, the founder of TFA (Teach for America, 2012). The program began with a corps of 500 volunteers. By 2012, 10,000 TFA volunteers provided classroom instruction to as many as 750,000 students. The program has been controversial from the very beginning, and for all of its success in attracting highly educated college graduates into teaching in some of the most challenging districts in the country, critics argue that the model could do more harm than good. The primary concern in the early 1990s, as it is 20 years later, was the amount of training volunteers receive—at that time, eight weeks of intensive training prior to entering the classroom—substantially less than a graduate of a teacher preparation program would receive (Darling-Hammond, 1994). It is difficult to measure the success of a program like TFA, and it is not our intent to weigh in on the specifics of the program, but it does underscore one reality that is clear: Many of the TFA members would not have entered education had it not been for the program. At the same time, a number of participants will leave education with a newfound appreciation for the challenges and complexities of trying to improve educational opportunity for all students.

TFA is an important touchstone for our discussion of paraprofessional staff because it laid the groundwork for thinking about alternative approaches to improving education, and it cast a broader net to attract new groups of college graduates to education. It is not a perfect model for understanding the role of paraprofessionals in college advising because the programs described here do not and cannot replace counselors. They play a different and complementary role to school counselors, and no attempts are made to train them otherwise. That is not the case in TFA, where volunteers are placed into classrooms that would otherwise be taught by traditionally certified teachers. For some, this may be a distinction without a difference. As we discuss toward the end of this chapter, any attempt to bring outside support into the school could be perceived as a threat to counselor jobs and the professionalism of the field. These are important conversations to have, and every attempt should be made to celebrate and reinforce the important role the school professionals play; it is a growing reality, in many of the persistently low-achieving (PLA) schools that we see, that there are simply too few resources to provide the level of support students and their families need to navigate the transition from high school to college.

The National College Advising Corps

In 2004, the Jack Kent Cooke Foundation funded a small but promising program at the University of Virginia to increase efforts to promote college participation among low-income, first-generation, and underrepresented minority students. The College Guide program placed 14 recent college graduates into high-need high schools to work with counselors and students to complete the college application and financial aid processes. Their initial success based upon that first grant resulted in a larger, more sustained investment in a multiyear project that became the National College Advising Corps (NCAC). The project was moved to the University of North Carolina–Chapel Hill and was expanded to serve many more students across several states and other university partners. The philosophy of the program is simple—the program employs "near peers" who are recent college graduates and who, in many cases, have come from the same communities or faced similar challenges to those they serve (National College Advising Corps, 2012). These graduates commit a year to serve in a high school and in some cases, students continue beyond the initial year.

The program operates as a partnership among three institutions—NCAC, the partnering postsecondary institution, and the high school that will serve as the home for the adviser. Each partner must commit something to the project—the school provides the space and the support where the college works with NCAC to provide the funding for the advisers. These are not volunteer positions because advisers are adequately compensated for their work, but most do not participate for the salary. Currently, 19 partnering colleges and universities are employing advisers to work with target schools across 13 states. In 2011, the state of Michigan alone placed 32 advisers across 40 high schools serving thousands of students (Michigan College Access Network, 2011). NCAC has contracted with researchers from Stanford to evaluate the impact of the adviser program, and initial findings suggest that students attending partner schools experience a boost in college participation of between 8–12% in comparison to similar schools without advising corps members.

The AmeriCorps Model

Service has been a national priority throughout U.S. history, but the focus on youth in service to achieve civilian priorities extends back to President Johnson's formation of the Volunteers in Service to America (VISTA) in 1964 (The Corporation for National & Community Service, 2012). In 1993, President Clinton signed the National and Community Service Trust Act, establishing the Corporation for National and Community Service and the AmeriCorps program. The program has been expanded in subsequent years and places thousands of volunteers across a range of service opportunities. In 2005, nearly 75,000 members provided more than 1.6 million hours of service to communities across the country, and one of the priorities is education (The Corporation for National & Community Service, 2012). AmeriCorps members received a living stipend of approximately $12,000 in 2012 and a tuition benefit of $4,500.

AmeriCorps has a range of programs at both the national and state levels, and partnering institutions have some discretion regarding how best to use members in service. A number of communities have identified AmeriCorps as a partner in their efforts to create a corps of college advisers, similar to the NCAC. The difference is that members used in this way do not receive the same level of compensation and are not provided the same coordinated training program. Instead, local partners assume responsibility for training volunteers tailored to the roles they play in school. Partnering organizations pay a portion of the cost (approximately $8,000 per member) and agree to provide members with the resources they need to perform their work (e.g. office space, computer, phone). AmeriCorps has become an increasingly important part of the staffing plans for pre-college outreach programs as they experience cuts at both the national and state levels, and in a few cases, partnering programs like the College Success Center discussed earlier, have employed members to work in schools as college advisers. This model has not been formally evaluated, but it is similar to the NCAC version, so it is likely to demonstrate similar levels of success to the degree that the work is similar and volunteers are effectively trained.

These models all appear very promising, but they are not without their drawbacks. Consistent with the experience of Teach for America, teachers, counselors, and administrative staff may be justifiably skeptical of asking relatively undertrained and unskilled volunteers into the school to provide services that are otherwise provided by trained educators. This is a particular concern in schools that are forced to cut teachers and staff as enrollments decline and budgets are cut. These are valid concerns and have to be addressed in partnership with schools. As soon as it appears that paraprofessionals are being used to supplant trained and experienced educators, their chances for successful collaboration are compromised. Our experience suggests that the model is not right for every school, but it may work well for schools that recognize the problem, trust that the services provided in partnership are complementary and not intended to replace qualified staff, and are so resource strapped that few other alternatives exist.

It is important to put clearly defined parameters around what these paraprofessionals are asked to do and how they should be utilized in the school. Unlike TFA, where members are expected to lead a class and to serve effectively as a teacher, college advisers—either NCAC or AmeriCorps members—are not asked to serve as counselors. This group of recent college graduates is well positioned to help students navigate the college choice process because they understand two things particularly well—how to navigate the college choice and application process and how to succeed once a student attends college. So long as members and volunteers focus their energy on helping students in these clearly defined ways, we believe these partnerships can be valuable for schools.

Conclusion

In this chapter, we've highlighted some of the innovative strategies designed to help students in lower-performing schools navigate the college choice process. We have spent a good deal of our own time working with these programs and supporting efforts to bring as many caring and motivated adults into the lives of young students with fewer advantages in large urban districts as we can. However, we are also sensitive to the criticisms of both pre-college outreach programs and the use of paraprofessional staff. If we had a choice, we would prefer to see more counselors in schools and more time dedicated to college choice in the high school curriculum, but the reality today is that remains a privilege for a relative few. We are more concerned that even with all of the federal resources dedicated to TRIO and GEAR UP and the array of national, state, and local college access programs, those efforts reach a relatively small proportion of the target populations. We've provided one illustration of the GEAR UP program and a high school level pre-college outreach program that is institutionalized into the school building (the College Success Center), and we argue that this is perhaps the only way to bring these services to a larger proportion of the population. The tradeoff is that there are real benefits to bringing students to campus—we know that many students spend little if any time on college campuses, and those who have typically do so through one of the outreach programs. At the same time, we know that one of the critical barriers to their eventual success in college is their ability to successfully navigate college once they arrive. That includes both their ability to adjust to the academic rigor of college and to adjust socially to a very different educational environment.

Admissions professionals must recognize that the social network supporting students through the college choice process is larger, more complex, and more highly differentiated than ever before. In some ways, this is a promising development—it means more assistance for the students who need it most. It does create some new challenges and opportunities for admissions professionals. To start, it is in the best interest of everyone that pre-college outreach programs and paraprofessionals have all of the information they need to help students through the college choice process, and we believe this is an important role for admissions professionals. Second, these individuals will be referring students to colleges and universities, in much the same way as school counselors and independent consultants have always done; institutions want to maximize their social networks, and this is one area for potential growth—particularly for admissions staff at less selective colleges. Admissions professionals must know their terrain and find the new networks that are likely to help them in their work while also improving access to college.

8

THE NEW FRONTIER OF
WEB-BASED COLLEGE
ACCESS STRATEGIES

It is unlikely that any change in recent history has affected the college admissions and the college choice process as significantly as the development of the Internet. The days of paper college applications and financial aid forms have been replaced, in nearly all cases, by a dizzying array of web-based tools. And the phone book–size guidebooks make attractive trophies on counselor bookshelves, but the heavy lifting of the college search process can be accomplished much more efficiently by a dozen or more web portals—many like Petersons, previously produced the paper versions of the college guides.[1] The National Center for Education Statistics indicates that 74% of high school seniors seek information from websites, publications, and search tools to learn about going to college—second only to the percentage of students who talk to counselors, teachers, and coaches (84%) (Chen, Wu, & Tasoff, 2010). Paper materials continue to have a place, but as Armstrong and Lumsden (2000) note in focus groups of enrolled students at the University of North Texas, students do not perceive them to be influential on their enrollment decisions, and they are lost in a sea of materials students receive during the process.

The growth of college access web-based tools has been substantial and with good reason. Kane (1999) points out that information is not equally accessible to all students and parents. In particular, low-income, first-generation, and underrepresented minority students have historically had less access to college choice–related information. The Web has great potential to serve as a democratizing force in the college choice process, but Long (2004) notes that students and families know little about the costs of college or the availability of financial aid, and the problem is worst among low-income families. As we discussed in Chapter 6, families overestimate the cost of college and know very little about financial aid. These findings are consistent across a number of studies (Avery & Kane, 2004; Horn, Chen, & Chapman, 2003; Kirst & Venezia, 2004), confirming that students and parents overestimate the cost of college, but they also overestimate the economic benefits of degree attainment, which from a human capital perspective, should lead more students to pursue a college degree.

In the past, as these processes shifted to the digital environment, the barrier for many families was access to technology—too few low-income families had computers in their homes (Jones, 2002). By the turn of the 21st century, the costs of technology had dropped dramatically, nearly all schools maintain sufficient technology, and the vast majority of homes are Internet capable across the income distribution. Jackson (2003) noted that the digital divide by income level was a function of both the inaccessibility of technology and parents' lack of comfort with these new technologies. Venegas (2006a) found that while many low-income families have access to computers, there may still be a gap in terms of the quality of service they are able to access. Her data suggest that most households have computers at their disposal, but that many low-income, first-generation, and underrepresented minority families lack instrumental knowledge necessary to utilize these tools effectively.

The Pew Research Center has found that some of the largest gaps by income exist in in terms of willingness to purchase products, pay bills, or complete banking transactions online (Jansen, 2010). The reluctance of low-income families to actively utilize the Internet for e-commerce suggests they may be even less likely to complete the FAFSA, which requires a great deal more personal information than any of these other transactions. Access to information via the Web has a democratizing potential and is an important rationale for moving so much of the college choice process online, but it fails to account for institutional motivations. First, colleges and universities operate in highly competitive markets, and web access may be the difference in terms of attracting a broader pool of students. Consider the experience of the University of Michigan, which is among the most selective public universities in the nation with no shortage of applications for its incoming class. In 2011, more than 42,000 applications were submitted, and only 37% were accepted for admission to yield a class of approximately 6,300 first-year students. Michigan has not had a problem filling a class, and yet, in 2006 they contracted for the development of a virtual campus tour that would appeal to a variety of expanding markets, including international applicants who were unlikely to visit campus before choosing an institution to attend. The virtual campus tour was a digitized three-dimensional environment where prospective students and their families could see and experience the campus. Video game technology is a costly venture for an institution that is already a highly selective institution, but its value proposition was precisely that it could appeal to a larger cross-section of a very large pool of applicants, and it might make a difference in terms of whether they choose to attend. By the end of the tour, students could submit their applications electronically. All institutions are looking for ways to attract more and better students, and the Internet opens many possibilities (Gifford, Mianzo, & Briceno-Perriott, 2005)—some of which may benefit low-income students, and others that will not. The virtual campus tour could inspire a few students to attend college, but it is more likely to affect top students from around the world who already have many options among which they need ways to differentiate.

Second, colleges are always searching for ways to improve efficiency, and the Web has given them an opportunity to do just that. Today, virtually every piece of the college application can be completed and submitted online, which holds promise for eliminating paper and all of the time, energy, and resources admissions offices invest in processing. An entire industry exists to help colleges and universities manage their electronic applications, move their student recommendations online, and to extract student transcripts electronically from district- and school-level student information systems. Testing agencies send student scores electronically, and students can monitor the completion of their applications on the Web. Paper has not yet disappeared from the process, but institutions are certainly moving in that direction, and one can clearly see why. Consider the shift from a paper application; in the not too distant past, every application was mailed to the campus, opened, entered manually into a database, filed, and in many cases, copied for review. Data entry from handwritten applications was prone to errors and even typed applications took time to enter. An electronic submission eliminates some of the data entry needs by allowing the program to import student data directly into a data management system.

Efficiency is an important institutional goal, but it may raise concerns when the use of technology actually has a negative effect on students who may already be less likely to attend college (McDonough, 2005). Whether or not the Internet has a democratizing effect or whether it simply maintains social class is a question open for debate, and it has not really been addressed by the research community outside the study conducted by Venegas (2006b). High-income families and students whose parents attended college have always had an advantage in terms of access to information, and it is likely, in the absence of the array of online tools available today, that they would continue to find ways to access that information. To that extent, there is a ceiling on access to information, meaning that at the margins, the Internet may help some students catch up. However, if access to technology is uneven, if some families are more knowledgeable about how to use that technology, or if others are more reluctant to use or are mistrustful of that technology, then the movement of the college application process may have actually created more barriers than it eliminated. Our experience suggests that the movement of the application process has benefited institutions more than it has benefited students, and for those at risk of not attending college, it may actually be a deterrent. We will examine this more closely as we discuss how the process has evolved electronically.

By no means are we suggesting that institutions should abandon technological efficiencies or that they should maintain dual systems to continue a paper process. Efficiency, however it is achieved, is a good development for higher education, and it should result in less cost borne by students. What we do argue is that colleges and universities have created a system and benefited from it, and they have a special responsibility to make that system work for all students, families, and schools—not only the ones most likely to attend their institutions. That means partnering with high-need schools and finding ways to help more students operate in this environment and take full advantage of the tools at their disposal. We believe this is important not only to increase access to the virtual application process but also to prepare students for what is to come. As we will examine in Chapter 9, the college environment requires students to operate in similar ways, both in the classroom and beyond. Goode (2010) examines the role of technology in undergraduate education and views it as the "invisible academic prerequisite" (p. 584). If researchers at UCLA's Higher Education Research Institute (HERI) are correct, incoming college students are reporting the highest rates of technology usage over their 40 years of survey data (Pryor, Hurtado, Saenz, Santos, & Korn, 2007). The sooner we prepare high school students for that reality, the more likely they will be able to turn the corner from access to college success—it appears that those left on the sidelines of technology will find it increasingly difficult to make the transition.

Literature examining the role of technology in the college choice process focuses on three broad themes—(a) social marketing to promote postsecondary education and to inform students and parents on the college choice process; (b) electronic applications and the process of submission; and (c) college cost, financial aid, the Free Application for Federal Student Aid (FAFSA), and the developing net price calculators. In the sections that follow, we discuss how technology has changed the way students navigate the college choice process. In each section we highlight specific changes that illustrate how the process has changed. The chapter concludes by considering how these changes have shaped the process for students deciding whether or not college is a viable option.

College Access Marketing—Selling the Idea

Hartman (1997) notes, more than a decade ago, that college admissions professionals have long used the latest forms of technology to deliver formally constructed messages to parents and prospective students to promote their institutions. These technologies ran the gambit from audio and filmstrips to campus videos to CDROMs. Today, the Internet is the "new frontier" in the marketing of higher education. Even though it has been with us for more than 20 years, the array of available tools changes rapidly. Social media, for example, could fundamentally change how institutions engage prospective students, but most institutions are still trying to figure out how to harness its potential. Hartman (1997) also points out that the Internet has changed the game because it is more difficult for institutions to craft their message when so many other sources of information are readily available to anyone interested in looking. Hossler (1999) summarizes the dilemma of admissions professionals concisely,

> Enrollment managers are perpetually caught in the nexus of competing values. Each year we are asked to recruit more and better-qualified students to institutions whose major attributes remain unchanged each year. Each of us is constantly in search of a new marketing approach, a new financial aid program, or a creative spark that will give us a competitive advantage among our peer institutions. In addition, we are always looking for ways to reduce our costs. (p. 12)

He goes on to describe the potential of the Internet to address these competing values but also warns that the Internet fundamentally changes the way information is delivered, accessed, and processed, posing new challenges to the enrollment management community. As more information is available from a variety of sources, both formal and informal, it becomes more difficult for institutions to craft the image of the college in the minds of prospective students and their parents (Hossler, 1999). Before 2000, Hossler was skeptical that the Web would fundamentally change students' college search behavior due to advances in online technology, but he did suggest important economies to be achieved in enrollment management by moving follow-up communications from paper to electronic media (email at the time). In a controlled experiment on his campus, he found that email was a quick and effective alternative mode of communication with prospective students, suggesting an opportunity to increase efficiency while also improving communication.

The cornerstone of the web-based college marketing plan is the institutional website (National Association of College Admissions Counselors, 2012). It serves as the primary source of information about the institution, and users most frequently identify it as an important source of information in the college choice process. By 2000, students were already more likely to report relying on the Web for information about colleges and universities than more conventional paper marketing strategies (Abrahamson, 2000). Poock and Lefond (2001) found, in their review of existing literature on the use of websites in the college choice process, that eight characteristics are important to students: content, enjoyableness of the experience, organization of the site, utility of graphics, ease of navigation, uniqueness of site, focus on target audience, and speed of connection. Of these characteristics, the quality of the content, the organization of the site, and the ease of navigation were consistently the most highly rated in terms of importance by prospective students utilizing the Web.

Kittle and Ciba (2001) note that the use of the Internet in college marketing changed from focusing primarily on attracting new "customers" to developing sustained relationships with prospective students. Those in enrollment management recognize the importance of developing relationships from the first point of contact through degree completion and a sustained commitment of alumni to the institution. Kittle and Ciba (2001) use a five-level framework to assess the degree to which institutions develop mechanisms for genuine interaction between prospective students and institutions. Their analysis indicates that over time, colleges and universities increased the capability of their tools to be more interactive along three dimensions—the application process, the use of faculty to promote the institution, and the campus tour. The idea is simple—the more genuine opportunities for prospective students to engage with the institution, the more likely they will receive the information they need and develop a sense of identity related to the institution.

In recent years, the role of technology has evolved in terms of the marketing of higher education. At the turn of the 21st century, the Internet remained secondary to print material, and the digital divide was substantial. Recently, the role of technology has changed considerably. By 2008, more students report utilizing websites, social networking, email, texting, and blogs to receive information from institutions, and the expected returns on investment were greatest for emails, online forms, and text messaging (Lindbeck & Fodrey, 2009, 2010). Lindbeck and Fodrey (2010) note, however, that most of this communication flows in a single direction and may not be an effective catalyst for establishing relationships with students.

One of the more recent developments in online marketing strategies is the use of social networking tools to connect with prospective students. Hayes, Ruschman, and Walker (2009) illustrate the potential of social networking in the admissions process with the single case of Xavier University's Road to Xavier e-recruitment tool. This tool created a venue for prospective students to interact with the admissions office and to receive information from current campus students. Social networking creates new opportunities for institutions to develop relationships with students, but they note that these tools are more effective at managing relationships with students who apply but less useful as a recruitment tool. As such, it underscores the importance of utilizing multiple marketing strategies in enrollment management. Constantinides and Zinck Stagno (2011) conducted a market segmentation analysis of students in the Netherlands and found that prospective students cluster in one of three basic groups according to the degree to which they engage in online technologies—nonusers, moderate users, and informational users. The implication is that nonusers will seek different sources of information and support to navigate the college choice process, whereas the advanced "informational users" will find social networking tools useful in their process and will generate much of the new content.

The Growth of College Access Marketing

Colleges and universities have a vested interest in marketing their institutions to prospective students and their parents. They operate in highly contested marketplaces, and most institutions are heavily dependent upon enrollments to generate sufficient revenues to cover costs. As such, institutions focus their marketing attention and resources on those students already most likely to attend college. They spend more time visiting high schools with high application and yield rates, and they target their materials to the segment of the student market most likely to attend their institutions. They do not typically target their resources to students or schools for which the decision of whether or not to attend college is very much an issue. These students are by far the most time consuming and expensive to recruit and enroll. However, public priorities to grow human capital by increasing the proportion of adults with a college education has given rise to a growing movement to market college access above and beyond the institutions themselves. Since the 1990s, a number of interested parties have been developing tools to more actively promote college access by increasing students' access to the information they need to navigate the college choice process, and the target audience is increasingly the group of students less likely to attend college—low-income, first-generation, and underrepresented minority students. According to the Southern Regional Education Board (SREB) and the GO Alliance (2012),

> College Access Marketing (CAM) is a kind of "social marketing" that encourages people to continue their education. CAM campaigns try to reach specific audiences, such as children of parents who didn't go to college, and get them to take specific actions, such as finishing high school, securing financial aid, or applying to colleges. (para. 2)

All entities operate out of self-interest, and states are no exceptions. Nearly every state in the nation has developed a college access web portal (Daun-Barnett & Das, 2011), and their motivation is typically economic development. Throughout the first decade of the 21st century, policy makers focused their attention on creating jobs and growing their state economies. Most recognize that growing sectors in a knowledge-based economy require college-educated talent, and in order to attract those jobs, states must increase the proportion of students going to college and earning degrees. Access to information and support to navigate the college choice process is the most recent in a long line of policy initiatives designed by states to increase college access and success. Most states maintain an array of financial aid programs (as discussed in Chapter 5), and a growing number have either established or ratcheted up their academic expectations for high school graduates (Chapter 3). Some have turned to these web-based tools because they are relatively low cost, but others are concerned that students and parents are not routinely given useful and comparable information to make decisions among very different types of institutions. Recent calls for accountability at the state and national level underscore the latter (U.S. Department of Education, 2006a).

In this section, we illustrate with specific examples the nature and scope of the CAM phenomenon. College access was a key public policy priority throughout much of the 1990s and early 2000s, and while some of the energy has shifted to college success, access remains an important issue. All of the entities that market college access are, in some way, invested in the outcome. States care about economic growth; testing agencies are developing and selling more tests; loan guaranty agencies were charged with the responsibility of outreach and financial literacy. All of these groups are better served as more students go to college. As a result, all of them have weighed in to provide comprehensive resources to help students navigate the college and (financial) choice process, and we talk about a few of them below.

State Agencies and the North Carolina Experience

One of the earliest comprehensive efforts to improve college access through a multimedia initiative took place in North Carolina, and it was fueled, in part, by the development of a college access web portal. The University of North Carolina General Administration partnered with the Pathways of North Carolina, the North Carolina State Education Assistance Authority (NCSEAA), and the College Foundation, Inc. (CFI) to create a comprehensive web-based tool that could serve as "one place to plan, apply, and pay for college" (Tillery & English, 2009, p. inside cover). The Pathways of North Carolina initially contracted with Xap, Inc., in 1999 to create their comprehensive college access web portal. In 2001, Pathways entered into a formal partnership with NCSEAA and CFI to create what is now known as the College Foundation of North Carolina (CFNC). The current portal is independent of Xap, Inc., although its early roots are evident in the format and style.

Every student in the state is eligible to create an individual profile and portfolio for career planning and exploration, academic planning and preparation, and financial information. The signature feature of CFNC.org is the ability to submit applications to all 110 public and private institutions in their state (Tillery & English, 2009). North Carolina was able to do so partly because the state system was in full support but also because many institutions—public and private—were still developing their web presence, and the portal appeared as a viable option. No state since has been able to make so many applications broadly available to students in a single portal because most institutions had already developed their online application and web marketing presence by the time other states established web portals.

Loan Guaranty Agencies

Some of the early proponents of college access marketing were directly interested in features of the college choice process and, as such, had a vested interest in helping more students and families decide whether or where to attend college. State-based loan guaranty agencies were among this group. For more than 40 years, the federal government has been the primary source of loans to students for college expenses, and the loan guaranty agencies served as middlemen between the federal government and the banks originating the loans. The role of guaranty agencies was

> to reach out and educate state high school and college students about the availability of financial aid. The agency often reviewed and processed loan applications to take the burden off the private lenders, and assisted in the disbursement process to the college or university. However, the main responsibility of the guaranty agency was to pay private lenders if student borrowers defaulted on their loans. (Roos, 2010, p. 3)

Loan guaranty agencies were not government entities, but they worked closely with state agencies. They were nonprofits that, in many cases, were also the state education assistance agencies, like the Higher Education Services Corporation (HESC) in New York or the Pennsylvania Higher Education Assistance Agency (PHEAA). In 2006, as part of the Higher Education Reconciliation Act, loan guaranty agencies were required to provide information to students and parents about how to navigate the college choice process, with a particular emphasis on how to pay for college (Common Manual Governing Board, 2009). These agencies, under the auspices of the Common Manual Governing Board, came together to develop and fund a single web portal—*Mapping Your Future*—recognizing that in most ways, the information students and parents needed was similar, irrespective of state differences. According to the Common Manual Governing Board (2009),

> Sponsored by guarantors and supported by lenders and servicers, *Mapping Your Future* is a national collaborative, public-service organization of the financial aid industry—bringing together the expertise of the industry to provide free career, college, financial aid, and financial literacy services for schools, students, and families via the Web. (p. AF-3)

Mapping Your Future's mission is to enable individuals to achieve lifelong success by empowering students, families, and schools with free, web-based career, college, financial aid, and financial literacy information and services. These services include the following: Online Student Loan Counseling, Show Me the Future®, CareerShip, a deferment navigator, a budget calculator, a debt/salary wizard, a loan wizard, a student loan consolidation calculator, and other money management tools. *Mapping Your Future* was also responsible for creating an additional resource—going2college.org—that resembles other state-level web portals. In 2010, the Family of Federal

Education Loan Programs (FFELP) was eliminated in favor of direct lending from the federal government to students, and the guaranty function was eliminated. The outreach function continues in many states as the Education Assistance Agencies remain.

Testing Agencies

Perhaps the most robust set of tools for navigating the college choice process has been developed by the testing industry, particularly The College Board. The College Board is a multifaceted enterprise with revenues topping $660 million in 2010 and whose products and services—including the SAT, PSAT, and Advanced Placement tests—are paid for and used by over seven million students each year (Lorin, 2011). It is also a not-for-profit organization committed to excellence and equity in education. The College Planning and College Search sites received more than 54 million visits in 2010 (The College Board, 2011b). The College Board tools—most recently the *bigfuture* tool—all emphasize academic planning and preparation, and they are the source of support for those preparing for the SAT or any of the other testing products (e.g. PSAT, ReadiStep). The ACT Student website offers a similar menu of features as The College Board Student site, but they do not appear to offer as many complementary resources (ACT Inc., 2012).

In October 2011, The College Board added a new website that is less information rich but that is more aesthetically engaging in terms of videos, graphics, and student experiences. The *YouCanGo!* site provides video testimonials from college students who experienced significant barriers to college but were not "held back" from attending college irrespective of costs, family responsibilities, high school grades, or overwhelming choices. Two additional tools are tied to students' use of the PSAT. All students who take the preliminary version of the SAT are given access to a diagnostic tool to help them understand the mistakes they made and to learn how to answer similar questions in the future. With a College Board login and a test code, students can access the *My College Quickstart* tool to begin their preparation for the SAT. *MyRoad* is a more robust version of The College Board student site that focuses more specifically on career exploration. Those who do not take the PSAT can access the site, but they are charged a fee for access to the service.

Advocacy Organizations

College access web portals take a number of different forms, and those developed by advocacy organizations differ from those already discussed. One of the more prominent initiatives was the national media marketing campaign launched in 2007 by the American Council on Education (ACE) in partnership with the Ad Council and the Lumina Foundation for Education

(Daun-Barnett & Das, 2011). While the prior initiatives focused on providing a single point of entry for all college choice information and much of the admissions process, the *Know How 2 Go* campaign was designed to change both hearts and minds about whether college was the right next step. Instead of assuming access to information was the problem, social marketing campaigns assume that, even with high expectations for college, many students do not know the steps to take and that messaging from peers to peers is the most effective vehicle to deliver that message. The campaign, at its height, was launched in 15 states and two large metropolitan centers. The media campaign materials were created and updated several times, and those materials were made available to anyone. Partnering organizations also received technical support to implement the campaign at the state and local levels, and those partners were responsible for developing the resources to maintain the effort in their states. The campaign was still in existence in 2012, but it will no longer be funded for development and technical support.

College.gov (which became a part of Federal Student Aid in 2012) was a similar, though shorter-lived, effort initiated by the federal government. The U.S. Department of Education (2011a) launched their web-based college access portal and social marketing campaign in 2009. According the development team, the site was developed to

> motivate students with inspirational stories and information about planning, preparing and paying for college. With students' input and participation, College.gov was created for high school students and their families as a comprehensive online resource with the help and tools students need to get started. (para. 2)

College.gov was a social marketing initiative, first and foremost. Their materials were vetted through student focus groups, and the messages and methods of delivery were tested as well. The federal campaign was reminiscent of the *Know How 2 Go* campaign. The Department of Education developed Public Service Announcement (PSA) materials, toolkits for counselors and teachers, and video clips for both students and parents, and has developed messages tailored to an audience of traditional-aged students and their families. In 2012, College.gov was folded into a more comprehensive information portal under Federal Student Aid. The information and many of the links remain the same, but it has lost its youthful edge and aesthetic appeal.

The proliferation of marketing online by both institutions of higher education and the interest groups described above has made information more broadly available than ever before, but it comes at a cost. Not all information is created equal, and not all students will be able to find the right information at the right times to address their own unique circumstances. Access to information, however, is not the only piece of the college choice puzzle. Below we discuss the evolution of two key features in the college choice process—the college application and the Free Application for Federal Student Aid (FAFSA). Each has changed significantly since the 1990s, and those changes have implications for students and their families.

Managing the College Application Online

In a recent December assembly, students at one of the high-need high schools in our local area were asked whether they had completed at least one of their college applications. More than half of the 65 students in the cafeteria raised their hands, which was a respectable proportion for a school that typically sends a majority of their graduates to the local community colleges with rolling admissions. One of the school counselors followed up by asking how many of them had requested their transcripts to follow those applications, and all but three hands went down. In that instant, it was clear that seniors in this high school, like in many lower-performing schools, were not fully informed about the college application process or what it took to complete a college application.

In districts across the country, high schools have built entire courses around completing the application process. These courses are typically taught during the first half of the senior year, where students complete career assessments, identify potential college majors, search for schools, write college essays, solicit teacher and counselor recommendations, compile their list of activities, engage in community service, complete their application forms and supplemental applications, and request their official high school transcripts. Many students sit for a second attempt at their college admissions tests, though these courses seldom allow time to cover test preparation. In some cases, every piece of the college application is transmitted electronically. Nearly every institution has its application form online; testing agencies send test scores directly to the college or university; the capability exists to extract transcripts from student information systems at high schools and import them to colleges; and a growing number of colleges are asking for student recommendations to be submitted through secure online systems. In turn, colleges allow applicants to monitor the completion of their application package online. Even with these courses in place, some students find it difficult to manage the array of materials, web tools, and deadlines.

Colleges and universities spend a good deal of time, energy, and resources to manage the application process as efficiently and effectively as possible. For many students, families, and schools, these changes have made the college application process easier to navigate. Parents who have attended college in the past may not be familiar with all of the web-based tools but generally understand the sequence of events along the way. Students who were already likely to attend college, by virtue of their parents' education, family income, or quality of high school experience, will be able to submit more applications quickly while managing the flow of applications, essays, transcripts, recommendations, and test scores to a larger number of institutions in a shorter amount of time.

We are concerned, however, about the smaller but still significant proportion of high school graduates who are less likely to have college-educated parents and who may attend underperforming schools, where their chances for postsecondary success are limited. More to the point, we are concerned about the additional burden these new processes may impose upon school counselors working with low-income, first-generation, and underrepresented minority students—these counselors are already stretched thin by added administrative responsibilities, and some of the new admissions systems make their job more difficult. For many, the simple task of sitting with students who lack the instrumental knowledge to effectively utilize technology may require counselors to spend more time teaching students the technology than counseling them through the process.

One of the more significant changes in the admissions application process is the gradual transformation from a paper academic transcript to an electronic version. Today, there are two directions colleges and universities have pursued, and both have the potential to make the system more efficient but potentially at the expense of counselors' time. A number of states and institutions have sought partnerships with private corporations to create electronic transcript exchanges between high schools and colleges—an entire technology industry has grown out of this idea, and a growing number of colleges are moving in this direction. Docufide by Parchment (2012), for example, boasts that in the past year they processed seven million electronic transcripts from 7,800 high schools and transferred them to 1,800 colleges and universities. Pearson Data Solutions (2012) claims that their National Transcript Service (NTC) serves more than 25,000 institutions representing more than 14 million students.

These systems are intuitively appealing. At their essence, they simply extract data from one system, translate it, and import it into another system without the necessary exchange of paper. We suspect the technology works well and that it has the potential to simplify the exchange of data over time. However, these systems rely heavily on the school or district for the data to be accurate. As the counselors we have spoken to will tell you, data stored in these systems is frequently inaccurate, which may yield inaccurate transcripts when they are extracted by the exchange. Counselors also express concern that, even with sophisticated systems like these, they are not always easily adapted to each state or district, and they require a good deal of training.

There is another, less frequently discussed concern among schools regarding electronic transcripts. Schools take great pride in not only the education they provide but also in how they present their student records to the world. The student transcript is not only a document indicating what students have accomplished at a school; it is also a reflection of the school itself. The aesthetics of the document are important, but perhaps more important is the issue of how the student GPA is calculated. When the transcript is extracted from the student information system, it is stripped of the formality of the school, and it leaves open the possibility for schools to consider only what they deem to be important, when calculating a student's GPA. For example, eliminating weighting for particular classes or including only core classes in the calculation of the overall GPA. Some colleges and universities recalculate grades as a matter of principle to ensure that students are compared against a consistent standard, and it would be easier for other institutions to do with ready access to the raw data. Unless clearly stated and defined, colleges have an enormous task in interpreting widely disparate grading and weighting systems reported on high school transcripts. Some e-transcript systems provide an alternative, allowing for the transfer of a PDF version of the transcript, but that reduces some of the efficiency from the exchange.

The other system growing in popularity is the use of self-reported transcripts. New York has been testing the SUNY Online Academic Record (SOAR), which allows students to report their own transcript information electronically as part of the SUNY common application process. An official transcript is required from the high school once the student chooses to attend the institution—thus eliminating a large proportion of the transcripts typically sent to SUNY Central. The University of Illinois and Rutgers University have both implemented similar self-reporting transcript systems (Rutgers University Office of Enrollment Management, 2012; University of Illinois Urbana-Champaign Office for Undergraduate Admissions, 2012). These systems have been found to result in surprisingly accurate self-reported data, and the process shifts data entry to the student.

What these systems seem not to take into account is how this change affects the work of high school counselors. Admissions professionals argue that the shift to self-report places the additional time burden on students, but our experience in schools suggests that at least some of this work is shifting to counselors as well. They print unofficial transcripts for students as they complete the SOAR and then are required to send a copy of the transcript to the institution a student chooses to attend. In some cases, counselors also spend time sitting with students to assist them in using the SOAR. The time saved by admissions professionals appears to shift some of that time spent to students and their counselors, and this may have a disproportionate impact on the students most at risk of choosing not to attend college. While the shift to an electronic submission process may impose some additional barriers for low-income, first-generation, and underrepresented minority students, the FAFSA may pose an even greater challenge for everyone involved.

Simplifying the FAFSA

In 2006, the paper FAFSA form was five pages long and asked students and parents a combined 127 questions about individual and family finances from income, deductions, and withholdings to demographic and school enrollment information. Dynarski and Scott-Clayton (2006) point out that the FAFSA asks for 33 additional sources of income that are not indicated on a W-2 form. Ironically, while the IRS estimates between 8–16 hours to complete the paper version of one's taxes, the U.S. Department of Education suggests the average FAFSA filer will take approximately one hour to apply for financial aid. One hour is an ambitious estimate, particularly for first-time filers. For the past decade, financial aid advocates have called for a simplified form. In 2005, the Advisory Committee on Student Financial Assistance (ACSFA) issued a series of recommendations to simplify the financial aid process and to provide greater certainty to students and parents.

Dynarski and Scott-Clayton (2006) make a compelling case that the complexity of the FAFSA is regressive in the sense that it may prevent otherwise eligible families from applying for aid. They also show that the complexity is unnecessary or, at very least, not worth the cost of compliance. In an analysis of data on FAFSA filers, they found that four items (adjusted gross income, marital status, family size, and number of family members in college), out of more than 70, account for three-quarters of the variation in Pell Grant awards, and they improve the formula to 90% with fewer than 10 total questions. They argue that all of the information needed to make reasonably accurate estimates of families' ability to pay for college could fit on the back of a postcard (Dynarski & Scott-Clayton, 2007).

Simplification is not only a matter of making the process easier—though many families would appreciate that. Rather, as Dynarski and Scott-Clayton (2006) point out, a complicated system makes it difficult for students and their families to estimate the net cost of college because they cannot reasonably account for federal, state, or institutional aid in their calculations. One of the additional challenges is the amount of time families have to complete the FAFSA, consider aid alternatives, and make a reasonable choice about the right institution to attend (based in part upon what they can afford). The FAFSA is available to file beginning January 1 of the year a student intends to enroll in college. Families will complete their taxes typically between early February and April 15, but the timeline accelerates for those who are applying for financial aid. Some families will begin the process (if they file online) by calculating estimates from last year's tax information, but many wait to submit their FAFSA until the current year's taxes are completed (to avoid having to complete major sections of the form more than once). The IRS requires that employers issue W-2 income statements by the end of January, and other tax forms for untaxed income, interest, and deductions follow close behind.

Assuming that families complete their taxes as soon as all of their forms are received, they will file their FAFSA by the end of February. The online form gives the student an estimate of the federal aid they may receive, based upon the data submitted, but these numbers are not certain until the Student Aid Report (SAR) is received by the college or university where an aid package inclusive of federal, state, and institutional aid is assembled. The SAR may take as long as 4–6 weeks to reach an institution. This window is important because many colleges either maintain rolling aid packaging or priority deadlines around March 1 for institutional aid eligibility. If students and their families complete all of these steps as quickly as possible, they may meet the priority deadline. In turn, the college will assemble its aid packages in a couple of weeks. Families may receive aid award notifications from colleges through March and April with the expectation that enrollment decisions will be made and confirmed by May 1. Families who complete the process quickly will have as much as a month to weigh financial aid packages and personal priorities to make an informed decision about which college to attend. For many others who are delayed at some point in the process, they will be required to make one of the most important investment decisions in their lives without much time to weigh the alternatives.

Simplification could improve the process in two ways. Most directly, a simplified form would take less time to complete for families and presumably less time to process at the U.S. Department of Education. Shortening the 4–6 week window may give families more time to make an informed choice. Second, a simpler process would allow families to more easily estimate their own potential aid packages based on the prior year's taxes. The current SAR is indecipherable to families, but if fewer than 10 questions could provide families with an estimate of the federal aid (perhaps state aid as well), they would have more and better information entering into the application and decision-making process. Further, allowing families to submit their actual FAFSA with last year's tax information would allow institutions to accelerate award notifications and give families more time to consider alternatives. Recently, several changes have been made to the process, but there is more work left to do.

To begin, the form has been simplified in its online version. It is not a postcard yet, but it is a start. A number of questions have been eliminated. The online application employs skip logic that allows families to avoid questions that will not pertain to their situation—meaning less time will be spent laboring over the meaning of questions and their applicability. Third, and perhaps most important, in 2011, the IRS has made tax information available for electronic retrieval through the FAFSA. Once taxes are verified and accepted by the IRS (a process that could take a couple of weeks), families can enter the FAFSA website and ask to retrieve their tax information. They will still be asked a number of additional questions regarding family finances, but most of it will be done automatically. Even with these changes, the window between filing the FAFSA and weighing financial aid options remains short. As such, two additional tools have been created.

In 2007, the U.S. Department of Education launched the FAFSA4caster—an online tool to estimate financial aid eligibility. The tool has been refined and can now provide families with reasonable estimates of federal aid eligibility, depending upon the reliability of the information families enter and the estimated costs of attendance. Second, through the reauthorization of the Higher Education Act, colleges and universities are now required to make net cost calculators available on their websites. The Department of Education has created minimum guidelines for these tools and makes templates available, but they leave the tool largely to the discretion of the institutions. The advantage of the cost calculator, theoretically, is that it can take into account both state aid programs and tuition discounting by institutions, but because the tools are not uniform across the board, the gains made by including state and institutional aid may be offset by the lack of comparability from one institution to the next.

At first glance, it might appear that such a concerted effort by so many interested parties to make more and better information available to students and parents who are engaged in the college choice process is a good thing; it is certainly better than having no information available at all! Unfortunately, in the process of creating more and better information, educators and policy makers may have lost sight of the impact on students and their parents. How are students and their parents expected to sift through the sheer volume of all that is now available, evaluate the quality of those sources, find the information they need, and then make informed decisions as a result? Many web-based college access tools are sponsored by states, testing agencies, loan guarantors, and advocacy groups; others provide links to institutional sources. More than a few savvy for-profit colleges have either purchased space at the top of the search or figured out how to game the search algorithm like FAFSA.com. Similar to the real estate analogy at the beginning of the book, consumers are at a disadvantage with this information because they may only engage in the search process once or twice in their lives, and each time the process will be very different. Today, school counselors, pre-college outreach providers, and independent consultants are the closest parallel to the buyer's agent. Aside from independent consultants who make it their business to know the process, these advocates for students are, at times, only slightly better informed about how to find the information students and parents need when they need it.

In order to improve students' chances for successfully navigating the college choice process from the search to the final enrollment decision, school counselors, pre-college outreach providers, and independent consultants who work with at-risk students must be empowered to employ a growing number of technological tools to the benefit of their students. Currently, those college admissions professionals who are least likely to have regular access to other college admissions professionals who can share their knowledge and insights about the evolving process are precisely those working with students who will wrestle with whether or not to attend college. It will not be an easy task overcoming these realities because it will require admissions professionals to spend more time providing professional development and reaching out to schools that may not otherwise be a part of their feeder network. The effort has to be made by the colleges and universities, and it may be that rapidly developing providers like pre-college outreach professionals can serve as the appropriate bridge to link the knowledge of admissions professionals with counselors to access more students.

We recognize that efficiency is an important goal, and the Web has allowed colleges and universities to create a much more efficient application and review process for their campuses and for many students. This is a positive development for higher education, but we must be diligent to ensure that these advances do not place some schools and students at a greater disadvantage as a result. We believe that the imbalance can be offset if the admissions community collectively develops a strategy to provide more comprehensive collaboration with the lowest-performing schools in their service regions. As a nation, we need more of their students attending college, and we expect that as more students have the information they need and their schools are more effective developing a college-going culture, more students will make a successful transition from high school to college, which increases the pool of students from which all institutions will draw. This may be a task more easily accomplished by state systems or professional school counselor networks that operate locally, statewide, or at the national level.

Suggestions for Admissions Professionals

What does all of this mean for college admissions professionals? In order to answer this question, we suggest that admissions professionals, particularly those new to the field, take some time to actually navigate the process as a student would do. That might actually require that you sit with students who are going through the process at a variety of schools. Assume that you know nothing about going to college and follow the many pathways high school seniors consider in their college choice process. Spend some time exploring the dizzying array of recruitment tools, promotional materials, college access marketing campaigns, and electronic processes and procedures students will navigate along the way. We believe that by examining these processes from the perspective of end users, admissions professionals can develop a fuller appreciation of what the implications—both good and bad—are for helping students navigate the process and go to college.

Next, we suggest that admissions professionals ask their partner schools how these tools affect their work. This is a different question than asking them whether or not the processes are effective for their students—which will probably yield a different response. If, for example, counselors respond that the SOAR systems require more time and energy on their part because they need to print unofficial transcripts for students or even sit with them to ensure they complete the process, then we may need to think about ways that our colleges and universities can provide these schools with some assistance to simplify that process on the school end as well. At very least, colleges or state systems that implement these changes should provide schools with real support to build greater capacity in the schools. Training may be one piece of it, but that solution leaves the responsibility for utilization in the hands of school counselors.

It may be time for us to rethink how admissions professionals utilize their time in schools or with pre-college outreach professionals. School visits may continue to be a critical piece of the fall travel season, but perhaps those visits are used to walk groups of students (and counselors) through the online application—this is a fairly common practice among community colleges and for-profit colleges that conduct instant admissions on-site. Perhaps more time can be spent connecting with counselors, pre-college outreach providers, and independent consultants in a virtual environment where more regular conversations can occur. For example, during the fall, it may be useful to have staff on-call and in virtual chat space to assist students with the application process so that admissions staff can provide this technical support rather than students relying on counselors, who as we have noted, do not have time to provide this level of support for all of their students.

Finally, we recommend that admissions professionals take time to develop some expertise in utilizing the tools that may not be central to their work, but are critical to students and parents. For example, if your districts utilize Career Cruising or Naviance or any of the college choice portals, know and understand how those systems work and think about how those are most effectively utilized to complete the process for your institution. Spend time to complete the FAFSA and any state applications for financial aid. For some families, cost is the first question on their minds, and the more knowledge and insight you can share with students and families about those processes, the better prepared they will be to apply for financial aid and attend college. The same advice applies for the web portals provided by the testing agencies. If your students are required to submit scores for an admissions test, then it will be valuable to you and to your college access partners that you remain up-to-date on the features of those tools and that you share that expertise with your college access peers who may not have the time or the resources to remain current in the developments across the field.

9

PLANNING FOR COLLEGE SUCCESS

In this chapter, we introduce a topic that could fill an entire volume—what it takes for students to be successful once they arrive at college. To this point we have focused on the role admissions professionals can play to help students overcome barriers to college, particularly through the network of college access professionals. For some students, access remains a central issue; for many more, the question is one of success. If college admissions professionals are successful in moving more students through the transition from high school to college, but those students fail to earn a credential of value—whether that includes a degree, certificate, or a set of transferrable skills to a vocational setting—then we have done little more than offer a false promise. In fact, some institutions have used predicted probabilities of success in their admissions decisions processes, recognizing the importance of college success. What may be more concerning is that failure to deliver on the promise may burden students and their families with added debt without the higher salary to meet that obligation. Throughout this volume, we have identified four essential barriers to college access that can be addressed through collaboration among admissions professionals, school counselors, pre-college outreach providers, and independent consultants—academic preparation, college affordability, social networks of support, and the use of technology. These challenges do not simply disappear once students enroll in college. Students and parents frequently cannot anticipate these challenges once they arrive on a college campus, and we believe that lack of knowledge is likely to prevent some from achieving success in college.

We are continually surprised by how little high school students know about college, given that so many plan to attend. In our small corner of the country, we are surrounded by 21 colleges and universities, six of which are located in the metropolitan center. Many of the urban high schools are within several miles of a college campus, yet few of their students report spending any time on their campuses. Those that have visited a campus typically do so through one of the many pre-college outreach programs operating throughout the district. Access to college campuses is different for students in rural communities. In some communities across the region, the nearest college may not be close enough to take advantage of social and recreational opportunities, and it may require that students or their families make a concerted effort to visit. While the challenges may differ, the results are the same—too few prospective college students spend time on college campuses and, as a result, do not know what to expect once they arrive.

The campus might as well be a foreign country to many students. Few high schools prepare students for the autonomy of choosing their own major or a general education curriculum. Many students leave high school ill prepared to utilize technology to the extent that it is used on college campuses. And many students are shocked by the amount of work they are expected to complete. These are the challenges students often know to expect. They may not know what it looks like, but they know academic expectations are going to be different. Fewer students are prepared to manage the changing lifestyle. They are confronted by new ideas and different perspectives; they engage with students from different cultural, ethnic, and religious experiences; they are forced to manage their finances as well as their academic and social calendars. These adjustments are greatest for those students who are not surrounded by family or friends who have attended college. In this chapter, we cannot hope to address all of the challenges students face when they arrive on campus, but we try to address some of the more important issues and particularly those that confront students early in their college careers. We also focus on issues that admissions professionals can address in their interactions with their college access counterparts in schools and community settings. And we remind admissions professionals that while they may not always pay full attention to the student experience once they matriculate, they are in the best position to understand that experience and to share those insights with their college access peers.

Academic Integration and College-Level Work

Most students have been forewarned that the academic expectations in college will far exceed those most students experience in high school. Beyond that, few have any idea what "different" means. In a standard orientation session by a faculty member, incoming college students will be told that for every hour in class, they should spend an additional two to three hours outside of class—for a 15-credit-hour semester, students would be committed to an additional 30 to 45 hours of out-of-class work, meaning that college is the equivalent of a full-time job. In reality, many students do not commit this amount of time to academic work, but they are working more hours and in different ways than in high school. The first step many students take in their academic transition is the college placement test, which provides an indication of whether students are prepared to complete college-level work or whether they will require remedial coursework.

151

Placement Testing and Remediation

The first barrier to college access we discussed was the degree to which students are academically prepared to attend college. High schools anticipate the courses students may be required to complete in order to gain admission to a given college, but the placement test is the final arbiter of college preparation. As we described in Chapter 2, there is frequently a gap between what high schools expect of students in order to earn their diploma and what colleges expect in the admissions process. One indicator of this gap is the prevalence of remedial education in college. According to the National Center for Education Statistics (NCES) (2011a), as many as a third of all students require remediation in one or more subjects, and that number rises to 42% among community college attendees. All of these students either completed high school or earned a General Equivalency Diploma (GED), suggesting that the high school completion standard does not adequately prepare some students for college.

Rosenbaum, Deil-Amen, and Person (2006) found that community college students were frequently unaware that remedial coursework would not count as college credit toward their degree. For some students, remediation can extend their college career for up to a year at considerable expense, both in terms of the cost of enrolling and the opportunity costs of foregone wages. Remediation might seem worth the effort if students' chances for postsecondary success improved. The findings on this question have been mixed, but recent research suggests that students in remedial courses are no more likely to demonstrate academic success than similar students with no remedial coursework (Attewell et al., 2006; Calcagno & Long, 2008; Levin & Calcagno, 2008; Martorell & McFarlin, 2007).

Students are commonly placed into remedial or credit-bearing courses in math and writing composition according to their scores on internally developed or nationally standardized placement exams, like Accuplacer and COMPASS. Colleges decide which tests to administer and what scores constitute adequate preparation for college-level work. In most cases, the placement decision is not binding or exclusive, meaning that some students will elect to forego remedial coursework. At other institutions, students may be required to complete remedial coursework before the take college-credited courses. The contentious policy questions revolve around whether remedial education should be offered at all and, if so, at what sort of institution. Policy makers in particular would rather not subsidize students and colleges for providing a level of education they believe should have been mastered in high school. Some states and postsecondary systems have pushed remediation out of 4-year institutions and onto community colleges (Boylan, Saxon, & Boylan, 1999; California State University, 2010; Gumport & Bastedo, 2001; Levin & Calcagno, 2008).

As Rosenbaum et al. (2006) point out, high school students lack two important pieces of information—the fact that they will be required to take a placement exam and that they might be required to complete non-credit-bearing courses that will not earn them credit toward their college degree. This is important information for students and their families as they make decisions about whether or where to attend college. It may also be useful information to share with schools regarding how well prepared their graduating seniors are for college-level work. A number of community colleges have attempted to bridge this gap by introducing their placement exam into high school for juniors or rising seniors.

Using placement tests as an early warning indicator in high school has merit, but it also has two possible consequences. In the absence of effective follow-up, the school may not know how to use the results in a constructive manner to maximize students' senior year. Additionally, the results of the test can leave students feeling they are not equipped for college, and this may actually depress their postsecondary aspirations and reduce the likelihood that they attend college. We suggest that—if colleges choose to provide early placement testing—it has to be a first step in a more comprehensive strategy to engage schools in conversations about how best to align the high school curriculum (in math and writing composition in particular) with postsecondary expectations. That strategy might also include conversations between high school math and English Language Arts (ELA) teachers and college professors on how best to bridge the high-school-to-college curriculum gap. Admissions professionals can play an important role in facilitating these conversations by sharing information with school counselors about how their students perform once they arrive on campus. Typically, this information is not difficult to access, but it has not normally been incorporated into the work of admissions professionals unless they are part of enrollment management offices at smaller campuses.

Academic Success Courses

A critical piece of the student orientation process is the academic success course, sometimes known as nature of inquiry or methods of inquiry. Most colleges and universities outside of the most selective across the country find that some proportion of their students is not adequately prepared to succeed in the classroom. For some students, the result is remedial coursework, but for others, including those who did well in high school, it may be that they never learned effective study strategies, how to structure a cogent argument, or write a comprehensive research paper. In most cases, they have not learned how to utilize the range of available library resources, and they may have little understanding of how faculty assess student learning in college.

In college, the expectations are different, and many students struggle with developing effective strategies for learning. A number of institutions offer courses designed to teach students to develop strategies for studying effectively. The content of these courses may include how to read, what to read, how to take notes, how to ask good questions, or how to utilize library resources.

These are all skills that high school students could benefit from developing as well, but they are critical to postsecondary success. Methods of inquiry courses teach students some of the theoretical and philosophical underpinnings of student learning and cognitive development. They also provide a set of strategies to manage their academic coursework, take and review lecture notes, read and review academic texts, and demonstrate mastery of course content. For some, the most important feature of these courses is that students are expected to practice these techniques in their other courses throughout the semester and are given feedback on their implementation of those strategies. These courses are an important complement to the university experience courses discussed later that focus greater attention on the social and developmental dimensions of the transition to college.

Managing the Cost of College

As we described in Chapter 5, being able to afford the cost of a college education weighs heavily on the minds of many students and their families, particularly those from low-income households (Heller, 1997). The net price of college, after all forms of financial aid and institutional tuition discounting are accounted, affects the choices students make about whether or where to attend college. Tinto (1993), whose work is most frequently cited in research on student persistence and success in college, concluded in his earlier work that affordability was not a significant factor in college success, as it was addressed when students made their choices about access and choice of institution. Others have argued that cost remains a relevant issue for college students as well, though it may operate in different ways (St. John, Andrieu, Oescher, & Starkey, 1994). In this section, we address two cost-related issues that have important implications for students—their decisions to work while in school and the level of debt they assume.

Working While in College

For many students, the decision regarding whether or not to work while in college is not even open for discussion. According to the National Center for Education Statistics (Aud et al., 2012), approximately 40% of full-time and 73% of part-time undergraduates work while in college—approximately 17% of whom spend more than 20 hours per week working. Students may work to avoid assuming high levels of debt to finance their college education or they may simply be offsetting the cost of living while they attend. Research examining the effects of work on student success is mixed. Early concerns were raised that students who worked were less likely to be successful in college, but subsequent research in this area found that the effects are a bit more complex. Students who work are less academically engaged, and they report spending less time studying—both of which have a negative effect on students' achievement and persistence (Pascarella & Terenzini, 2005). However, the same body of research suggests there is no direct relationship between working behavior and student success. Other research suggests working while in school may have positive effects until students exceed 15–20 hours per week. The effects of work are not conclusive, but a couple of general principles seem useful.

Working will be the reality for many students, and, when done in moderation, the effects appear to be positive (or at least not a barrier to success). As most institutional policies require, students should not work more than 20 hours per week or it may begin to affect their academic success. Even though the research is not clear on this point, we recommend that students work on campus if they are able. Campus employers offer two benefits beyond those off campus—they provide greater flexibility because they are easy to get to and they are accustomed to building their schedules around student course schedules, and they provide an opportunity for students to be more actively engaged in the campus community and/or with a group of college student peers.

Assuming Loan Debt

Deciding whether or not to apply for loans to pay for school is a very personal and in many cases, a difficult decision for students and families. It is clear to see why. For the first time in our nation's history, student loan debt exceeds credit card debt at more than $1 trillion. Among students who take out student loans, the average debt burden is more than $27,700 by the time they leave college. Assuming students are employed in reasonably well-paying jobs once they graduate, $30,000 in student loans is manageable over the typical 10-year repayment period. But what students and families need to understand is that, like any investment, there are risks. As students have learned firsthand since the 2008 recession in the United States, a college degree is not a guarantee for a well-paying job. Table 9.1 provides estimates for monthly payments depending upon the amount of money a student borrows and the interest rate of the loan, assuming a 10-year repayment schedule.

It should be clear from Table 9.1 that assuming some debt is reasonable and will likely pay off in the long run. Even for students who do not earn a degree, if they worked full time at $10/hour, they would earn $400 per week before taxes, meaning that even $20,000 in loans would cost a student less than 20% of their monthly salary. We are not suggesting a particular threshold for loan debt, but we do suggest that students consider real numbers to estimate what is a reasonable amount of debt to assume. A student entering a nursing program, for example, may expect a median salary of $66,000 per year (Salary.com, 2013), where the average associate's degree earns only $41,000 (U.S. Bureau of Labor Statistics, 2012). Different debt levels are appropriate depending upon the potential wages students are likely to earn.

Table 9.1 Estimated Monthly Payments by Principal and Interest Rates

	Interest Rates				
Principal	3.4%	4.5%	5.6%	6.0%	6.8%
$3,500	50	50	50	50	50
$5,500	54	57	59	61	63
$11,500	113	119	125	127	132
$15,500	152	160	168	172	178
$21,500	211	222	234	238	247
$31,500	310	326	343	349	362
$41,500	408	430	452	460	477
$51,500	506	533	561	571	592

One of the more promising developments in student loans is the establishment of an income-based repayment (IBR) option. Students with loans through the federal direct lending program have an option when they finish their postsecondary work to pay their loans based upon a proportion of what they earn. Participants in IBR may choose to pay 10% of their salary until the loan is repaid or until they have been paying consistently for 20 years. Assuming students remain in good standing and do not default on their loans, the remaining principal will be forgiven at the end of 20 years. IBR serves as sort of a social safety net that is relatively recent in the United States—specifically since the Family of Federal Education Loan Programs (FFELP) was eliminated in favor of direct lending by the federal government to consumers. Prior to 2011, direct lending was modest relative to loans originated by private banks through FFELP, and as such, relatively few students were eligible for IBR. Now that all federal student loans originate with the federal government, all new loans will be eligible.

Social Integration and the Transition to Campus Life

In our visits with high school students, we expect to talk about financial aid, including student loans, involvement on campus, resources to improve academic success, and student support programs available to help students make the transition to college. Those are important issues to consider, but they are not the questions we hear from students attending schools where college access is very much an open question. Instead, students are more interested in the social life of the campus: what the residence halls are like, whether the food is good, and whether there are parties to attend. For students who have spent their entire academic careers in single-building schools, the fact that even a small campus will have a dozen or more buildings can create anxiety.

In this section, we discuss some of the salient social transitions students face as they arrive on campus.

Living the Life

Those who choose to study abroad know to anticipate the "culture shock" of living in a new and different society under a new set of norms, rules, and expectations. They may not know what differences to expect, but they appreciate that it will be different in some way. What many study abroad offices—and students who spend an extended period of time outside the country—will tell you is that the return home also involves a sort of culture shock. When done well, a study abroad experience forces one to view the world from a different perspective and to see oneself and one's culture through a different lens. When students return home, they frequently find that while their perspectives have changed a great deal, very little has changed at home. This adjustment becomes more difficult for those whose families and friends have never experienced something similar. It is difficult to describe how one's worldview changes to family and friends who have never experienced such a shift or who may even be resistant to change of that magnitude. Students whose family or friends have spent time abroad will experience this differently because those around them will be able to relate to their experiences. They will know what to anticipate, what questions to ask, and what support they may need. Students without the same network will find it more difficult to anticipate or to describe.

We believe the same is true for students who make the transition from high school to college. They may anticipate that life will be different in college, but they may have no idea how it will be different or in what ways. Those whose parents, siblings, or friends have gone to college will be at an advantage during this transition because this information will flow throughout their social network. The transition may not be easy, but they will know what to expect, what questions to ask, and who can be most helpful along the way. Similarly, many low-income, first-generation, and underrepresented minority students may struggle with the "shock" of both learning to operate in a new cultural context and then finding their place as they return home for the first time. Even in a few short months, they will change in both subtle and significant ways, while those at home will frequently remain relatively unchanged.

The transition from high school to college is not a student issue alone. Enrollment managers recognize the importance of retaining students who choose to attend; deans, provosts, and presidents are aware that retention and degree attainment are important markers of prestige; and alumni/development officers appreciate the value of the student experience to the likelihood current students will turn into future donors. In short, colleges and universities care as much about the success of students as students themselves do. There are really two ways to think about what happens to students once they leave high school and begin their postsecondary career. The first is reflected in the enormous body of research examining how colleges affect students. Pascarella and Terenzini (2005) have spent the better part of the past 30 years summarizing the literature regarding how colleges affect students, from cognitive and moral development to psychosocial development and civic engagement to retention and degree completion.

The second major theme, which is a subset of the research on college effects, focuses on student persistence and an examination of the reasons why students leave. The seminal work in this area was published by Vincent Tinto (1993), who likened the departure patterns of students to some of the early work done by sociologists on suicide—essentially departing from society. His theory and those who have followed (Braxton, 2000; Dey & Astin, 1993; Fike & Fike, 2008; Oseguera & Rhee, 2009; Seidman, 2005; Singell, 2010) recognize student success is a function of both individual characteristics and the structure and function of postsecondary institutions. From this perspective, social and academic integration are critical to the eventual success of the student. It would be impossible to summarize these two bodies of research in the space we have, but we will highlight some of what we know about helping students succeed in college that college access professionals should be prepared to anticipate for their students.

Embracing Cultural Differences

The culture of each college or university is unique in many ways, and we are cautious about attempting to distill that uniqueness into a set of common principles. We can, however, help students recognize the characteristics of institutions that may influence their experiences while in college. One of the first realities that students face when they arrive on campus is that they are now surrounded by other students from very different socio-cultural experiences than their own. Despite generations of debate over integration in K12 schools, the majority of high school students in the United States attend schools with students who are racially, ethnically, and socio-economically similar. Stated differently, schools remain highly segregated, meaning that college may be the first time many students interact with students different from themselves. Racial and ethnic differences are some of the more visible differences when students arrive, but they must also contend with differences by class, religion, sexual orientation, and nation of origin.

Not every college campus is equally diverse, but the reality is that a greater proportion of current college students are lower-income, first-generation, and underrepresented minority students attending college directly out of high school. At the same time, demographic shifts remind us that the fastest growing population in the United States is Hispanic, with estimates suggesting the United States will be a majority minority nation by 2050 and that

Hispanics will comprise 29% of the population (Passel & Cohn, 2011). What this means for students is that they must be prepared to reflect upon their own experiences, assumptions, and biases and learn to engage with peers who may differ from them in any number of ways.

One way to reduce the fear of the unknown is to do what most admissions professionals recommend as a matter of course—visit campus. The campus visit is an important indicator to admissions professionals regarding the likelihood that an individual will apply and whether they will accept an offer and attend the institution. Of course, not all students can visit college campuses. Students in rural communities may live too far away from a campus to do so easily, and the psychological distance between high schools and colleges in metropolitan centers can be as great a barrier for some as the actual distance for students in rural areas. This is when the recruitment function for admissions offices becomes so important—in the absence of being able to bring every prospective student to campus, college admissions professionals must paint a picture for a student or family with whatever tools they have at their disposal, including print materials, DVDs, virtual campus tours, and alumni interviews.

We have found that these visits occur much less frequently at schools for which college access, or even high school completion, is low. We encourage admissions professionals to spend more time in high-need schools and pre-college outreach programs serving low-income students, but our goal is slightly different. Most of these visits by admissions staff are made to feeder schools from which a larger number of students are already likely to attend the institution or which has a large pool of students meeting the college profile. These visits make sense in terms of achieving some measure of advantage in the competition for enrollments. We suspect that expanding that network of schools to include lower-performing schools in existing recruiting regions can open up larger markets of students by empowering the staff at those schools with the information they need to help their students prepare for college participation. In a less tangible way, we also expect that these visits can help to contribute to the creation of a college-going culture in these lower-performing schools. In some cases, colleges adopt high-need high schools in their districts and assume some responsibility for helping them build a college-going culture. We believe this is a step in the right direction, but it might require that each admissions counselor adopt a school in order to change the system.

Student Ambassador Programs

One alternative utilized by many college campuses is to develop and nurture student ambassador programs, particularly among students from high-need schools and districts. While all colleges structure these programs slightly differently, they typically recruit, train, and empower (and in some cases pay) students to return to their high schools as informal recruiters. Many recent high school graduates do this on their own, as they want to share their experiences with friends, counselors, and teachers at their former schools. The challenge of expanding this network of ambassadors to reach high-need schools is twofold. First, there are few of these students enrolled at many institutions already. Second, students from high-need schools may require additional financial support themselves, meaning they may be working to support themselves through school. If we hope to make these networks effective for these schools, then we must find ways to engage more of these students, perhaps in work–study positions or other paid positions in addition to their roles promoting college participation in their former schools.

Summer Orientation

The first formal academic exposure many students have on campus occurs during new student orientation, either during the summer or directly preceding the start of the fall semester. Orientation programs attempt to provide students and families with all the information they need to navigate their college career and find the resources that will help them succeed. Typically, they include discussions of academic success from faculty; college placement testing; campus activities fairs; meetings with academic advisers; conversations about health, safety, and wellness; and course registration. Along the way, orientation aids (current college students) create social opportunities for students to meet new people and to begin forging relationships that help students feel more comfortable with this new environment.

Campuses structure summer orientation in a variety of different ways. Some large campuses hold separate 2-day orientation sessions throughout the summer and use that time to acclimate students in smaller batches to the institution. Other institutions will organize orientation immediately preceding the start of the academic year. The advantage of the latter is that first-year students are also given an opportunity to move in and adjust to campus life before other students return. Student affairs professionals recognize that it is difficult for students to absorb all they need to know in a few short days or without any context. As a result, many campuses offer courses to extend the orientation period throughout the first semester of their freshman year.

University Experience Courses

A number of colleges and universities recognize that there is simply too much material to include in a relatively short period of two or three days, and they have implemented college experience courses. These courses are taught by a combination of staff, faculty, and students and tend to earn college elective credit for the purposes of full-time status, but they do not count toward major or degrees. University experience courses provide the institution more time to help students adjust to college and give them an opportunity to reflect on their experience and ask questions along the way. The introduction to college course may discuss the array of resources and support services on campus, time management, alcohol and drug use, student conduct, academic integrity, and generally the social adjustment to college. In most cases, these courses spend very little time on what it takes to succeed academically at the institution.

New students face a number of important choices, such as whether to live on campus, how to get involved on campus, and whether to work while in school. Some of these choices are more or less prevalent depending upon institutional type. For example, a much smaller proportion of a community college population will live on campus, and a greater proportion will work while enrolled in school. Other colleges may require students to live on campus for some portion of their undergraduate career, which may affect which students choose to attend the institution. All colleges deal with these questions differently. A number of small colleges, for example, are finding new ways to employ students on campus to cover their family contribution to the cost of college—these efforts extend beyond what federal work–study programs cover.

Identifying the Right Support Services

Perhaps the greatest adjustment students make is the shift from a prescriptive high school environment to a permissive postsecondary institution. In high school, students have very little discretion in terms of how they use their time. They set their schedules with their counselors; they fill every period of every day with required or elective courses, study halls, or co-curricular experiences; they eat when they are told; and they frequently do only what is necessary to earn the grade they desire. In college, by contrast, they are responsible for their own time. They choose the classes they wish to take; they create their own schedule, which may give them large chunks of unscheduled time during the day or days off during the week; and they are responsible for seeking any help they may need, which requires them to recognize when they actually need help. If a student performs poorly in high school, a teacher will notice, and a counselor or academic intervention specialist may intervene; the school counselor may call a student to the office to check in and see why the student is struggling. Seldom is this the case in any but a few of the smaller liberal arts colleges—and even then the supports are unlikely to compare to what students receive in high school.

College educators view this change as part of developing autonomy and individual identity, and students move through this process at different rates. Colleges and universities simply make the range of services available, and those who need them can seek them out. This flexible strategy is more cost effective for two reasons. First, to achieve recommended high school student-to-counselor ratios of nearly 250:1, larger institutions would need to hire many more counselors. A campus of 20,000 students might reasonably need at least 80 counselors. Second and perhaps more challenging, it would be impossible to achieve that scale with the variety of counseling functions available on campus. The role most similar to the school counselor may be the academic adviser on a college campus. Academic advising is accomplished in a variety of different ways, from centralized advising services to TRIO and other college success programs to the intensive supports provided by Division I athletics programs. At some institutions, the faculty provides academic advising, particularly once students enter a major or a graduate program.

In addition to academic advising, students may seek out mental health counseling, career counseling, and financial aid counseling, not to mention the admissions counseling they received on their way into the institution. At some institutions, students may receive health and nutrition counseling or life coaching. All of these counseling support services are provided by most campuses in one form or another, and they all require fairly specialized knowledge. Students also tend to seek them out at different points along their academic careers. Academic advising is most intentional during the early years of a college career, while career counseling is typically sought out at the end of a degree program. Financial aid counseling is relevant as students enter the institution and also when they leave, particularly if they have assumed loans along the way. A growing feature of many student support service areas is disability or accessibility services. These offices tend to be small and focused on students with a particular set of physical, learning, or behavioral challenges.

An important distinction between high schools and colleges is the fact that school counselors are used more as generalists and are asked to perform a variety of functions, including but not limited to mental health counseling, academic advising on course selection, college and career counseling, and student discipline. From a student perspective, this approach may be more efficient because one person can attend to the variety of needs a student has, and it is clear to the student whom they can ask for support. But it also means that counselors must be trained to serve students in a number of important capacities, and it is unlikely that they are highly trained in more than one or two of these domains. Alternatively, colleges differentiate their roles and expect staff to specialize in particular areas. As a consequence, postsecondary counselors are much more expert in financial aid or career counseling or mental health, but they do not know much about other functional areas on campus.

162

Embracing Technology in College

We've committed all of Chapter 8 to the changing role of technology in the college choice process, and we expressed concern that the shift to the virtual environment has a disproportionate effect on low-income, first-generation, and underrepresented minority students. We have suggested that increasing access to information and shifting the college choice process to the Internet has complicated the transition from high school to college for some. Not everyone we talk to on college campuses is concerned about the increasing use of technology in the college choice process. Those working on college campuses recognize that technological IQ is critical for student success once they arrive on the college campus. Some college and university leaders believe that if students are not prepared to navigate the web-based college choice process, then they will be ill equipped and underprepared for the technology employed on college campuses. There may be some truth to that concern. Even among a generation of students who are digitally native, too few have spent the time to develop instrumental knowledge to navigate the college choice process (Venegas, 2006a).

A 2012 study of undergraduates' use of technology in the United States and abroad illustrates how technologically advanced students are expected to be on college campuses. Today, more than 85% of undergraduate students report owning a laptop, and an increasing proportion are reporting the use of smaller portable devices (e.g. tablets and smartphones) (Dahlstrom, Dziuban, & Walker, 2012). The presence of technology has increased dramatically over 20 years, but the same is true in K12 schools as well. Many schools, even those with the highest needs, have fully functioning computer labs, smartboard technology, and wireless access. The difference is the degree to which students are expected to employ technology for the range of academic and social applications. Pryor et al. (2007) report that more than 80% of college students use the Internet for research or homework. Increasingly, colleges utilize course management systems that serve as a virtual environment unique to each class. In that space, faculty may post materials, communicate with students, assess their learning, and create opportunities for students to communicate with one another.

Through the same system(s), students may also have the opportunity to access their academic and administrative records, register for courses, request transcripts, monitor academic progress, and learn about available opportunities on campus. Today, nearly every part of a college student's academic life is managed online. We have already discussed the importance of the FAFSA and the online application process—a form that students will continue to complete each year they enroll in college. In addition, students register for courses electronically; they can order transcripts with the click of a button or review their academic records. Students manage email and their calendars online, they apply to their major programs online, and they research which courses to take as they progress through their academic programs. Much of the information students need to navigate their academic careers is available electronically, and at many institutions, paper resources are increasingly scarce.

One of the largest technological differences between high schools and colleges for many students is the proliferation of digital resources that are quickly replacing more tangible paper journals, newspapers, and bound volumes. We have not systematically examined the variety of resources available to students across the board, but in our experience, students do not always have adequate time dedicated to learning how to utilize Library Information Sciences (LIS) technology if they are given the opportunity to engage in extensive research and writing. In our experience, most schools have technology available in their libraries, but they are not always equipped with the full array of research tools and may lack adequate staff to train all students on how to use this technology well. At many colleges and universities, students will actually be required to complete a library skills certification. Students at such institutions may either complete the requirement in orientation or at the beginning of their academic career. In some cases, the option is left to students, and they may complete the requirement at any time during their undergraduate career, whereas some institutions may place a check stop on a student account to prevent them from registering for classes if they do not complete the requirement within a certain amount of time.

Conclusion

In this chapter, we only scratch the surface in terms of what admissions professionals need to know about student success in college. We know that many students will find the academic transition difficult to manage, and the sooner they are aware of the differences, the sooner they can begin to develop the right habits and study skills. We also recognize that students cannot simply turn on a switch and move from doing no homework in high school to spending several hours per day on independent work. It takes time to build that sort of endurance. For some, the transition from high school to the local community college can help to make a more gradual transition to the academic requirements of a 4-year institution.

We have not weighed in on whether students should work while in school, and we suspect that most will have to assume some level of debt to finance their educations, but our general conclusion is that the threshold for work and debt is similar. We recommend everything in moderation. Most campuses have policies in place limiting the number of hours students can work in on-campus jobs (they typically are not aware of employment off campus). Work is a reality for many students, and the research is suggestive that working on campus for 20 hours or less may serve some students well. Debt is a different issue, but again, moderation is essential. The price of college is rising at a time when a greater proportion of low- and middle-income students are choosing to attend college. Student loans have made college more affordable for many students who would not otherwise have an opportunity to attend, but students and families should be mindful of how much debt they assume relative to the income they are likely to earn when they enter the workforce.

In our experience, students express anxiety about the social transition from high school to college. Even students who are involved in high school can find it more difficult to discover their place at postsecondary institutions that are many times larger than the schools they left. We do not discuss it in great depth here, but living on campus or independently for the first time can be a difficult transition for students. One of the real advantages of intervention programs and living learning communities on college campuses is that they provide regular opportunities for students to connect to the social fabric of the institution. We do not spend any time here reviewing the research on campus involvement—far too much has been written to do it justice. Instead, we suggest that students find their social and academic support systems, wherever they may exist. We know that involvement on campus is generally associated with positive student outcomes, but not every student has the same opportunities to participate. We do recognize, however, that one of the real advantages of engagement is the sense of community and the development of a social support network.

Finally, students must be aware of the important place technology plays in the academic life of colleges and universities. It is nearly ubiquitous in terms of its usage on campus for the exchange of information, formal and informal communication, and the development of the social network. Those who have not yet learned to employ technology in their academic work will be at a disadvantage when they arrive on campus. There is always time to make the adjustment, but the more students can anticipate, the better off they will be. The role of technology is complicated by the high degree of autonomy students experience for the first time on campus. This is a natural part of student development, but we are reminded that the greater the level of challenge students face, the more support they will need to make a successful adjustment.

Implications for Admissions Professionals in College Success

College admissions professionals are boundary-spanning individuals who serve as the primary point of connection between colleges and universities and their external environments, particularly in relation to the most important institutional input—student enrollments. To some degree, operating in this space requires that they are expert in both what it takes for students to make the successful transition into college and what it will require for them to achieve success once they arrive. Traditionally, admissions professionals focus only on the former, assuming the responsibility for success rests with others on campus. To a certain degree that is true, but in order for students to make informed decisions about which institution to attend, they need to know what to anticipate in college, and admissions staff are in the best position to provide that information.

School counselors and school administrators care a great deal about the eventual success of their students, but they have no idea what happens once they leave high school. Some districts have subscribed to the National Student Clearinghouse Student Tracker—a system nearly 95% of colleges and universities use to outsource enrollment verification—to follow their students into college, but this information will only indicate whether a student enrolled in a given term and whether they maintained full-time status. Admissions professionals should make it a part of their work with schools to report back on the success of their students—how many enroll, are they successful earning degrees, and do they require remedial coursework? This information serves two purposes. First, it provides the schools with real information they can use to think about how to improve their work to help more of their students succeed. Second, it demonstrates the institution's commitment to a genuine partnership where information flows in both directions and their belief that long-term relationships are more important than near-term enrollment successes.

Finally, admissions professionals must cultivate future enrollments in schools by helping their college access partners to engage students more actively in the information-gathering process earlier in high school. That means more active promotion of the opportunities already available, like shadow and ambassador programs. It might also mean developing new programs to help students understand how to manage time, study effectively, find the right mix of engagement opportunities and academic and social supports. For example, many campuses make faculty lectures available to prospective students, but perhaps these experiences should be made more broadly available online for students who may not be able to visit campus. One of the features of the virtual campus tour at the University of Michigan was the chat feature that allowed students to interact with admissions staff in real time and to ask questions along the way. The social networking capabilities of these tools can be expanded to include engagement with current students on campus. Some of these features are common for students who have applied or committed to the institution, but we suggest that they can be expanded to reach a broader pool of students and should be done earlier in the process. Ultimately, we believe it may be time to think differently about how we engage with secondary school partners and other college access professionals, and this begins by finding out what they need and developing new strategies to address those needs.

10

EMPOWERING ADMISSIONS PROFESSIONALS AS COLLEGE ACCESS ADVOCATES

Admissions professionals operate in a highly contested and competitive environment with real pressures to enroll an incoming class; achieve critical social and academic benchmarks for the class profile; and serve as the face of the institution for students, parents, school counselors, and pre-college outreach programs. They alternate between spending long hours on the road, moving from school to school and from one admissions fair to the next in the fall, and in the spring existing in virtual isolation, harvesting the fruits of their labor in the form of completed applications for review. The work is long, sometimes hard, and certainly not for everyone. If the only thing we accomplish with this volume is to help new admissions professionals better understand key aspects of their role, then we believe we have made an important contribution to the profession.

Of course, we set our sights a little bit higher by suggesting that college admissions professionals are a part of a much larger network of college access professionals and that they are critical to the viability of that network to support a greater number of students as they decide whether and where to attend college. We have situated admissions professionals as critical sources of information and support for three groups of college access professionals who spend much of their time with high school students—and prospective college applicants—school counselors, pre-college outreach providers, and independent consultants. All three groups rely on admissions professionals to figure out how best to support their students as they navigate the college choice process. Admissions professionals recognize the value of this network, and they cultivate those relationships most likely to result in more student applications. We have suggested that, while these relationships are important and valuable, existing networks leave out many of the professionals who work with students who need more support and encouragement than any other—low-income, first-generation, and underrepresented minority students attending schools that send very few students to college.

The second contribution we make in this volume, then, is to begin to extend that network by first helping admissions professionals understand the roles other college access professionals play, how they do their work, and what barriers exist that can be addressed to increase college access for many more high school students. We also hope to provide a glimpse of how the admissions process affects other college access professionals. Admissions professionals manage the information that school counselors, pre-college outreach providers, and independent consultants need—what it takes for their students to be admitted to the institution and to be successful once they arrive. In turn, these professional groups manage the resource most valuable to college admissions offices—access to students as prospective college enrollees. The challenge we face attempting to recast college admissions staff as college access professionals is that they continue to operate in competitive markets, and the high schools serve as a competitive space where each institution is attempting to find their competitive advantage. So long as that script dominates, it will be difficult to shift attention from the contest for high-achieving, college-ready students to those not yet certain of their postsecondary plans. In this concluding chapter, we distill what we believe are the most salient themes throughout the book, and we turn our attention to a set of recommendations for improving college access by engaging college admissions staff in the broader network of college access professionals.

Focus on System Alignment at the Local Level

John Dewey noted near the turn of the 20th century that aligning high schools and colleges would be complicated by both the structure and function of the different types of institutions and the history and evolution of each "system" along separate trajectories (Orrill, 2001). Comprehensive high schools did not yet exist, but educators were wrestling with the organization of schools by grade levels, with a dizzying array of grade-level permutations. During this time, some community colleges grew as an extension of high school, while others evolved out of the junior college. There were not as many variations of either schools or colleges then as exist today, but even then the notion of aligning the two systems was difficult to conceptualize.

The challenges to system alignment are more complex today, but the pressures to find solutions have increased. Postsecondary education is becoming a necessity to enter many careers that lead to a middle-class lifestyle, and alignment may be one of the structural remedies to the problem. P16 councils and coordinating structures have developed in states across the country. The assumption among policy makers is that there are essentially two public systems of education in states and that they are misaligned to the extent that students receive conflicting messages about academic success and the cost of pursuing a college education. The solution necessarily becomes an issue of state- and system-level policy to make the connections between high schools and colleges seamless.

We are not optimistic about system-level alignment as a college access strategy for two reasons. First, there exists far too much variation in schools and in postsecondary institutions to allow for simple one-to-one connections. Within comprehensive schools there are at least three common paths (or tracks), each serving different types of students, depending upon whether they are likely to pursue a college path, a vocational path, or a less certain though flexible general path. In addition to the comprehensive high school, students may attend themed schools (e.g. honors, arts, technology), charter schools, early and middle college high schools, or an array of private high schools. Meanwhile, colleges and universities are highly differentiated across sectors, with community colleges maintaining lenient academic standards for open enrollment to all students with an ability to benefit; regional public and private colleges serving local students; flagship public universities serving state, national, and global student bodies; and elite private colleges educating the most academically talented and the wealthiest students in the country.

For as hard as educators and policy makers have tried to create a single standard through state-level high school graduation requirements, state-mandated tests, and common core standards, it has been impossible, and impractical, to expect that one standard could be acceptable to all schools or all colleges. State college and university systems have tried as hard, in some cases, to improve alignment among postsecondary institutions with standardized general education curricula, common course numbering, and standardized placement exams. These efforts may move institutions incrementally, but they have by no means resolved the problems college students face as they consider transferring from one college to another.

We suggest that alignment is a critical goal and that it should be pursued over the long term at the state level in a way that reflects the complexity of the system—but in the near-term, alignment is really most effective at the local level, in conversations between admissions professionals and school counselors, to start. These are the conversations that already happen in some places, and it has been the most common form of alignment since the accreditation of high schools first began at the University of Michigan during the late 19th century. In fact, this form of alignment gives us the notion of feeder institutions. Over time, colleges come to rely upon a number of high schools to enroll a high proportion of their graduating seniors. These relationships evolve because both institutions are invested in the relationship and both benefit from it. Colleges attract students they know are prepared to succeed at their institution, and high schools leverage those relationships to establish a college-going culture that attracts future students to their school. These shared expectations have evolved over time and developed in collaboration. Most colleges can identify a network of feeder institutions, and admissions professionals spend a good deal of time cultivating relationships with counselors and others at those schools. These relationships allow for regular communication about how expectations change and evolve, and this works to the advantage of students at those schools.

We are suggesting that a new set of relationships between high schools and colleges is needed and that college and university admissions professionals serve as the front line of engagement. To the extent that P16 implies that postsecondary education is a right—or at very least a necessity—state systems must bear the responsibility of working with the highest-need schools to help them better prepare the next generation of students for college and work. Developing relationships and sharing information is a starting point, but we imagine the relationships between admissions professionals and school counselors serve as a bridge that allows others to engage in conversations over curricular alignment, student life, and academic success. Colleges and universities have an incentive to develop these relationships in order to achieve their enrollment goals, and a sustained effort to expand the pool of students prepared to enter postsecondary education will benefit both the institution and the larger system.

In order to include lower-achieving high-need high schools in this broader network, we need to solve a sort of collective action problem. Current feeder networks have developed gradually and with sustained commitment on both sides. They are easy to develop because both sides benefit in clear and measurable ways; high schools develop a reputation for placing students in colleges, thus attracting more similarly capable high school students, and colleges enroll students appropriately prepared to succeed at the institution. There is no simple way to identify which colleges take responsibility for reaching out to which high-need schools because there are no incentives for colleges to do so in the existing system. The benefits operate collectively, meaning that if the higher education community works more actively with these high-need schools, then over time, the pool of college-ready students will grow, placing upward pressure on all enrollments. The collective benefits are possible to achieve, but only if the higher education community coordinates to more actively identify and engage these schools. We suggest that this may be a role for state affiliates of the National Association of College Admissions Counselors (NACAC) or another comparable organization that can bring the array of higher education partners to the table.

Understand the Roles of College Access Professionals

In our varied experiences in schools and colleges, we have found that these groups operate in relative isolation and, as a consequence, seldom understand the nature of the contributions other college access professionals make. Even among the authors who come from these different perspectives, it has taken several years and countless conversations for us to develop a shared understanding of these four separate worlds. We have found, for example, that school counselors are increasingly asked to do more with less, and that includes college counseling as a relatively small part of their overall portfolio. They serve as more flexible administrators, assuming responsibilities for scheduling, student conduct, testing, mental health, and career planning. Most school counselors have very little formal training in the college choice process, and they figure out what they can from whatever sources are available. They care about the lives of their students after college, but they have no idea what happens to them once they leave.

Pre-college outreach programs are deeply committed to leveling the playing field for students attending schools where opportunities are limited. They have the time, energy, and passion to work with students who demonstrate potential but who require some attention and additional support to achieve their full potential. In many ways, we believe, this is the key to meeting the needs of students who are currently less likely to attend college. Based upon some of our interviews, admissions professionals estimated that 80% of the college counseling that occurs in New York City, for example, is provided by these outreach programs, located either in community agencies or postsecondary institutions. New York City may not be typical of many communities, as it is home to famed programs like the Harlem Children's Zone, Prep for Prep, and many others, but it does suggest the important role these professionals might play in other contexts. These programs attempt to provide supplemental instruction for students who are falling behind in core subject areas, they expose students to college and university campuses, and they provide hands-on support to help students navigate the college choice process. Many of these programs offer summer experiences on college campuses that give students a rare opportunity to see what college might be like if they choose to attend.

Pre-college outreach programs rely on soft money—state, federal, and private philanthropic dollars—and have experienced sustained cuts over time. As a result, they are trying to serve more students with fewer resources, meaning that each student receives less of what he or she needs. Clearly, these programs need additional resources to continue their work, but they also need access to the information admissions professionals manage and to students in their partnering schools. We suggest that one of the roles admissions professionals could play in a more systematic way is to develop sustained relationships with these programs in their respective service regions and to take an active role in helping them to connect with their local schools and with the resources on college campuses. The first responsibility a new admissions professional will have to these groups is to listen to what they do, how they do it, and what they need.

One of the recommendations we make is for admissions professionals to create regular and systematic opportunities—like advisory committees—to listen to school counselors and pre-college outreach providers. These consultative bodies do two things. First, they provide admissions offices the opportunity to hear from the professionals who work with students on a regular basis. It is an opportunity to understand more fully what these professionals do on a day-to-day basis and how the admissions staff might be helpful to their respective students. Second, it is a symbolic gesture that the college or university is listening to the local community. For all but a small and highly selective pool of institutions, the community is an important feeder of college enrollments.

Articulate Clear Academic Expectations

In Chapter 4, we discussed in detail how complicated the question of academic preparation has become. High school completion is a useful starting point, but it is clear that simply earning a high school diploma does not mean a student will be prepared to complete college-level work. Most admissions professionals will know by the end of their first full enrollment cycle what the "typical" student looks like academically at their college or university, or even what the minimum threshold might be, and they can communicate that to counselors who can plant the seeds early with students. Admissions staff can tell, in general terms, that a certain GPA from a given school, combined with a slate of core academic courses will, on average, predict a student's likelihood of success at the institution. In our experience, these conversations take place between admissions professionals and school counselors, but there are several conditions that limit the strength of this network. First, colleges and universities are constantly attempting to improve their academic profiles, meaning that academic preparedness is a slow-moving target at many institutions. Second, entry-level admissions positions experience relatively high turnover rates, meaning these relationships with schools begin anew every few years. Third, as we have described, school counselors and pre-college outreach professionals are continually doing more with less, meaning they have less time to stay current on admissions trends on their own. All of these conditions make it difficult to communicate academic expectations clearly to students.

This is actually one area where our recommendations are not for admissions professionals. Even if they find more and better ways to communicate these expectations to counselors and pre-college professionals, the metrics they know well are imperfect proxy measures for real curricular alignment. If we hope to achieve greater alignment between high school curricular expectations and preparation for postsecondary work, then we need to begin a set of conversations among high school teachers and college professors. Admissions counselors are unlikely to play a role in this strategy, but directors of admissions or enrollment managers may help to facilitate connections between the two groups. Admissions professionals may be helpful in the early stages by sharing their placement exams and cut scores with school counselors. In our experience, an increasing number of colleges are utilizing standardized placement exams like the COMPASS test or Accuplacer. Some community colleges have already seen this as an opportunity to go into local schools to administer the test and to provide students with information about whether they will be prepared for entry into college-level coursework. Only occasionally do these efforts include conversations between English and math teachers in schools and professors in those subjects at the local colleges. We believe this is where the real work must be done to clarify academic expectations. Telling students or school counselors whether students are prepared is a useful diagnostic starting point, but to improve preparation, professionals responsible for the academic content must work more closely together. The real work is to develop strategies that help high-need high schools to move students from operating at below grade level in math and English Language Arts (ELA) to college preparedness in four years.

Clarify Price and Demystify Student Aid

For many students and families, the most important—and most confusing—part of the college choice process is understanding price. In particular, families struggle to understand the difference between sticker price and net price. They can identify quickly what an institution charges for tuition, fees, room, and board, but it can be difficult for families to assess what they will actually pay. This ambiguity happens to be the cornerstone of competitive advantage for colleges and universities in a highly contested marketplace. There are few incentives for colleges and universities to be clear about net price. Like realtors, colleges intend to "sell" enrollments at the highest price students are willing to pay, and they don't want to suggest any amount less. The more recent move toward greater transparency in college prices is changing the playing field a bit, but colleges will continue to try to maintain their competitive advantage by keeping their tuition discounting practices close to the vest.

There are efforts among policy makers at the federal and state levels, in particular, pushing strategies to clarify net cost for students and families. For example, the federal requirement that all colleges post net cost calculators on their websites is a step toward better estimates of price. The FAFSA4caster published by the U.S. Department of Education is another potentially effective tool for figuring net price by approximating eligibility for federal aid, but it is still limited because it cannot account for state aid programs or institutional tuition discounting practices. The State University of New York (SUNY) system has recently developed a standardized "shopping sheet" to be sent to students in their financial aid package. For all SUNY and participating private institutions, the system will send students identical sheets that will make it easier to compare financial aid packages. These are all important steps that will likely improve students' information about price without requiring anything additionally of the admissions staff.

It will be easier for public institutions than many of their private counterparts to adopt these more standardized practices regarding net price because they discount tuition at much lower rates and for a smaller proportion of students. The signals sent by Harvard, Princeton, and the handful of highly selective privates who guarantee to replace loans with grants are the notable exception. They have been clear that admitted students below a certain income threshold will not pay anything for tuition and fees. These programs are feasible because relatively few low-income students are academically prepared to be admitted, and these colleges maintain enormous endowments that make it possible to discount tuition in these targeted ways.

If we hope to improve college enrollment rates among high school graduates at high-need high schools, then we need to address issues of college prices much earlier in the college choice process than is currently the case. Many students begin to engage actively in their search process in the 11th grade, and some wait until their senior year. For students who know they will attend college, relative prices may not matter in terms of whether they will attend, but it will certainly influence their choice of institution. For students from low-income families, price—real or perceived—may influence aspirations and the decisions students make about their academic path in high schools. We need more effective strategies to help these students and their parents understand sticker price, net price, and financial aid in the freshman or sophomore year when it is still possible to affect a student's academic trajectory. The role of admissions counselors may be less direct, providing better information to school counselors and pre-college outreach programs and embracing tools that more faithfully approximate net price for students.

We also suggest that admissions professionals, in concert with their financial aid counterparts, develop outreach efforts to help more students understand student loans. Low-income families are justifiably debt averse when it comes to student loans, and they have reason to be concerned. In the cases where students qualify for full federal need-based grant aid (Pell Grant), families may earn less than the loans for which their students are eligible. In relative terms, loans of that magnitude seem irrational, knowing how difficult they would be to pay at a similar income. Others may be inclined to take more loans than they need because they are available, without much attention to repayment over time. The result may be excessive loan debt that may result in higher rates of default—a situation that colleges want to avoid because the federal government is concerned about high default rates. For-profit colleges in particular have come under close scrutiny for the high default rates among their students.

One of the important recent developments in federal student loans is the income-based repayment (IBR) option, which provides students who leave college with high loan debt with a choice. They can either attempt to pay their loans according to the predetermined payment schedule, or they can extend the period to 20 years and pay only what they can afford—set at 10% of their annual earnings. At the end of the extended pay period, and assuming they maintain their payments over the entire time, any remaining balance at the end of 20 years is forgiven. This program provides a safety net for debt-averse students and their families, and this may be one of the programs low-income families will find appealing as encouragement to consider attending college, even when loans are a part of the financial aid package.

Admissions professionals must develop strategies to more systematically communicate prices and financial aid options. Many of the new transparency and accountability initiatives are making the information more readily available to families. The New York State Shopping Sheet requires colleges and universities to use the same template to report sticker price, financial aid, and net costs to students and their families. These initiatives are far removed from the day-to-day interactions between admissions professionals and students, but they could be effective if admissions staff embrace this approach to educating students on college cost.

Own the Complexity of the College Choice Process

Admissions professionals need to recognize that they have created the admissions process and that their efforts to increase efficiency for their institutions have made the process easier and more accessible for some but, at the same time, more complex for students and families who are already less likely to attend college. There are certainly larger forces at work that extend beyond the college, but institutions are responsible for their shift online with much of the college choice process. We believe the benefits of the digital shift outweigh the costs, but that in so doing, college admissions professionals must assume responsibility for helping students, families, school counselors, and pre-college outreach providers to understand the process and to provide additional support to help students complete the process. Currently, it operates as an effective sorting mechanism, keeping less prepared or less motivated students out of the admissions pipeline—something that can streamline the work of admissions offices but may reduce the overall number of students in the pool. We recognize that to make this process simpler could undermine the efficiencies to be gained by allowing the process to self-select students out of applying, but that should be a tradeoff worth making.

The one example that underscores the conflict admissions offices face is the growth in participation in the Common App. In many ways, the Common App is designed to simplify the process for students by allowing them to submit one application that is distributed to many institutions. Presumably a simpler process might expand the total pool of potential student college applicants, but it is more likely to increase the number of potential choices students identify, meaning more applications per student, not more students. At the same time, an application shared with hundreds of other institutions makes it difficult for institutions to differentiate the process in order to attract the students they seek. Currently, more than 450 institutions participate in the Common App, or approximately 10% of colleges in the United States. Most of these institutions require a supplemental application. Common App has addressed this by making the supplemental application part of the initial process, but that means a student may fill out a different supplemental for each institution just to complete the application process. Colleges want to be included in an application that may result in additional submissions beyond their traditional feeders, but they are not willing to do so without maintaining their own unique variations on the application.

We do not expect that admissions professionals, alone, are in a position to make the process less complex, though they could in some ways. Rather, we argue that admissions professionals can be more honest and transparent about the application and decision-making process. For example, a number of colleges that are even moderately selective will recalculate high school GPA in order to more accurately compare students across institutions. Not all institutions share this practice openly because they recognize that schools apply weights and encourage students to take a range of courses in an effort to improve their high school GPA. Stripping these features from the student transcript effectively undermines the advantages schools attempt to provide to their graduates. Admissions professionals need to be clearer about these practices so that school counselors all understand the rules of the game and can make the appropriate adjustments as they serve the needs of their students.

The same may be true for how colleges deal with AP, dual enrollment, and transfer credit. Not all colleges accept these credits easily or in the same ways. For example, the University of Michigan and Michigan State University both maintain policies that would not allow students to double-dip—earn credit for both high school and college from the same course. If the course earned a student credit toward his or her high school diploma, then the course would not be given credit in college. Others use AP courses to waive required courses without changing the number of credits students need to earn. Dual enrolled classes pose an additional challenge because those credits are frequently considered transfer credits and are subject to the policies applied to traditional transfer students. That may mean that credits earned and accepted at one institution will not be accepted by another institution the student hopes to attend. One of the more specific examples we have seen in high-need high schools is the growth in dual enrollment offerings by community colleges and for-profit colleges. These credits are earned either for free or at a substantially reduced cost, but, depending upon the course and the grade, they may or may not be accepted by other colleges. Admissions professionals may need to think about educating school counselors and pre-college outreach providers about dual enrollment and transfer credit policies so that students can make informed choices about enrolling in these courses.

Listen to College Access Professionals

If there is one theme that we hope will stick with readers, it is that college access is the collective responsibility of at least four key groups of professionals— college admissions professionals, school counselors, pre-college outreach providers, and independent consultants. Certainly, others are instrumental, including parents, teachers, coaches, ministers, and peers—but these are the professionals charged with some direct responsibility for helping students transition from high school to college. That collective responsibility can only be achieved with a strong network, which we believe begins with a common understanding of the roles others play. In Chapter 3, we described these roles briefly to help readers begin to see how these roles are defined, how they do their work, and what incentives influence what they do and how they do it. While this is a useful place to start, we recommend that admissions professionals take it a step further. In our experience, the best way to understand the experience of others is to experience their work with them. We also believe that the time spent learning from others must be substantial and mutually beneficial. To that end, we suggest that admissions professionals should spend time shadowing school counselors and pre-college outreach professionals. One of the challenges is to find a time when the work of admissions professionals is more flexible and when their presence might benefit the other groups. For example, the summer may be a great time for admissions professionals to work with a pre-college outreach program. Many of these federal TRIO and state-sponsored programs offer summer experiences that bring students right to campus. The program would benefit by having someone from admissions spending a day a week shadowing, observing, participating, and sharing their knowledge with students, parents, and staff. In exchange, the admissions counselor begins to understand what these programs do, how they work to the benefit of at-risk students, and how these programs might serve as potential feeders to the institution.

With school counselors, the shadow experience may be more difficult to achieve. The fall is the best time for school counselors because this is the time of year they are working with seniors to complete the college application process. This coincides with the travel season for most admissions staff. We suggest that one way to accomplish the goals of a shadowing experience would be to spend an entire day at a single high school and shadow the school counselors. More often this time is spent meeting with a handful of students or a brief conversation with the school counselor, but if the expectation is set that the admissions person is visiting simply to learn, even a single day of shadowing could be instructive. We recommend that admissions professionals incorporate this practice into their annual schedule and that they be intentional with the schools they identify—from regular feeder schools to local and regional schools that serve a high proportion of students who typically do not attend college.

We also recommend that the shadow experience should be reciprocal. In other words, admissions offices should create opportunities for school counselors and pre-college outreach providers to see how the admissions process works and in particular, how admissions decisions are made. Some institutions already do this, but one suggestion is to identify some number of school counselors from one's service region to spend the day—or several days—reviewing student applications, listening to deliberations over admissions decisions, and actually participating in the decision-making process. The admissions process is mysterious to many school counselors and pre-college outreach providers, and this insight will help them more effectively work with their students and understand what your institution values in the admissions process. For counselors at preparatory schools and wealthy public districts, making time for these activities may be relatively easy. In order to include those working in high-need districts or in pre-college outreach programs, it may mean the admissions office must find some way to reduce the cost of that experience for those who may not have the professional development support to engage in this way.

Increase, Expand, and Target Professional Development for College Access Professionals

In our conversations with school counselors in particular, few of them receive any training in college counseling during their graduate degree programs or internship experiences. As a result, they rely more heavily on informal training opportunities. Many of them are "self-taught," meaning they've sought out answers to the questions students most commonly pose, and over time, they have developed a set of knowledge and tools that informs how they serve students. Others report participating in professional conferences or district-sponsored professional development training programs. Conferences are the most targeted strategy, and NACAC-sponsored events at both the state and national levels are potentially valuable outlets, but few districts have the resources to send school counselors to these meetings. In some states, the public system provides similar training opportunities at substantially reduced cost, but even those are difficult to attend during an academic year.

Those who can attend these events do, but in many cases, those left behind are the counselors working in high-need districts where fewer students are attending college and where many other issues beyond college and career readiness confront school counselors regularly. In order to reach this population of counselors, admissions offices, state systems, and professional organizations must shift away from making these opportunities available (passive) to bringing the training right to counselors in schools (active). There is no simple solution here, but we know that when left to the discretion of counselors, they will seek out professional development on the issues that consume the greatest amount of their time—in college preparatory schools, that means college choice, but for other districts the focus may be on more challenging mental health issues or training on information technologies. The result, of course, is that counselors in high-need schools will not have the same access to professional development around college choice and as a result will be comparatively less prepared to help their students through the college choice proces

One approach we suggest is to create college success centers in schools that are intended to complement the work of school counselors by assuming responsibility for the administrative aspects of the college choice process— SAT registration and fee waivers, college admissions applications, PSAT review, FAFSA completion—and serving as a conduit between the school and the range of external resources that may be leveraged in support of students and counselors. Colleges and universities have the resources to create these sorts of initiatives, and they provide a regular mechanism to connect school counselors with the knowledge and resources they need from the college admissions community. Structurally, what we are proposing is not all that new. Many schools have college and career readiness centers, frequently staffed by a school counselor or an administrative assistant. The model we discussed in Chapter 7 is one of several strategies and utilizes faculty from the school of education, graduate students from a higher education administration program, and AmeriCorps volunteers. These centers might employ work–study students from local colleges, peer leaders from within the school, or even parents of enrolled students. In all cases, we suggest that the center serve as a point of connection between the schools and the resources that can be most helpful to counselors, students, and parents who are engaged in the college choice process.

Conclusion

The admissions landscape is changing, and with that change comes a realignment of incentives. The network of college access professionals has always been an important element of admissions work, but today the incentives are even greater for admissions professionals to tap into and expand the professional network to schools that might not have made the priority list in the past. Colleges and universities of all types are enrollment driven, and competition for the "traditional" college student has grown fierce as the size of the age cohorts decline and many colleges and universities intend to grow in size or prestige. The reservoir of untapped potential rests in the schools where many students still do not choose to attend college or are less successful when they arrive. The challenge we see is finding a way to act collectively across postsecondary education to bring more school counselors, pre-college outreach providers, and independent consultants into the fold and to develop genuine relationships that are bidirectional—which is to say that all parties recognize their mutual self-interest in the expansion of these networks. We have suggested that the two keys to aligning high schools and colleges in this way are to develop a full understanding of what each of these professionals does and then to develop a shared sense of the challenges students and parents face as they navigate the college choice process. This book lays the foundation for both, but it also requires time, energy, and sustained commitment on the part of all parties, beginning with admissions professionals, to nurture and sustain these networks. College admissions is a business, and we should never lose sight of that—but it is a business with a broader public purpose, and admissions professionals are key to helping their institutions live that purpose.

NOTES

7 PRE-COLLEGE OUTREACH PROGRAMS AND STRATEGIES

1. Participating states include California, Indiana, Maryland, Minnesota, New Mexico, Rhode Island, Vermont, Washington, and Wisconsin.
2. States identified with outreach programs included California, Florida, Georgia, Indiana, Minnesota, New Jersey, New York, Oklahoma, Rhode Island, Vermont, Washington, and Wisconsin.
3. More recent evidence suggests that there are only eight service regions remaining in 2012 (State of Indiana, 2012).

8 THE NEW FRONTIER OF WEB-BASED COLLEGE ACCESS STRATEGIES

1. We have defined college access web portals in prior work as more interactive web resources that require participants to log in to some or all of the features and that provide multiple audiences with information they need to navigate the college choice process.

REFERENCES

Abrahamson, T. (2000). Life and death on the Internet: To Web or not to Web is no longer the question. *Journal of College Admission, 168*(Summer), 6–11.

Academic Senate for California Community Colleges. (1995). CSU policy to eliminate remedial education. Retrieved April 28, 2012, from http://www.asccc.org/node/175079

ACT, Inc. (2012). *Why go to college?* Iowa City, IA: Author.

Adelman, C. (1999). *Answers in the tool box: Academic intensity, attendance patterns, and bachelor's degree attainment* (p. 124). Washington, DC: U.S. Department of Education.

Adelman, C. (2004). *The toolbox revisited: Paths to degree completion from high school to college.* Washington, DC: U.S. Department of Education.

Allensworth, E., Nomi, T., Montgomery, N., & Lee, V. (2009). College preparatory curriculum for all: Academic consequences of requiring Algebra and English I for ninth graders in Chicago. *Educational Evaluation and Policy Anlaysis, 31*(4), 367–391.

American Diploma Project. (2002). Ready or not: Creating a high school diploma that counts. Executive Summary (pp. 8). Washington, DC: Achieve, Inc., The Education Trust, Thomas B. Fordham Foundation.

American Indian Higher Education Consortium. (2007). AIHEC AIMS fact book 2007—Tribal colleges. Retrieved March 20, 2012, from http://www.aihec.org/resources/AIMS.cfm

American Indian Higher Education Consortium. (2010). AIHEC history and mission. Retrieved March 20, 2012, from http://www.aihec.org/about/historyMission.cfm

American School Counselor Association (ASCA). (2004). ASCA national standards for students. Alexandria, VA: American School Counselor Association.

American School Counselor Association (ASCA). (2007). School counseling standards: School counselor competencies. Alexandria, VA: Author.

American School Counselor Association (ASCA). (2010). Student-to-counselor ratios. Retrieved July 12, 2013, from http://www.schoolcounselor.org/files/Ratios10-11.pdf

American School Counselor Association (ASCA). (2013). The role of the professional school counselor. Retrieved 2/20/2013, 2013, from http://www.schoolcounselor.org/content.asp?contentid=240

American Youth Policy Forum. (2001). Raising minority student acheivement. Retrieved March 20, 2012, from www.aypf.org/publications/rmaa/pdfs/Tribal-Colleges.pdf

Angus, D., & Mirel, J. (1999). *The failed promise of the American high school: 1890–1995*. New York: Teachers College Press.

Antonio, A. L., & Bersola, S. H. (2004). Working toward K-16 coherence in California. In M. W. Kirst & A. Venezia (Eds.), *From high school to college: Improving opportunities for success in postsecondary education* (1st ed., pp. xii, 424). San Francisco, CA: Jossey-Bass.

Archibald, R. B., & Feldman, D. H. (2011). *Why does college cost so much?* New York: Oxford University Press.

Armstrong, J. J., & Lumsden, B. (2000). Impact of universities' promotional materials on college choice. *Journal of Marketing for Higher Education, 9*(2), 83–91.

Attewell, P., Lavin, D. E., Domina, T., & Levey, T. (2006). New evidence on college remediation. *Journal of Higher Education, 77*(5), 886–913.

Aud, S., Hussar, W., Johnson, F., Kena, G., Roth, E., Manning, E., . . . Nachazel, T. (2012). *College student employment: The condition of education* (Vol. 2012, pp. 89–116). Washington, DC: National Center for Education Statistics.

Aud, S., Hussar, W., Kena, G., Bianco, K., Frohlich, L., Kemp, J., & Tahan, K. (2011). *The condition of education 2011 (NCES 2011–033)*. Washington, DC: U.S. Department of Education, National Center for Education Statistics.

Avery, C., Hoxby, C., Jackson, C., Burek, K., Poppe, G., & Raman, M. (2006). Cost should be no barrier: An evaluation of the first year of Harvard's financial aid initiative. *NBER Working Paper Series* (12029), 24. Retrieved from http://www.nber.org/papers/w12029

Avery, C., & Kane, T. (2004). Student perceptions of college opportunities: The Boston COACH program. In C. M. Hoxby (Ed.), *College choices: The economics of where to go, when to go, and how to pay for it* (pp. 355–391). Cambridge, MA: National Bureau of Economic Research.

AVID.org. (2012). What is AVID? Retrieved June 4, 2012, from http://www.avid.org/abo_whatisavid.html

Bailey, T. (2009). Challenge and opportunity: Rethinking the role and function of developmental education in community college. *New Directions for Community Colleges, 145*, 11–30.

Bailey, T., & Mechur Karp, M. (2003). Promoting college access and success: A review of credit-based transition programs (pp. iii–35). New York, NY: Community College Research Center.

Ball, H. (2000). *The Bakke case: Race, education, and affirmative action*. Lawrence: University Press of Kansas.

Barro, R., & Lee, J.-W. (2011). Educational attainment in the adult population (Barro-Lee data set). Retrieved June 29, 2011, from http://go.worldbank.org/8BQASOPK40

Baum, S. (2004). *A primer on economics for financial aid professionals*. New York: College Board.

Baum, S., & Ma, J. (2007). Education pays: The benefits of higher education for individuals and society. *Trends in Higher Education Series* (pp. 48). New York: College Board.

REFERENCES

Baum, S., & Ma, J. (2012). Trends in college pricing: 2011. *Trends in Higher Education Series* (pp. 32). New York: College Board.

Baum, S., & Payea, K. (2012). Trends in student aid: 2011. *Trends in Higher Education Series* (pp. 32). New York: College Board.

Bell, A. D., Rowan-Kenyon, H. T., & Perna, L. W. (2009). College knowledge of 9th and 11th grade students: Variation by school and state context. *The Journal of Higher Education, 80*(6), 663–685.

Bettinger, E., & Long, B. T. (2005). Addressing the needs of under-prepared students in higher education: Does college remediation work? *NBER Working Paper Series* (11325), 30. Retrieved from http://www.nber.org/papers/w11325

Blackmer, A. R., Bragdon, H. W., Bundy, M., Harbision, E. H., Seymour Jr., C., & Taylor, W. H. (1952). *General education in school and college.* Cambridge, MA: Harvard University Press.

Bornstein, D. (2004). *How to change the world: Social entrepreneurs and the power of new ideas.* Oxford and New York: Oxford University Press.

Bowen, H. R., & Carnegie Council on Policy Studies in Higher Education. (1977). *Investment in learning: The individual and social value of American higher education* (1st ed.). San Francisco: Jossey-Bass Publishers.

Bowen, W. G., Kurzweil, M. A., & Tobin, E. M. (2005). *Equity and excellence in American higher education.* Charlottesville, VA: University of Virginia Press.

Boylan, H. R., & Saxon, D. P. (1999). Outcomes of remediation: Prepared for the league for innovation in the community college (pp. 25): National Center for Developmental Education.

Braxton, J. M. (2000). *Reworking the student departure puzzle* (1st ed.). Nashville: Vanderbilt University Press.

Bridgeland, J., & Bruce, M. (2011). *National survey of school counselors: Counseling at a crossroads.* New York: Civic Enterprises with Hart Research for the College Board.

Brint, S. G., & Karabel, J. (1989). *The diverted dream: Community colleges and the promise of educational opportunity in America, 1900–1985.* New York: Oxford University Press.

Calcagno, J. C., & Long, B. T. (2008). The impact of postsecondary remediation using a regression discontinuity approach: Addressing endogenous sorting and noncompliance. *NBER Working Paper Series* (14194), 40. Retrieved from http://www.nber.org/papers/w14194

California State University. (2010). Fall 2007 regularly admitted first time freshman remediation statewide. Retrieved November 22, 2012, from http://www.asd.calstate.edu/performance/combo/2007/index.shtml

Carnegie Commission on Higher Education. (1973). *Continuity and discontinuity: Higher education and the schools.* New York: McGraw Hill Book Company.

Cavell, L., Blank, R. K., Toye, C., & Williams, A. (2005). *Key state education policy indicators: 2004* (pp. 57). Washington, DC: Council of Chief State School Officers.

Chen, X., Wu, J., & Tasoff, S. (2010). The high school senior class 2003–04: Steps toward postsecondary enrollment. *Issue Tables.* Washington, DC: Institute for Education Sciences.

Chu, K. (2009). Average credit card debt rises with fees, tuition. *USA Today Money.* Retrieved from http://usatoday30.usatoday.com/money/perfi/credit/2009-04-12-college-credit-card-debt_N.htm

Clinedinst, M., Hurley, S. F., & Hawkins, D. A. (2011). *State of college admissions: 2011* (pp. 35). Alexandria, VA: National Association for College Admissions Counselors.

Clinedinst, M., Hurley, S. F., & Hawkins, D. A. (2012). *State of college admissions: 2012*. Alexandria, VA: National Association for College Admission Counseling.

Clune, W. H., & White, P. A. (1992). Education reform in the trenches: Increased academic course taking in high schools with lower achieving students in states with higher graduation requirements. *Educational Evaluation and Policy Analysis, 14*(1), 2–20.

Cohen, A. M., & Brawer, F. B. (2003). *The American community college* (4th ed.). San Francisco: Jossey-Bass Publishers.

Cohen, A. M., & Kisker, C. B. (2010). *The shaping of American higher education: Emergence and growth of the contemporary system* (2nd ed.). San Francisco, CA: Jossey-Bass.

Coleman, J. S. (1988). Social capital in the creation of human capital. *The American Journal of Sociology, 94*(Supplement), S95–S120.

College Summit. (2012). College Summit: Connect to your future. Retrieved June 4, 2012, from http://www.collegesummit.org/

Commission on the Reorganization of Secondary Education. (1918). *Cardinal principles of secondary education* (pp. 32). Washington, DC: National Education Association & Department of the Interior.

Committee on Prospering in the Global Economy of the 21st Century, & Committee on Science Engineering and Public Policy. (2007). *Rising above the gathering storm: Energizing and employing America for a brighter economic future.* Washington, DC: National Academies Press.

Common Core State Standards Initiative. (2010). Common Core State Standards for mathematics. Retrieved December 12, 2010, from http://www.corestandards.org/

Common Manual Governing Board. (2009). The Common Manual: Unified student loan policy. Retrieved January 13, 2010, from http://www.commonmanual.org/doc/ECMarchive/ECM2009.pdf

Conant, J. B. (1959). *The American high school today.* New York: McGraw Hill Book Company.

Conley, P. (1995). The allocation of college admissions. In J. Elster (Ed.), *Local justice in America* (pp. 25–79). New York: Russell Sage Foundation.

Constantine, J., Seftor, N. S., Martin, E. S., Silva, T., & Myers, D. (2006). *A study of the effect of the Talent Search program on secondary and postsecondary outcomes in Florida, Indiana and Texas.* Washington, DC: Mathematica Policy Research, Inc.

Constantinides, E., & Zinck Stagno, M. (2011). Potential of the social media as instruments of higher education marketing: A segmentation study. *Journal of Marketing for Higher Education, 21*(1), 7–24.

Cornwell, C., & Mustard, D. B. (2004). Georgia's HOPE scholarship and minority and low-income students: Program effects and proposed reforms. In D. Heller & P. Marin (Eds.), *State merit scholarship programs and racial inequality.* Los Angeles: The Civil Rights Project.

Council of Chief State School Officers. (2008). *Key state policies on PK-12 education: 2008* (p. 42). Washington, DC: Author.

Croninger, R. G., & Lee, V. E. (2001). Social capital and dropping out of high school: Benefits to at-risk students of teacher's support and guidance. *Teachers College Record, 103*(4), 548–581.

Cunningham, A., Redmond, C., & Merisotis, J. (2003). Investing early: Intervention programs in selected US states. (pp. 1–70). Washington, DC: Institute for Higher Education Policy.

Curs, B. R., Singell, L. D., & Waddell, G. R. (2007). The Pell program at thirty years. In J. Smart (Ed.), *Higher education: Handbook of theory and research* (Vol. XXII, pp. 281–334). The Netherlands: Springer.

Dahlstrom, E., Dziuban, C., & Walker, J. D. (2012). *ECAR study of undergraduate students and information technology, 2012* (p. 38). Educause Center for Applied Research. Retrieved July 12, 2013 from http://www.educause.edu/library/resources/ecar-study-undergraduate-students-and-information-technology-2012.

Darling-Hammond, L. (1994). Who will speak for the children? How "Teach for America" hurts urban schools and students. *Phi Delta Kappan, 76*(1), 21–34.

Darst Williams, S. (2008). The downside of International Baccalaureate. *Show and Tell for Parents.* Retrieved from http://www.showandtellforparents.com/wfdata/frame161–1017/pressrel45.asp

Daun-Barnett, N. (2008). *Preparation and access: A multi-level analysis of state policy influences on the academic antecedents to college enrollment.* PhD dissertation, University of Michigan, Ann Arbor, MI.

Daun-Barnett, N. (2011). The Kalamazoo Promise: A new twist on tuition guarantees. *Journal of Student Financial Aid, 41*(1), 28–37.

Daun-Barnett, N., & Das, D. (2011). College access and the web-based college knowledge strategy: Analysis of the *Know How 2 Go* campaign. *Enrollment Management Journal, 4*(3), 42–65.

Daun-Barnett, N., & St. John, E. P. (2012). Constrained curriculum in high schools: The changing math standards and student achievement, high school graduation and college continuation *Education Policy Analysis Archives, 20*(5), 1–20.

Dawes, P. L., & Brown, J. (2005). The composition of consideration and choice sets in undergraduate university choice: An exploratory study. *Journal of Marketing for Higher Education, 14*(2), 37–59.

DePaul University. (2012). History and timeline. Retrieved October 12, 2012, from http://www.depaul.edu/about/history-and-timeline/Pages/default.aspx

Dey, E. L., & Astin, A. (1993). Statistical alernatives for studying college student retention: A comparative analysis of logit, probit, and linear regression. *Research in Higher Education, 34*(5), 569–581.

Dika, S. L., & Singh, K. (2002). Applications of social capital in educational literature: A critical synthesis. *Review of Educational Research, 72*(1), 31–60.

Docufide. (2012). Leader in eTranscript exchange. Retrieved January 3, 2013, from http://www.docufide.com/

Dynarski, S. M. (2003). Does aid matter? Measuring the effect of student aid on college attendance and completion. *American Economic Review, 93*(1), 279–288.

Dynarski, S. M., & Scott-Clayton, J. E. (2006, April). *The cost of complexity in federal student aid: Lessons from optimal tax theory and behavioral economics* (pp. 1–50). Cambridge, MA: Harvard University, Kennedy School of Government & National Bureau of Economic Research.

Dynarski, S. M., & Scott-Clayton, J. E. (2007). College grants on a postcard: A proposal for simple and predictable federal student aid. *The Hamilton Project: Advancing opportunity and growth* (pp. 1–54). Washington, DC: The Brookings Institution.

Ehrenberg, R. (2007). The economics of tuition and fees in American higher education. *Working Paper*, 15. Retrieved from http://digitalcommons.ilr.cornell.edu/workingpapers

Ehrenberg, R. G. (2002). *Tuition rising: Why college costs so much.* Cambridge, MA: Harvard University Press.

Ellis, B. (Producer). (2011a, June 18). Average student loan debt tops $25,000. *CNN Money.* Retrieved from http://money.cnn.com/2011/11/03/pf/student_loan_debt/index.htm

Ellis, B. (Producer). (2011b, June 18). More colleges charging $50,000 or more a year. *CNN Money.* Retrieved from http://money.cnn.com/2011/10/28/pf/college_tuition/index.htm

Farmer-Hinton, R. L., & Adams, T. L. (2006). Social capital and college preparation: Exploring the role of counselors in a college prep school for Black students. *Negro Educational Review, 57*(1–2), 101–116.

Federal Student Aid. (2012). Income based repayment plan. Retrieved June 10, 2012, from http://studentaid.ed.gov/PORTALSWebApp/students/english/IBRPlan.jsp

Fike, D. S., & Fike, R. (2008). Predictors of first-year student retention in the community college. *Community College Journal, 36*(2), 68–88.

Finn, J. D., Gerber, S. B., & Wang, M. C. (2002). Course offerings, course requirements, and course taking in mathematics. *Journal of Curriculum and Supervision, 17*(4), 336–366.

Fletcher, J. M., & Tienda, M. (2008). High school peer networks and college success: Lessons from Texas. Retrieved July 12, 2012, from www.sole-jole.org/882.pdf

Freedman, J. (2000). *Wall of fame: One teacher, one class, and the power to save schools and transform lives.* San Diego, CA: AVID Academic Press.

Gandara, P. (2002). A study of high school LaPuente: What we have learned about preparing Latino youth for postsecondary education. *Educational Policy, 16*(4), 474–495.

Gandara, P., & Maxwell-Jolly, J. (1999). *Priming the pump: Strategies for increasing the achievmeent of underrepresented minority undergraduates* (p. 129). New York: The College Board.

Geiser, S., & Santelices, V. (2004). The role of advanced placement and honors courses in college admissions. *Research and Occasional Paper Series, CSHE.4.04.*

Georgia Student Finance Commission. (2012). Scholarship and grant award history. Retrieved January 10, 2013, from https://www.gsfc.org/GSFCNEW/SandG_facts.CFM?guid=&returnurl=http://www.gacollege411.org/Financial_Aid_Planning/HOPE_Program/Georgia_s_HOPE_Scholarship_Program_Overview.aspx

Gifford, D., Mianzo, F., & Briceno-Perriott, J. (2005, Summer). Pen to mouse: Web-based technology's impact on college admission applications. *Journal of College Admission*, 17–18.

Goode, J. (2010). Mind the gap: The digital dimension of college access. *Journal of Higher Education, 81*(5), 583–618.

Greene, J. P., & Forster, G. (2003). *Public high school graduation and college readiness rates in the United States* (p. 24). New York: Manhattan Institute.

Gullatt, Y., & Jan, W. (2003). How do pre-collegiate academic outreach programs impact college-going among underrepresented students? Retrieved July 7, 2012, from http://www.inpathways.net/precollegiate.pdf

Gumport, P. J., & Bastedo, M. N. (2001). Academic stratification and endemic conflict: Remedial education policy at CUNY. *Review of Higher Education*, 24(4), 333–349.

Hagenbaugh, B. (2002, December 12). U.S. manufacturing jobs fading away fast. *USA Today*. Retrieved from http://usatoday30.usatoday.com/money/economy/2002-12-12-manufacture_x.htm?False

Hall, G. S. (1901). How far is the present high-school and early college training adapted to the nature and needs of adolescents? *The School Review*, 9(10), 649–681.

Hartman, K. E. (1997). College selection and the Internet: Advice for schools, a wake-up call for colleges. *Journal of College Admission*, 154, 22–31.

Hayes, T., Ruschman, D., & Walker, M. (2009). Social networking as an admission tool: A case study in success. *Journal of Marketing for Higher Education*, 19(2), 109–124.

Hearn, J. C. (2001). The paradox of growth in federal aid for college students, 1965–1990. In M. B. Paulson & J. Smart (Eds.), *The finance of higher education: Theory, research, policy, and practice* (pp. 267–320). New York: Agathon Press.

Heckman, J. J., & LaFontaine, P. A. (2010). The American high school graduation rate: Trends and levels. *Review of Economics and Statistics*, 92(2), 244–262.

Heller, D. E. (1997). Student price response in higher education: An update to Leslie and Brinkman. *Journal of Higher Education*, 68(6), 624–659.

Hines, S. E., & Whitaker, V. (2005). *AVID evaluation: Newport News public schools equity and accountability*. Newport News, VA: Evaluation, Research, and Testing Division, Newport News School District.

Hispanic Association of Colleges and Universities. (2012). HACU member Hispanic-serving institutions (HSIs). Retrieved March 20, 2012, from http://www.hacu.net/assnfe/CompanyDirectory.asp?STYLE=2&COMPANY_TYPE=1,5&SEARCH_TYPE=0

Hodum, R. L., & James, G. W. (2010). An observation of normative structure for college admission and recruitment officers. *The Journal of Higher Education*, 81(3), 317–338.

Holland, N. E. (2011). The power of peers: Influences on postsecondary education planning and experiences of African American university students. *Urban Education*, 46(5), 1029–1055.

Holmes, D., Verrier, D., & Chisholm, P. (1983). Persistence in student affairs work attitudes and job shifts among master's program graduates. *Journal of College Student Personnel*, 24(5), 438–443.

Horn, L., Chen, X., & Chapman, C. (2003). Getting ready to pay for college: What students and parents know about the cost of college tuition and what they are doing to find out. In N. C. f. E. Statistics (Ed.), *Statistical analysis report*. Washington, DC: U.S. Department of Education.

Hossler, D. (1999). Using the Internet in college admission: Strategic choices. *Journal of College Admission*, 162, 12–19.

Hossler, D., Schmit, J. L., & Vesper, N. (1999). *Going to college: How social, economic, and educational factors influence the decisions students make*. Baltimore, MD: Johns Hopkins University Press.

House, R. M., & Martin, P. J. (1998). Advocating for better futures for all students: A new vision for school counselors. *EDUCATION-INDIANAPOLIS, 119,* 284–291.

Housel, M. (2011). The truth about the great American manufacturing decline. *The Motley Fool.* Retrieved June 29, 2011, from http://www.fool.com/investing/general/2011/02/25/the-truth-about-the-great-american-manufacturing-d.aspx

Indiana Commission for Higher Education. (2011). Indiana's Twenty-first Century Scholars program: Years of impact. Retrieved June 12, 2012, from www.in.gov/che/files/21st_Century_Scholar_Report.pdf

Ingels, S. J., Curtain, T. R., Kaufman, P., Naomi Alt, M., & Chen, X. (2002). *Coming of age in the 1990s: The eighth grade class of 1988 12 years later* (p. 172). Washington, DC: U.S. Department of Education, National Center for Educational Statistics.

Ingels, S. J., Planty, M., & Bozick, R. (2005). *A profile of the American high school senior in 2004: A first look—Initial results from the first follow-up of the Education Longitudinal Study of 2002 (ELS:2002) (NCES 2006–348).* Washington, DC: U.S. Department of Education.

Institute for Higher Education Policy. (1998). *Reaping the benefits: Defining the public and private value of going to college* (p. 26). Washington, DC: Institute for Higher Education Policy.

International Baccalaureate Organization. (2012a). About the International Baccalaureate. Retrieved May 4, 2012, from http://www.ibo.org/general/who.cfm

International Baccalaureate Organization. (2012b). The IB Diploma Programme. Retrieved May 4, 2012, from http://www.ibo.org/diploma/

International Baccalaureate Organization. (2012c). The IB Diploma Programme: Preparation for university in the 21st century. Retrieved May 4, 2012, from http://www.ibo.org/recognition/

Ironbridge Systems, Inc. (2010). An evaluation of college summit outcomes (pp. 1–9). Washington, DC: Social Impact Exchange.

Jackson, C. (2003). Divided we fall: The federal government confronts the digital divide. *Journal of Student Financial Aid, 33*(3), 21–39.

Jacob, B. (2001). Getting tough? The impact of high school graduation exams. *Educational Evaluation and Policy Analysis, 23*(2), 99–121.

Jansen, J. (2010). Use of the Internet in higher-income households. *Pew Research Center's Internet & American Life Project* (pp. 1–41). Washington, DC: Pew Research Center.

Johanek, M. C. (2001). *A faithful mirror: Reflections on the College Board and education in America.* New York: College Board.

Johns Hopkins University School of Education. (2012). Four pillars of transformation. Retrieved June 4, 2012, from http://www.tdschools.org/about-talent-development-secondary/four-pillars-of-transformation/

Johnstone, D. B., & Del Genio, B. (2001). College-level learning in high school: Purposes, policies, and practical implications. In D. Humphreys (Ed.), *The academy in transition.* Washington DC: AACU.

Jones, S. (2002). The Internet goes to college: How students are living in the future with today's technology. In P. R. Center (Ed.), *Pew Internet & American Life.* Washington, DC.

Jordan, D. S. (1904). The high school of the twentieth century. *The School Review,* *12*(7), 545–549.

Jump, J. (2004). Admission, heal thyself: A prescription for reclaiming college admission as a profession. *Journal of College Admission, 184,* 12–17.

Kane, T. J. (1999). *The price of admission: Rethinking how Americans pay for college.* Washington, DC: Brookings Institution Press.

Katz, M. B. (1968). *The irony of early school reform: Educational innovation in mid-nineteenth century Massachusetts.* Cambridge, MA: Harvard University Press.

Kemple, J. J., Herlihy, C. M., & Smith, T. J. (2005). Making progress toward graduation: Evidence from the Talent Development high school model. New York, NY: MDRC.

Kim, D. H., & Schneider, B. (2005). Social capital in action: Alignment of parental support in adolescents' transition to postsecondary education. *Social Forces,* *84*(2), 1181–1206.

Kirst, M., & Venezia, A. (2004). *From high school to college: Improving opportunities for success in postsecondary education* (1st ed.). San Francisco, CA: Jossey-Bass.

Kitchens, R., Gross, D., & Smith, H. (2008). *Community capitalism: Lessons from Kalamazoo and beyond.* Bloomington, IN: AuthorHouse.

Kittle, B., & Ciba, D. (2001). Using college web sites for student recruitment: A relationship marketing study. *Journal of Marketing for Higher Education, 11*(3), 17–37.

Klopfenstein, K. (2004). The Advanced Placement expansion of the 1990s: How did traditionally underserved students fare? *Education Policy Analysis Archives,* *12*(68), 1–15.

Krug, E. A. (1964). *The shaping of the American high school.* New York: Harper & Row Publishers.

Lareau, A., & Horvat, E. M. (1999). Moments of social inclusion and exclusion race, class, and cultural capital in family-school relationships. *Sociology of Education,* *72*(1), 37–53.

Lautz, J., Hawkins, D., & Perez, A. B. (2005). The high school visit: Providing college counseling and building crucial K-16 links among students, counselors and admission officers. *Journal of College Admission, 188,* 6–15.

Lazerson, M. (2001). The College Board and American educational history. In M. C. Johanek (Ed.), *A faithful mirror: Reflections on the College Board and education in America* (pp. xxv, 400). New York: College Board.

Lee, J. B. (1980). *State student incentive grants: Issues in partnership* (pp. 1–174). Boulder, CO: Education Commission of the States.

Lee, M. A., & Mather, M. (2008). *Population bulletin: U.S. labor force trends* (Vol. 63, pp. 20). Washington, DC: Population Reference Bureau.

Lee, V. E., Croninger, R. G., & Smith, J. B. (1997). Course-taking, equity, and mathematics learning: Testing the constrained curriculum hypothesis in U.S. secondary schools. *Educational Evaluation and Policy Analysis, 19*(2), 99–121.

Leonard, J. P. (1953). *Developing the secondary school curriculum* (rev. ed.). New York: Rinehart and Company.

Leslie, L., & Brinkman, P. (1987). Student price response in higher education: The student demand studies. *Journal of Higher Education, 58*(2), 181–204.

Levin, H., & Calcagno, J. C. (2008). Remediation in the community college: An evaluator's perspective. *Community College Review, 35*(3), 181–207.

Levitt, S. D., & Dubner, S. J. (2005). *Freakonomics: A rogue economist explores the hidden side of everything* (1st ed.). New York: William Morrow.

Lewin, T. (2010, July 2). International program catches on in U.S. schools, *The New York Times.* Retrieved from http://www.nytimes.com/2010/07/03/education/03baccalaureate.html?pagewanted=print

Lewin, T. (2011, July 1). Court overturns michigan affirmative action ban. *The New York Times.* Retrieved from http://www.nytimes.com/2011/07/02/education/02michigan.html

Lin, N. (2001). *Social capital: A theory of social structure and action.* New York: Cambridge University Press.

Lindbeck, R., & Fodrey, B. (2009, Summer). Using technology in undergraduate admission: Current practices and future plans. *Journal of College Admission,* 25–30.

Lindbeck, R., & Fodrey, B. (2010, Summer). Using technology in undergraduate admission: A student perspective. *Journal of College Admission,* 10–17.

Linsenmeier, D. M., Rosen, H. S., & Rouse, C. E. (2002). Financial aid packages and college enrollment decisions: An econometric study. *NBER Working Paper Series* (9228), 45. Retrieved from http://www.nber.org/papers/w9228

Long, B. T. (2004, July). *The role of perceptions and information in college access: An exploratory review of the literature and possible data sources.* Boston: The Education Resources Institute (TERI).

Long, B. T., & Riley, E. (2007). Financial aid: A broken bridge to college access? *Harvard Educational Review, 77*(1), 39–63.

Lorin, J. (2011). Not-for-profit College Board getting rich as fees hit students. *Bloomberg News.* Retrieved October 10, 2011, from http://www.bloomberg.com/news/2011-08-18/not-for-profit-college-board-getting-rich-as-fees-hit-students.html

Mahoney, J. (2001). Perception of the profession is a cause for concern. *Journal of College Admission, 170,* 40–43.

Martorell, P., & McFarlin, I. (2007). Help or hindrance? The effects of college remediation on academic and labor market outcomes. Retrieved from http://www.utdallas.edu/research/tsp-erc/pdf/wp_mcfarlin_2010_help_or_hindrance_college_remediation.pdf

Mathews, J. (2010, July 15). Class struggle: The untruth about International Baccalaureate. *Washington Post.* Retrieved from http://voices.washingtonpost.com/class-struggle/2010/07/post_5.html

Matthay, E. R. (1992). The professional development needs of secondary school counselors. *Journal of College Admission, 135,* 7–12.

Matthews, C. M. (2012). *Federal support for academic research* (Vol. R41895, p. 26). Washington, DC: Congressional Research Service.

McDonough, P. M. (1997). *Choosing colleges: How social class and schools structure opportunity.* Albany: State University of New York Press.

McDonough, P. (2005). *Counseling and college counseling in America's high schools* (p. 40). Los Angeles: National Association of College Admissions Counselors.

McElroy, E. J., & Armesto, M. (1998). TRIO and Upward Bound: History, programs, and issues—Past, present, and future. *Journal of Negro Education, 67*(4), 373–380.

McNeal, R. B. (1999). Parental involvement as social capital: Differential effectiveness on science achievement, truancy, and dropping out. *Social Forces, 78*(1), 117–144.

Michigan College Access Network. (2011). *2011 annual report: Working to increase college participation and completion rates in Michigan* (pp. 1–8). Lansing, MI: Author.

Miller-Adams, M. (2008). *The Kalamazoo Promise: Building assets for community change*. Kalamazoo, MI: Upjohn Institute for Employment Research.

Miron, G., & Cullen, A. (2007). Trends and patterns in student enrollment in Kalamazoo Public Schools: Evaluation of the Kalamazoo Promise. *Working Paper No. 4*. Kalamazoo, MI: Western Michigan University Evaluation Center.

Mitchell, J., & Jackson-Randall, M. (2012, March 22). Student loan debt tops $1 Trillion. *Wall Street Journal*. Retrieved July 12, 2013 from http://online.wsj.com/article/SB10001424052702303812904577295930047604846.html

Musoba, G. D. (2004). *The impact of school reform on college preparation: A multilevel analysis of the relationship between state policy and student achievement*. PhD dissertation, Indiana University, Bloomington, IN.

National Association of College Admissions Counselors (NACAC). (1979). NACAC history: 1979. Retrieved 2/21, 2013, from http://www.nacacnet.org/about/history/Pages/1979.aspx

National Association of College Admissions Counselors (NACAC). (2012). *State of college admissions annual report*. Washington DC: Author.

National Association of State Student Grant and Aid Programs (Producer). (2011, June 12). 41st annual report on state-sponsored student financial aid. Retrieved from http://www.nassgap.org/viewrepository.aspx?categoryID=3

National Association of Student Financial Aid Administrators. (2011). *National student financial aid: 2010 national profile of programs in the Title IV of the Higher Education Act* (pp. 1–27). Washington, DC: Author.

National Center for Education Statistics. (1996). Table 152.—State requirements for high school graduation, in Carnegie units: 1980 and 1993. Retrieved August 10, 2004, from http://nces.ed.gov/programs/digest/d96/D96T152.asp

National Center for Education Statistics. (2005). Digest of Education Statistics, 2005 Retrieved June 1, 2006, from http://www.nces.ed.gov/pubs2005/digest2005/

National Center for Education Statistics. (2011a). Digest of education statistics, 2010. Retrieved October 11, 2012, from http://nces.ed.gov/programs/digest/d10/ch_1.asp

National Center for Education Statistics. (2011b). Fast facts: College enrollment. Retrieved June 12, 2012, from http://nces.ed.gov/fastfacts/display.asp?id=98

National Center for Education Statistics. (2012). IPEDS data center. Retrieved October 12, 2012, from http://nces.ed.gov/ipeds/

National Center for Higher Education Management Systems. (2010). Progress and completion: Graduation rates. Retrieved June 14, 2010, from http://www.higheredinfo.org/dbrowser/index.php?measure=20

National College Advising Corps. (2012). History of the Corps. Retrieved October 6, 2012, from http://www.advisingcorps.org/about-ncac/history-of-the-corps

National Commission on Excellence in Education. (1983). *A nation at risk* (p. 26). Washington, DC: Department of Education.

National Education Association. (1894). *Report of the committee of ten on secondary school studies.* New York: American Book Company.

National Math and Science Initiative. (2008). The National Math & Science Initiative. Retrieved March 3, 2008, from http://www.nationalmathandscience.org/node/936

National Office for School Counselor Advocacy (NOSCA). (2011). *Eight components of college and career readiness counseling* (Vol. 2012, pp. 1–8). Washington, DC: The College Board.

Nelson, L. (2011, June 15). The new Perkins Loan. *Inside Higher Ed.* Retrieved from http://www.insidehighered.com/news/2011/06/15/panel_discussion_looks_at_changes_to_perkins_loan_program

New York State Education Department. (2011). Science and Technology Entry Program (STEP). Retrieved October 20, 2012, from http://www.highered.nysed.gov/kiap/step/

New York State Higher Education Services Corporation (Producer). (2012, June 12). New York's Tuition Assistance Program—A history. Retrieved from http://www.hesc.com/content.nsf/CA/Appendix_E_New_Yorks_Tuition_Assistance_Program_A_History

Niu, S. X., & Tienda, M. (2010). Minority student academic performance under the uniform admission law: Evidence from the University of Texas at Austin. *Educational Evaluation and Policy Analysis, 32*(1), 44–69.

Oakes, J. (1992). Can tracking research inform practice? Technical, normative, and political considerations. *Educational Researcher, 21*(4), 12–21.

Obama, B. (2010). Remarks of President Barack Obama—As prepared for delivery address to joint session of congress. Retrieved March 5, 2010, from http://www.whitehouse.gov/the_press_office/remarks-of-president-barack-obama-address-to-joint-session-of-congress/

Office for Civil Rights. (1991). Historically Black colleges and universities and higher education desegregation. Retrieved March 30, 2012, from http://www2.ed.gov/about/offices/list/ocr/docs/hq9511.html

Organisation for Economic Co-operation and Development. (2010). *Education at a glance 2010: OECD Indicators* (Vol. 2011). Paris, France: Author.

Orrill, R. (2001). Grades 11–14: The heartland or the wasteland of American education? In M. C. Johanek (Ed.), *A faithful mirror: Reflections on the College Board and education in America* (pp. xxv, 400). New York: College Board.

Oseguera, L., & Rhee, B. S. (2009). The influence of institutional retention climates on student persistence to degree completion: A multilevel approach. *Research in Higher Education, 50*, 546–569.

Oswald, K. J. (2002). *The AVID program in AISD: Program evaluation report, 2000–01* (p. 36). Austin, TX: Austin Independent School District.

Ou, D. (2009). To leave or not to leave? Regression discontinuity analysis of the impact of failing high school exit exam. *Economics of Education Review, 29*(2), 171–186.

Parsad, B., Alexander, D., Ferris, E., & Hudson, L. (2003). *High school guidance counseling (NCES 2003–015)* (p. 124). Washington DC: Institute of Education Sciences, U.S. Department of Education.

Pascarella, E. T., & Terenzini, P. T. (2005). *How college affects students: A third decade of research* (2nd ed.). San Francisco: Jossey-Bass Publishers.

Passel, J., & Cohn, D. V. (2011). *U.S. population projections: 2005–2050* (p. 55). Washington DC: Pew Research Hispanic Center.

Pearson Data Solutions. (2012). Electronic student records and transcripts. Retrieved November 12, 2012, from http://www.pearsondatasolutions.com/transcripts

Perna, L. W. (2006). Studying college access and choice: A proposed conceptual model. In J. Smart & M. Paulsen (Eds.), *Higher education: Handbook of theory and research*. Memphis, TN: Springer.

Perna, L. W., & Swail, W. S. (2001). Pre-college outreach and early intervention. *Thought & Action, 17*(1), 99–110.

Perna, L. W., & Titus, M. A. (2005). The relationship between parental involvement as social capital and college enrollment: An examination of racial/ethnic group differences. *The Journal of Higher Education, 76*(5), 485–518.

Plank, S. B., & Jordan, W. J. (2001). Effects of information, guidance, and actions on postsecondary destinations: A study of talent loss. *American Educational Research Journal, 38*(4), 947–979.

Poock, M. C., & Lefond, D. (2001, Summer). How college-bound prospects perceive university web sites: Findings, implications, and turning browsers into applicants. *College and University Journal, 77*(1), 15–21.

Powell, A. G., Farrar, E., & Cohen, D. K. (1985). *The shopping mall high school: Winners and losers in the educational marketplace*. Boston: Houghton Mifflin.

President's Commission on Higher Education. (1947). *Higher education for American democracy*. New York: Harper & Brothers.

Pryor, J., Hurtado, S., Saenz, V., Santos, J. J., & Korn, W. (2007). *The American freshman: Forty year trends*. Los Angeles, CA: Cooperative Instituional Research Program.

Quist, A. (2007). The International Baccaalureate curriculum. *Education News*, 9.Retrieved from http://www.educationnews.org/articles/the-international-baccalaureate-curriculum.html

Ravitch, D. (1974). *The great school wars, New York City, 1805–1973: A history of the public schools as battlefield of social change*. New York: Basic Books.

Reardon, S., Atteberry, A., Arshan, N., & Kurlaender, M. (2009). *Effects of the California high school exit exam on student persistence, achievement, and graduation* (Vol. 2011). Palo Alto, CA: Institute for Research on Education Policy & Practice.

Reese, W. J. (2005). *America's public schools: From the common school to No Child Left Behind*. Baltimore, MD: Johns Hopkins University Press.

Roos, D. (2010). How financial aid organizations work. Retrieved October 12, 2012, from http://money.howstuffworks.com/personal-finance/college-planning/financial-aid/state-financial-aid-organizations3.htm

Rosenbaum, J. E., Deil-Amen, R., & Person, A. E. (2006). *After admission: From college access to college success*. New York: Russell Sage.

Rudolph, F. (1962). *The American college and university, a history*. New York: Vintage Books.

Rutgers University Office of Enrollment Management. (2012). Self-reported academic record. Retrieved January 3, 2013, from https://www.ugadmissions.rutgers.edu/srt/Login.aspx

Sadler, P., Sonnert, G., Tai, R., & Klopfenstein, K. (2010). *AP: A critical examination of the Advanced Placement program.* Cambridge, MA: Harvard Education Press.

Salary.com. (2013). Nursing salaries by job title. Retrieved March 12, 2013, from http://www1.salary.com/registered-nurse-Salary.html

Savitz-Romer, M. (2008). The urban challenge. *ASCA School Counselor, 46*(2), 13–19.

Say Yes to Education. (2012). Say Yes to Education scholarships and grants. Retrieved October 26, 2012, from http://buffalo.sayyestoeducation.org/college-scholarships/scholarship-types

Schiller, K. S., & Muller, C. (2003). Raising the bar and equity? Effects of state high school graduation requirements and accountability policies on students' mathematics coursetaking. *Educational Evaluation and Policy Analysis, 25*(3), 299–318.

Schimmel, C. (2008). School counseling: A brief historical overview. Retrieved from http://wvde.state.wv.us/counselors/history.html

Sebring, P. A. (1987). Consequences of differential amounts of high school coursework: Will the new graduation requirements help? *Educational Evaluation and Policy Analysis, 9*(3), 258–273.

Seftor, N. S., Mamun, A., & Schirm, A. (2009). *The impacts of regular Upward Bound on postsecondary outcomes 7–9 years after scheduled high school graduation: Final report.* Washington, DC: Mathematica Policy Research Inc.

Seidman, A. (2005). *College student retention: Formula for student success.* Westport, CT: Praeger Publishers.

Singell, L. D. (2010). Modeling retention at a large public university: Can at-risk students be identified early enough to treat? *Research in Higher Education, 51,* 546–572.

Sipple, J. W., Killeen, K., & Monk, D. H. (2004). Adoption and adaptation: School district responses to state imposed learning and graduation requirements. *Educational Evaluation and Policy Analysis, 26*(2), 143–168.

Smith Morest, V., & Mechur Karp, M. (2006). Twice the credit, half the time. In T. W. Bailey & V. S. Morest (Eds.), *Defending the community college equity agenda.* Baltimore: Johns Hopkins University Press.

Sokatch, A. (2006). Peer influences on the college-going decisions of low socioeconomic status urban youth. *Education and Urban Society, 39*(1), 128–146.

Southern Regional Education Board, & GO Alliance. (2012). What is College Access Marketing? Retrieved October 13, 2012, from http://collegeaccessmarketing.org/whatiscam_ektid34.aspx

St. Clair County Community Foundation. (2010). The SCC plan: Creating a path toward higher education. Retrieved October 12, 2012, from http://www.stclairfoundation.org/knowhow2go

St. John, E. P., Andrieu, S., Oescher, J., & Starkey, J. B. (1994). The influence of student aid on within-year persistence by traditional college-age students in four-year colleges. *Research in Higher Education, 35*(4), 455.

St. John, E. P., Daun-Barnett, N., Fisher, A. S., Lee, M., & Williams, K. (2008). Indiana's Twenty-first Century Scholars program: A statewide story with national implications. *Results and reflections*. Indianapolis, IN: Lumina Foundation for Education.

St. John, E. P., Daun-Barnett, N., & Moronski, K. (2012). *Public policy in higher education*. New York: Routledge.

St. John, E. P., & Musoba, G. D. (2006). Academic access. In E. P. St. John (Ed.), *Education and the public interest: School reform, public finance, and access to higher education*. New York: Springer.

St. John, E. P., Musoba, G. D., & Simmons, A. B. (2003). Keeping the promise: The Indiana Twenty-first Century Scholars Program. *The Review of Higher Education, 27*(1), 103–123.

St. John, E. P., Musoba, G. D., Simmons, A. B., & Chung, C.-G. (2002). *Meeting the access challenge: Indiana's Twenty-first Century Scholars program* (p. 60). Indianapolis, IN: Lumina Foundation for Education.

Stanley, M. (2003). College education and the midcentury GI Bills. *The Quarterly Journal of Economics, 118*(2), 671–708.

Stanton-Salazar, R. J., & Dornbusch, S. M. (1995). Social capital and the reproduction of inequality: Information networks among Mexican-origin high school students. *Sociology of Education, 68*(2), 116–135.

State of Indiana. (2012). 21st Century Scholars service regions. Retrieved October 11, 2012, from http://www.in.gov/ssaci/2500.htm

Steinberg, J. (2002). *The gatekeepers: Inside the admissions process of a premier college*. New York: Viking.

Stevens, M. (2009). *Creating a class: College admissions and the education of elites*. Cambridge, MA: Harvard University Press.

Stewart, D. (1998). Perspectives on educational reform. In C. Swann & S. Henderson (Eds.), *Handbook for the college admissions profession* (p. 1). Westport, CT: Greenwood Publishing Group.

Swann, C. (1998). Admissions officer: A profession and a career. In C. Swann & S. Henderson (Eds.), *Handbook for the college admissions profession* (pp. 29–35). Westport, CT: Greenwood Publishing Group.

Swann, C., & Henderson, S. (1998). *Handbook for the college admissions profession*. Greenwood Publishing Group.

Swanson, C., & Chaplin, D. (2003). *Counting high school graduation when graduation counts: Measuring graduation rates under the high sctakes of NCLB* (p. 52). Washington, DC: Urban Institute.

Swanson, J. (2008). *An analysis of the impact of high school dual enrollment course participation on post-secondary academic success, persistence and degree completion*. PhD dissertation, University of Iowa, University Heights, IA.

Tabor, A. (2011). *Evaluation report: Advancement via individual determination* (pp. 1–18). San Francisco, CA: San Francisco Unified School District.

Teach for America. (2012). Our history. Retrieved October 5, 2012, from http://www.teachforamerica.org/our-organization/our-history

Teitelbaum, P. (2003). The influence of high school graduation requirement policies in mathematics and science on student course-taking patterns and achievement. *Educational Evaluation and Policy Analysis, 25*(1), 31–57.

The Center for Higher Education Policy Analysis. (2005). The impact of peers on college participation: A review of the literature. Retrieved March 12, 2012, from http://www.uscrossier.org/pullias/research/publications/

The College Board. (1983). *Academic preparation for college: What students need to know and be able to do.* New York: College Entrance Examination Board.

The College Board. (2003). A brief history of the Advanced Placement program. Retrieved April 30, 2012, from http://about.collegeboard.org/history

The College Board. (2011a). Annual AP Program Participation, 1956-2011. Retrieved July 12, 2013, from http://media.collegeboard.com/digitalServices/pdf/research/AP-Annual-Participation-2011.pdf

The College Board. (2011b). YouCanGo! web portal. Retrieved December 18, 2011, from http://youcango.collegeboard.org/

The College Board. (2012). The college completion agenda. Washington, DC: Author.

The Corporation for National & Community Service. (2012). About AmeriCorps: History, legislation, and budget. Retrieved October 6, 2012, from http://www.americorps.gov/about/ac/history.asp

Thelin, J. R. (2004). *A history of American higher education.* Baltimore: Johns Hopkins University Press.

Tierney, W. G., Corwin, Z. B., & Colyar, J. E. (2005). *Preparing for college: Nine elements of effective outreach.* Albany: State University of New York Press.

Tierney, W. G., & Jun, A. (2001). A university helps prepare low income youths for college. *Journal of Higher Education, 72*(2), 205–225.

Tillery, C., & English, D. (2009). *An evaluation of North Carolina's college planning web portal.* Chapel Hill, NC: College Foundation of North Carolina.

Tinto, V. (1993). *Leaving college: Rethinking the causes and cures of student attrition* (2nd ed.). Chicago and London: University of Chicago Press.

U.S. Bureau of Labor Statistics. (2012). Education pays. Retrieved June 5, 2011, from http://www.bls.gov/emp/ep_chart_001.htm

U.S. Census Bureau. (2000). The graduates: Educational attainment, 2000. Retrieved October 22, 2005, from http://www.census.gov/population/pop-profile/2000/chap09.pdf

U.S. Census Bureau. (2010). State and county quick facts. Retrieved August 16, 2012, from http://quickfacts.census.gov/qfd/states/00000.html

U.S. Department of Education. (1998). National Early Intervention Scholarship and Partnership (NEISP) program. Retrieved March 30, 2012, from http://www2.ed.gov/PDFDocs/FinAidHB/ch9_s4.pdf

U.S. Department of Education. (2003). *National evaluation of GEAR UP: A summary of the first two years.* Washington, DC: Policy and Programs Studies Service.

U.S. Department of Education. (2006a). Spellings Commission on the Future of Higher Education final report. Retrieved June 15, 2006, from http://www.ed.gov/about/bdscomm/list/hiedfuture/about.html

U.S. Department of Education. (2006b). *A test of leadership: Charting the future of U.S. higher education.* Washington, DC: Author.

U.S. Department of Education. (2010). Developing Hispanic serving institutions program—Title V. Retrieved March 20, 2012, from http://www2.ed.gov/programs/idueshsi/index.html

U.S. Department of Education. (2011a). Federal Student Aid. Retrieved September 14, 2012, from http://studentaid.ed.gov/redirects/college-gov

U.S. Department of Education. (2011b). Talent Search. Retrieved September 23, 2012, from http://www2.ed.gov/programs/triotalent/index.html

U.S. Department of Education. (2011c). Upward Bound—Applicant information. Retrieved March 17, 2012, from http://www2.ed.gov/programs/trioupbound/applicant.html

U.S. Department of Education. (2011d). Promise Neighborhoods. Retrieved August 16, 2011, from http://www2.ed.gov/programs/promiseneighborhoods/index.html

U.S. Department of Education. (2012a). Federal Pell Grant program. Retrieved June 10, 2012, from http://www2.ed.gov/programs/fpg/funding.html

U.S. Department of Education. (2012b). Federal work study program. Retrieved January 12, 2013, from http://www2.ed.gov/programs/fws/index.html

U.S. Department of Education. (2012c). Gaining Early Awareness and Readiness for Undergraduate Programs (GEAR UP)—Purpose. Retrieved June 15, 2012, from http://www2.ed.gov/programs/gearup/index.html

U.S. Department of Veterans Affairs. (2012). Post-9/11 GI Bill (Chapter 33) payment rates for 2013 academic year. Retrieved January 12, 2013, from http://www.gibill.va.gov/resources/benefits_resources/rates/CH33/Ch33rates080113.html#TUITION

University of Illinois Urbana-Champaign Office for Undergraduate Admissions. (2012). Self-reported academic record FAQ. Retrieved January 3, 2013, from http://admissions.illinois.edu/faq/srar.html

University of North Carolina at Chapel Hill. (2012). Carolina Covenant. Retrieved July 12, 2013, from https://carolinacovenant.unc.edu/

University of Virginia. (2011). AccessUVA makes it happen. Retrieved June 12, 2012, from http://www.virginia.edu/financialaid/access.php

University System of Georgia. (2012). How HOPE changes will affect USG students. Retrieved January 20, 2013, from http://www.usg.edu/student_affairs/students/how_hope_changes_will_affect_usg_students

Venegas, K. M. (2006a). Internet inequalities: Financial aid, the Internet, and low-income students. *American Behavioral Scientist, 49*(12), 1652–1669.

Venegas, K. M. (2006b). Low-income urban high school students' use of the Internet to access financial aid. *Journal of Student Financial Aid, 36*(3), 4–15.

Warren, J. R., Jenkins, K. N., & Kulick, R. B. (2006). High school exit examinations and state-level completion and GED rates, 1975 through 2002. *Educational Evaluation and Policy Analysis, 28*(2), 131–152.

Wechsler, H. S. (2001). Eastern standard time: High school-college collaboration and admission to college, 1880–1930. In M. C. Johanek (Ed.), *A faithful mirror: Reflections on the College Board and education in America* (pp. xxv, 400). New York: College Board.

Wellman, J., & Vandal, B. (2011, July 21). Five myths of remedial education. *Inside Higher Ed.* Retrieved from http://www.insidehighered.com/views/2011/07/21/wellman_vandal_5_myths_about_remedial_education

Willingham, W., & Breland, H. (1982). *Personal qualities and college admissions.* Princeton, NJ: College Board.

Wraga, W. G. (1994). *Democracy's high school.* Lanham, MD: University Press of America.

INDEX

Note: Locators in italics indicate material found in figures and tables.

INDEX

technology, student use of 163–4
Ternzini, P. T. 158
testing agencies 64, 133, 140
Thelin, J. R. 19, 25
Tienda, M. 113
Tierney, W. G. 108, 124–5
Tinto, Vincent 158
Titus, M. A. 107, 109
trainers, pre-college outreach providers
as 52–3
transcript services 105, 143–4
transfer credit 176
transition, to campus life: cultural
differences and 158–9; "living the
life" 157–8; student ambassador
programs 159–60; summer
orientation 160; support services and
161–2; university experience courses
160–1
transportation, in undergraduate
budgets 81
travel season 40–1
Trends in College Pricing (The College
Board) 80–1
Trends in Higher Education (The
College Board) 80–1
Trends in Student Aid (The College
Board) 80–1
Tribal Colleges (TCs) 23–4
Tribally Controlled Community College
Assistance Act 23
TRIO program 12, 49, 115, 117–18,
120, 129, 162, 177
tuition and fees: enrollment decisions
and 103; growth in 78; in
undergraduate budgets 81
tuition discounting 79–80, 82–3, 94
Tuition Incentive Program 124
21st Century Scholars 122

UCLA's Higher Education Research
Institute (HERI) 134
undergraduate budgets, average
estimated 81
undocumented students 24
unemployment rates, college education
and 2
United States, educational attainment
in 1
universities/colleges, history of: access/
exclusion and 19–21; affirmative
action and 22–4; community
colleges 25–6; federal financial aid

and 26–7; Great Society and 26–7;
Servicemen's Readjustment Act
(1944) 21, 26
university experience courses 160–1
University of Chicago 26
University of Illinois 144
University of Michigan 23, 29, 132,
169, 176
University of North Carolina 96, 127,
138
University of Southern California 116,
124
University of Virginia 95–6, 127
Upward Bound: federal investment in
118; incentives and 14; standard
program 119–20
U. S. Department of Education 61,
120–1, 141, 147, 173

Venegas, K. M. 132, 133
Venezia, A. 7
Vesper, N. 104–5
veterans, educational benefits for 21
virtual campus tour 132–3
vocational education movement 30
Volunteers in Service to America
(VISTA) 128

wages, college education and 2
Walker, M. 136
web portals xii
websites (institutional) 135
Wesleyan College (Georgia Female
College) 21
Wilberforce University 22
William D. Ford Direct Loans *85*
women, affirmative action and 23
women's colleges 21
working while in school 154–5
work study *85*, 89
World War II: access to higher
education after 21; community
colleges after 26
Wraga, W. G. 30

Xap, Inc. 138

Yeshiva University 20
yield management 41
YouCanGo! 140

Zell Miller Scholarship 93
Zinck Stagno, M. 136